REGIONAL INNOVATION STRATEGIES

THE CHALLENGE FOR
LESS-FAVOURED REGIONS

REGIONS, CITIES AND PUBLIC POLICY SERIES

Series Editor: Ron Martin, Department of Geography, University of Cambridge

Throughout the industrialised world, economic transformation, rapid technological change and increasing globalisation are giving greater prominence to the nature and performance of individual regional and urban economies. The patterns and processes of regional and urban development are being fundamentally redrawn. At the same time, regions and cities are assuming an increased importance as arenas of public policy innovation and implementation and as new loci of social and economic intervention and regulation. *Regions, Cities and Public Policy* is an international series which aims to provide authoritative analyses of the new significance of regions and cities for economic development and public policy. It aims to combine fresh theoretical and empirical insights with constructive policy evaluation and debate, to provide a definitive set of conceptual, practical and topical studies in the field of regional and urban public policy analysis.

REGIONAL INNOVATION STRATEGIES

THE CHALLENGE FOR LESS-FAVOURED REGIONS

edited by

Kevin Morgan and
Claire Nauwelaers

Regions, Cities and Public Policy Series

London: The Stationery Office   *London*: Regional Studies Association

First published in the United Kingdom by The Stationery Office in 1999 *with* the Regional Studies Association (registered charity 252269).

A CIP catalogue record for this book is available from the British Library
A Library of Congress CIP catalog has been applied for

ISBN 0 11 702379 5

Printed in the United Kingdom by The Stationery Office
J0086961   C8   10/99   441906   19585

CONTENTS

LIST OF TABLES

LIST OF FIGURES

CONTRIBUTORS

MAURICE AVERY has worked in Quebec's University network for more than twenty-five years. In that time he has played a central role in university research policies at both institutional and governmental levels. He has participated in the setting-up of a number of research centres and has started up partnerships and collaborative programmes involving industrial firms and universities. In recent years he has been actively involved in regional strategic planning in science and technology and has contributed to the definition and implementation of the regional technology plan (RTP) for the Bas-Saint-Laurent region in Quebec. He has been a member of the Science and Technology Council of Quebec since 1996, as part of which he contributes to the definition of science and technology policies. As president of Soft Innove, he helps to shape strategies within the context of regional and national systems of innovation.

BELÉN BARROETA is senior consultant in Información y Desarrollo, SL (INFYDE) in Las Arenas, Vizcaya (Spain), and works as a specialist in regional development projects, in the areas of technological innovation, enterprise support, as well as evaluation of public policies.

PATRIES BOEKHOLT joined Technopolis in 1996 and is director of Technopolis BV in the Netherlands, focusing on science, technology and innovation policy at the regional, national and international level. She graduated from the Catholic University of Nijmegen and gained a doctorate from Aston Business School, UK. Previously she worked for several years as a senior researcher at the TNO – Centre for Technology and Policy Studies (STB-TNO), the major research and technology organisation in the Netherlands. She has conducted science and technology evaluations, international comparative studies on innovation issues, and cluster and network studies, and has participated in peer review exercises. Regional innovation issues have been one of her key areas in the past years. Her recent activities have included participation in Regional

Innovation and Technology Transfer Strategy (RITTS) projects (Berlin and Overijssel), the evaluation of the Regional Technology Plan for DG XVI of the European Commission, and an international comparative review of cluster policies for the Dutch Ministry for Economic Affairs and the OECD.

JAIME DEL CASTILLO is Professor in the Department of Applied Economics of the University of the Basque Country and is the director of the consulting company Información y Desarrollo, SL (INFYDE). He is an expert who works for the European Commission on feasibility studies and the evaluation of technological parks, and is process consultant to the Regional Innovation Strategies (RIS) and Regional Innovation and Technology Transfer Strategies and Infrastructures (RITTS). He has taken part as a specialist in the European Secretariat within the framework of support for the RTP pilot experiences. In this context, he has provided assistance in the Innovation Strategies for several regions in Southern Europe as well as in Latin America.

JAN COBBENHAGEN works at MERIT (Maastricht Economic Research Institute on Innovation and Technology), a scientific research institute of the University of Maastricht. He is the programme leader of MERIT's research programme 'Innovation Management in Firms and Regions'. Furthermore, he is part-time Associate Professor in Innovation Management at the University of Liège and coordinator of the study track 'International Innovation Management' at the University of Maastricht. His research experience is in innovation management, organisational change processes and regional innovation policy. As a process consultant, he is involved in several studies related to regional innovation policy (RITTS, RIS/RTP), including RIS Limburg (B), RITTS Iceland, RITTS Flanders and RTP Limburg (NL). He has published several books and articles on innovation management, regional innovation policy and organisational change.

DYLAN HENDERSON is a researcher at the Department of City and Regional Planning, Cardiff University. He is currently studying for a PhD looking at new forms of regional innovation policy in Wales. Between 1994 and 1995 he was principal researcher for the Wales Regional Technology Plan.

GRIGORIS KAFKALAS is Associate Professor at the Department of Urban and Regional Planning and Development, Aristotle University of Thessaloniki. He has written or edited many articles and books, including the edited volume *Cities and Regions in the New Europe* (with M. Dunford, London: Belhaven, 1992); *Urban and Regional Development: Theory, Analysis and Policy* (in Greek) (with P. Getimis and N. Maraveyias; Athens: Themelio, 1993); *Institutional Interventions in City Centres* (in Greek) (with K. Spiridonidis; Thessaloniki: Art of Text; 1994). He has directed and/or participated in many research and education programmes in cooperation with Greek and European academic and other institutions. In 1995–96 he was a member of the management unit of the Regional Technology Plan for Central Macedonia. His ongoing research includes the coordination of a project on the 'Mechanisms for the Internationalisation of European Cities' and the partnership in two Leonardo projects on intelligent regions and the training of training designers. His interests are in sustainable spatial development and the regional and spatial dimensions of European integration. He is a co-director of the Greek biannual scientific review *Topos: Journal of Urban and Regional Studies* (ISSN: 1105-3267).

NICOS KOMNINOS is Associate Professor of City and Regional Planning in the Aristotle University of Thessaloniki and his research focuses on innovation areas and planning (industrial clusters, urban renewal, science and technology parks, technopolises, innovative regions, and virtual innovation environment). He is the author of more than a hundred scientific works, including the books *Theory of Urbanity* (Athens: Synchrona Themata, 1986); *Capitalist Development and Crisis Theory: Accumulation, Regulation and Spatial Restructuring* (London–New York: Macmillan–St Martin's Press, 1989), *Technopolis and Development Strategies in Europe* (Athens: Gutenberg, 1993); *The Innovative Region: The Regional Technology Plan of Central Macedonia* (Athens: Gutenberg, 1998). He coordinates the Urban and Regional Innovation research unit and has participated in numerous European projects. He is an expert of the European Commission for the Action of Support to Science Parks (DG XIII), the Regional Innovation and Technology Transfer Strategies and Infrastructures (RITTS-DG XIII), and the Regional Innovation Strategies (RIS-DG XVI).

MIKEL LANDABASO is an economist and was Assistant to the Director General of the Basque Regional Development Agency (SPRI) before joining the Regional Policy Directorate General of the European Commission in 1990. He is currently responsible for the launching and management of pilot actions in the fields of innovation promotion (RIS – Regional Innovation Strategies – and RTTs – Regional Technology Transfer Projects) and information society (RISI – Regional Information Society Initiative) under Article 10 of the European Regional Development Fund.

KEVIN MORGAN is Professor of European Regional Development at the Department of City and Regional Planning, Cardiff University. His current research interests include regional innovation strategies, regional development agencies and sustainable food supply chains. He has published widely on various aspects of regional development and his most recent book (co-authored with Philip Cooke) is *The Associational Economy: Firms, Regions and Innovation* (Oxford University Press, 1998). In addition to his academic work he has acted as a consultant for many organisations, including the European Commission, OECD and Regional Development Agencies throughout Europe.

CLAIRE NAUWELAERS is an industrial economist and a senior research fellow at MERIT, the Maastricht Economic Research Institute on Technology and Innovation, at the University of Maastricht (NL). She graduated and worked previously at the University of Louvain (Belgium). At MERIT, she belongs to the 'Regional Innovation Strategies in Europe' research team. Her main area of research and expertise is on the functioning of regional innovation systems. She performs policy-oriented work on questions such as the evaluation of EU programmes aiming at regional innovation-oriented development, scientific support for the implementation of regional innovation and information society strategies in EU regions and the evaluation of ERDF operational programmes and the development of the methodological aspects of the evaluation of regional innovation support infrastructures. She has developed an extended expertise as process consultant for the RITTS, RTP/RIS and RISI operations of the European Commission, through which she advises regional governments for the design of their innovation policies.

SLAVO RADOSEVIC is a Lecturer at the School of Slavonic and East European Studies, University College London. He has been a Senior Fellow at SPRU (Science and Technology Policy Research) at the University of Sussex for more than six years, where he has researched changes in science, technology and industry policies in Central and Eastern Europe. He has acted as a consultant to UNIDO, the World Bank, the EU, TNO in Russia and to Ernst & Young in advising the Romanian government on science and technology policy. He has published extensively on science and technology issues in Central and Eastern Europe and is the author of *International Technology Transfer and Catch-up in Economic Development* (Edward Elgar, 1999).

ALASDAIR REID is an industrial and regional economist with ten years experience in the design, evaluation and implementation of programmes in the fields of regional innovation and industrial policy. Following previous posts with Coopers & Lybrand in Brussels, and as a Research Fellow at the Catholic University of Louvain, he is now a senior manager with an economic consultancy, ADE SA in Louvain-la-Neuve, Belgium, where he is responsible for projects in the field of regional development, evaluation of public policy and the transformation of Central and Eastern European countries. He has acted as an expert for a large number of services of the European Commission, including DGI (Phare), DGXII (Research & Development), DGXIII (Innovation Programme) and DGXVI (Regional Policy); as well as numerous regional and national governments in the EU and Phare countries. Since April 1996, he has been responsible within the Technical Assistance Unit of DGXVI of the European Commission for the support and supervision to the 20 Regional Innovation Strategies pilot projects being implemented throughout the European Union. In addition, he is currently responsible within ADE, in partnership with Zenit, Germany and

Enterprise Plc, UK, for the carrying out of a thematic evaluation of RTDI measures financed under Objective 2 of the Structural Funds on behalf of the Evaluation Unit of DGXVI.

STUART A ROSENFELD is president and founder of Regional Technology Strategies Inc., a non-profit organisation located in Chapel Hill, North Carolina, that researches, designs, implements and assesses technology-based development strategies and policies. His current interests include research and policy formulation for various states and regions on regional industry clusters and business networks and particular roles for technical colleges, all with an emphasis on less-populated areas. He has served on committees for the National Academy of Sciences, testified before and reported to more than a dozen US legislative and congressional and OECD committees, and published more than a hundred papers and books on networks, economic development, technology policy and vocational education, including *Competitive Manufacturing: New Strategies for Regional Development, Smart Firms in Small Towns, and Significant Others: Exploring the Potential for Manufacturing Networks, Industrial-Strength Strategies: Regional Clusters and Public Policy, and Overachievers: Business Clusters that Work.* He previously served as deputy director of the Southern Growth Policies Board, an inter-state compact representing the governments of 13 states and Puerto Rico, and as founder and director of its subsidiary, the Southern Technology Council.

JEAN SEVERIJNS studied economics at Tilburg University in the Netherlands, and from 1980 until 1986 worked in the economic department of the Rijnmond public authority in Rotterdam, which is a regional government. In that period he was responsible for policy-making regarding SME's, innovation and labour market issues. Since then he has worked for the Dutch Province of Limburg in different positions. He is currently deputy head of the Innovation Unit of the Province of Limburg, a visiting lecturer at EIPA (European Institute of Public Administration), a visiting lecturer at the Strathclyde European Partnership, a member of the strategic board of the University of Mendoza (Argentina) and adviser to the European Commission (DG XIII and DG XVI).

MEIRION THOMAS has degrees from the London School of Economics and the University of Wales. He worked in financial services, the motor industry and the private steel industry before establishing the Welsh Development Agency's Business Services Division in 1990. Since moving to the Cardiff Business School in 1995 he has established a new unit that carries out research and consultancy in the field of economic and business development. He is also a director of the Paris-based consultancy company CM International. He was Project Director for the Wales Regional Technology Plan (1994–96), and is an adviser to regional governments and organisations in Spain, Portugal, Greece and Scotland. He is also a member of the European Commission's Innovation and Growth Working Group.

ITZIAR URIZAR, former consultant in Información y Desarrollo, SL (INFYDE) specialises in the field of innovation policies and is currently a lecturer in the Department of Applied Economics of the University of the Basque Country.

INTRODUCTION

In preparing this book the contributors have been motivated by three over-lapping considerations. These are worth spelling out, in the belief that the context in which a book is conceived helps the reader to understand the perspective even if he does not accept the arguments. The fact that all the authors are in varying degrees engaged with the protean policy-making world – whether as academic-based policy analysts, as practising public administrators or as consultants who specialise in policy evaluation – helps to explain why our first motivation was to produce a book which at least tried to bridge the debilitating gap between theory and practice, a gap that has long bedevilled the debate on regional development to the detriment of theorists and practitioners alike.

Just as management gurus often fail to appreciate the prosaic world in which firms operate, where corporate behaviour is determined as much by habit and routine as it is by reason, so economic theorists often underestimate the institutional inertia and the turf struggles which can defeat the best-laid plans for economic regeneration in the less favoured regions. This discrepancy – between the perspective of the theorist and the concerns of the practitioner – emerged time and time again in the countless meetings which DG XVI (the Regional Policy Directorate of the European Commission) convened to discuss the impact of the Structural Funds. Whatever the shortcomings of the European Commission, it is worth saying that DG XVI in particular has played an immensely important role in breaking down the barriers between theorists and practitioners. In contrast to the stuffy and imperious traditions which dog many national bureaucracies, where civil servants rarely interact with either theorists or practitioners, DG XVI officials appear to be equally at home with both. Indeed, it was in seminars organised by DG XVI that many of our contributors met for the first time, and this book is the tangible outcome of that process of cross-fertilisation. It is our hope and belief that such cross-fertilisation has the potential to render theory more realistic on the one hand, while on the other hand making the professional world of practice more receptive to innovative ideas.

If the first motivation for this book was to try to bridge the gap between theory and practice then the second was to gain a better understanding of the new forms of regional policy – namely regional *innovation* policy – that were beginning to emerge in Europe and North America. In the European Union, for example, an important transition is underway in the focus of the Structural Funds, the main instrument for promoting social and spatial cohesion in the EU. Time was when the Structural Funds were largely geared to the provision of 'heavy' infrastructures in the less-favoured regions, like roads, buildings, land reclamation, basic training and so forth. In recent years, however, the emphasis has begun to shift to 'soft' infrastructures, like innovation-support services to foster the exploitation of research and technological development (RTD), and to promote themes like the information society, equal opportunities, the environment and new skill sets. This new focus is partly to be explained by the fact that the Commission is now more intent on addressing not just the symptoms of peripherality (like high unemployment and low GDP per capita for example), but also the causes, one of which is deemed to be a weak capacity to innovate (that is, the capacity to generate new products, new processes and new technologies, for example).

In so far as the pre-1994 Structural Funds addressed the problem of innovation in the less-favoured regions, as in the STRIDE programme for example, it did so in a very partial and one-sided fashion. As Landabaso and Reid argue in chapter 2, these first-generation regional innovation policies privileged supply-side measures over demand-side and treated innovation as though it were synonymous with RTD activities. In contrast, the new generation of regional innovation policy – in the shape of the RTP, RIS and RITTS programmes – tries to strike a more judicious balance between demand and supply and recognises that, of the two, it is far more difficult to shape the former than the latter.[1] These new regional innovation programmes also entertain a much broader understanding of what constitutes innovation, thus highlighting the role which a wide array of organisations can play in fostering innovation capacity.

Although it is still too early to judge whether these new initiatives will make a difference in the less-favoured regions, we have been struck by the difficulties they are already beginning to pose for the regional authorities which are charged with implementing them. Firstly, as we argue in chapter 1, the skills required to design and deliver regional innovation programmes are radically different from the skills involved in constructing basic infrastructure like a road, for example. The second difficulty is more of a political problem in the sense that these new regional innovation programmes require an uncommon amount of political maturity on the part of the regional authorities because the dividends, if there are any, are necessarily long-term in nature, and certainly longer than the electoral cycles which dominate the minds of most politicians. In other words, regional innovation policies do not satisfy the criterion of conventional regional policy, namely short-term job creation. As we argue in chapter 12, the way out of this conundrum is to give parity of esteem to job-creating measures and innovation-oriented measures because the less-favoured regions desperately need to promote both social cohesion and economic development.

The third motive behind this book was to highlight the point that innovation and economic development are collective social endeavours in which the capacity to collaborate, and in particular the ability to find joint solutions to common problems, is perhaps the most important asset of all. This is one of those intangible or relational assets which falls under the generic title of social capital, i.e. the norms and networks of trust and reciprocity which facilitate cooperation and coordination. While all the contributors to this volume are rightly sceptical when organisations parade their commitment to 'partnership', an overworked mantra which has launched a thousand mission statements, we nevertheless subscribe to the notion that relational assets like trust, voice and loyalty are a necessary (but not sufficient) ingredient in the recipe for regional renewal. Significantly, practitioners tend to be far less equivocal about this point than academic theorists, which may mean that those who are actively engaged in inter-organisational networks have a finer appreciation of what it takes to get ahead together. Being engaged at the sharp end, in other words, they may be in a better position to appreciate that, where it occurs, successful collaboration is very often the product of a process in which time and effort have been invested in getting to know each other, understanding each other and learning to trust each other. All of this is easier said than done, especially in the domain of inter-firm relations, because a competitive environment contains powerful incentives for deceitful, proprietorial and opportunistic behaviour. However, there are good theoretical and practical reasons for thinking that such forms of behaviour are unlikely to yield the more robust, high-trust networks which we believe are essential if less-favoured regions are to become something other than they are today.[2]

Whether we like it or not, less-favoured regions are under pressure to do more for themselves, not least because national governments are less inclined to sanction the transfer payments associated with classical welfarism and because EU Structural Funds will be more narrowly targeted in the years ahead. With the advent of Economic and Monetary Union (which circumscribes the monetary powers of national governments) and EU Enlargement (which dilutes the influence of the Structural Funds), the challenge facing the less-favoured regions seems set to become more daunting than ever before. If it is right and proper that less-favoured regions assume more control over their own affairs, this should not be seen as an opportunity for national governments to divest themselves of responsibility for the fate of their poorer regions. As we show in the following chapters, while the new regional innovation policies have made a promising start, by stimulating a more collaborative approach to problem-solving for example, this needs to be complemented by supportive measures from national governments and the EU, otherwise these 'little victories' can be wiped out. Since we are moving towards a more complex system of multi-level governance in the EU we would do well to remember that the sound principle of subsidiarity recommends *devolving* responsibility, not *shelving* it.

Having explained the motivations behind the book, it is time to outline the structure. The first two chapters offer general overviews. Chapter 1 reviews some recent arguments concerning the socio-spatial dynamics of innovation, including the debate about globalisation and localisation, and addresses the new role which is assigned to the state in this literature, while chapter 2 examines the evolution of regional innovation policy in the EU from the standpoint of the European Commission, where the authors are based.

Chapters 3 to 7 address the experiences of the regions – Wales, Limburg, Lorraine, Castilla y León and Central Macedonia – which were chosen to pilot the Regional Technology Plan, the new generation of regional innovation policies which the European Commission launched in 1994. Each of these chapters' authors have been intimately involved in the RTP process in these regions.

To complement the RTP regions we thought it would be instructive to examine the problems of developing a regional innovation strategy in other contexts, to this end chapter 8 examines the RITTS experience in South Brandenburg, part of the former East Germany, and chapter 9 addresses analogous issues in Central and Eastern Europe more generally. As an antidote to European parochialism we thought it would be useful to include a North American perspective, not least because the state level is frequently more experimental, more innovative than the federal level: therefore chapter 10 reviews the US experience of state-level strategies and chapter 11 examines the case of Quebec in Canada. Finally, chapter 12 seeks to distil some of the wider lessons of the new wave of regional innovation strategies.

NOTES

1. RTP refers to the Regional Technology Plan (a forerunner of RIS, which refers to Regional Innovation Strategies), while RITTS refers to Regional Innovation and Technology Transfer Strategies. For a full account of all these programmes see the European Commission's Practical Guide to Regional Innovation Actions (Brussels, 1997).

2. This argument is elaborated in more detail in Cooke and Morgan (1998).

1 A Regional Perspective on Innovation: From Theory to Strategy

INTRODUCTION

Something unusual is happening when high-ranking politicians take time and trouble to launch a modest regional development programme which brings in very little money and offers no immediate political reward. Yet this is precisely what has happened in Wales (UK), Norte (Portugal), Castilla y León (Spain) and many other regions of the European Union (EU) in recent years. The occasion for these unusual events, with which national politicians were keen to be associated, was the official launch of a new EU policy for lessfavoured regions called the Regional Innovation Strategies (RIS) programme. That these politicians involved themselves was due in large part to the fact that the European Commission had presented the RIS programme as an opportunity for a few regions to act as 'laboratories' for a new generation of regional policy and a chance, perhaps, for them to engage with the future before it arrived. In other words, there was a certain cachet attached to the exercise which compensated for the lack of traditional payoffs.

This might seem like an unconventional, indeed irrelevant, way to introduce a discussion on innovation. Far from being irrelevant, however, these political vignettes capture a major theme of this book – the urgent need to build new and wider constituencies through which to promote innovation. This is a terribly neglected issue and it reflects a much bigger problem, namely, the debilitating gap between theory and practice in the field of innovation, a gap which is particularly wide in less-favoured regions (LFRs), whose firms are often the last to benefit from product, process and organisational innovations. What compounds this situation is the fact that the collective institutions in these regions – regional governments, trade associations, chambers of commerce, labour unions and the like – are very often part of the problem. To the extent that these institutions are implicated in clientistic networks, in which status is privileged over knowledge, power over learning, the past over the present, they are ill-equipped to generate and disseminate new practices. Without strong political support for new innovation networks, there is little or no prospect of countering the conservative cultural routines which lie at the heart of this kind of institutional inertia, and the latter is as much a part of the regional problem as any conventional economic factor.

It is for this reason that we emphasise the inordinate significance of connecting the debate on innovation to the political process so that new interactions can take place between hitherto unconnected parties. The task of orchestrating the framework for interaction is largely the responsibility of politicians and, as we shall see later, this process of orchestration has been likened to a series of intersecting conversations in which the key issues are who talks to whom and what they talk about (Piore 1995). In other words public policy has an enormously important role to play in promoting innovation, but this is a radically different role from what has been practised in most European countries to date.

Programmes like RIS seek to give practical expression to the new theoretical thinking in innovation which has emerged over the past decade. A new and potentially rewarding dialogue is also beginning to emerge at the theoretical level between innovation researchers and economic geographers: roughly, we might say that the former are turning to geography to help to explain uneven patterns of innovation, while the latter are turning to innovation to help to explain uneven patterns of geography. For the most part, though, this convergence of interest has focused on *advanced* regions in the world economy, Southern California, Baden-Württemberg, Emilia-Romagna and the like, regions which are at the frontier with respect to technical and organisational innovation. What we hope is distinctive about this book, however, is that it focuses on the problems and prospects for innovation in the more *peripheral* regions of Europe and North America.

Just as there is no single template which explains the success of 'advanced regions', since each has its own specificity, so it is with LFRs. All too often, however, our mental model of what constitutes innovation is derived from the technological frontier – from activities like R&D, from places like Silicon Valley – even though most regions depend on more prosaic activities. Here we would do well to recall Nathan Rosenberg's excellent critique of the intellectual prejudices which litter the study of innovation. Among other things, he has argued, we confine our thinking about innovations to features which are likely to be true only of major innovations; we tend to focus disproportionately upon discontinuities and neglect continuities in the innovation process; we attach excessive importance to the role of scientific knowledge and insufficient importance to engineering and other 'lower' forms of knowledge; and we tend to privilege the early stages of the innovation process over the crucial later stages. He argued that these prejudices act as an intellectual barrier to a better understanding of innovation and economic development, because

> The factors which influence the productivity of resources in economic activity
> are numerous and prosaic. It is time to recognize that the intellectual division

of labour has given the economist a subject matter in which relatively grubby and pedestrian forms of knowledge play a disconcertingly large role. (Rosenberg 1976, p. 62)

If innovation is understood in the narrow sense, to mean the generation of new technologies or the ability to launch radical product innovations for example, then LFRs are clearly not innovative because they do not have the competence to do such things, indeed this is one of the reasons why they are peripheral regions. However, if innovation is understood in a broader sense, to include new methods of working in the factory, better and more effective networking relationships between firms in the supply chain, more dynamic synergies between public and private sectors and so forth, then it is not at all fanciful to speak of innovation in LFRs (Cooke and Morgan 1998). In the context of the least-developed regions, where firms see themselves and others in atomistic terms and where, consequently, there are low levels of social capital (e.g. norms of trust and reciprocity), the most significant innovation might be to develop voice-based mechanisms through which firms and public agencies can begin to interact locally so as to explore joint solutions to common problems.

At this point it is useful to invoke Albert Hirschman's perceptive, but sadly neglected, analysis of economic development strategy. In contrast to theories which stressed the scarcity of conventional factors, like capital, education and entrepreneurship for example, Hirschman argued that these 'scarce' factors could be reduced to a more fundamental scarcity, namely 'the basic deficiency in organization'. In particular he identified a shortage of 'the *cooperative* component of entrepreneurship', which involved among other things the art of agreement-reaching, conflict resolution and cooperation-enlisting activity. Hirschman's definition of development remains as important today, for both analysis and policy-making, as it was when first it appeared in 1958. Development, he argued, 'depends not so much on finding optimal combinations for given resources and factors of production as on calling forth and enlisting for development purposes resources and abilities that are hidden, scattered, or badly utilized' (Hirschman 1958, p. 5).

The principal advantage of this definition is that it focuses attention on the essential dynamic and strategic aspects of development. So, instead of concentrating exclusively on the husbanding of scarce resources for example, it highlights the need to look for what Hirschman called 'pressures' and 'inducement mechanisms' that might elicit and mobilise these resources for development purposes. Although he was writing about under-developed countries, Hirschman's analysis remains pertinent to the 'innovation deficit' of LFRs in developed countries, especially as regards the emphasis he placed upon agreement-reaching, conflict resolution and cooperation-enlisting activity. This reinforces our earlier point about the importance of the framework for interaction, the formal regulations and informal norms under which public and private agents interact in a more or less mutually beneficial way, a framework shaped largely by the state.

However, there is a much more important sense in which Hirschman is pertinent to the central concerns of this book. Always alive to new opportunities for progress, even in the most unpromising conditions, Hirschman sees human agents not as the powerless victims of structure but, rather like Marx did, as making their own history but not in the circumstances of their own choosing. In other words, agents always have choices, however circumscribed they may be, and this informed his intellectual argument in favour of a perspective which 'places the difficulties of development back where all difficulties of human action begin and belong: in the mind' (Hirschman 1958, p. 11).[1]

The pertinence of this remark was brought home to us during the original launch of the RTP (regional technology plan) programme, when an EU official contrasted the old and new regional policies of the European Commission. If the old regional policy was about opening roads, he said, the new approach was mainly 'about opening minds' (Landabaso 1994). That is to say, traditional regional policy had been about building physical infrastructure, while the new accent is on building social capital – that is, a relational infrastructure for collective action based upon trust, reciprocity and the disposition to collaborate for mutually beneficial ends, the so called 'intangible factors' which are deemed to play such an important role in innovation and economic development today (Doeringer and Terkla 1990; Storper 1995, 1997).

Traditional definitions of innovation make too much of the tangible technical dimensions and too little of the intangible social, organisational and relational dimensions. Thus instead of being conceived as a single act, innovation is now understood as a social process, as we see in more detail in the next section. Furthermore, while the firm is the key institution of innovation, recent theories have stressed the importance of a wide array of other public and private institutions, including networks, in promoting learning and innovation. In other words both the process and the agents of innovation are understood in a much broader sense than hitherto, and this helps to overcome the intellectual prejudices noted earlier.

In the following section we examine the socio-spatial dynamics of innovation, where we argue that firms are not nearly so impervious to geography as the globalisation thesis would have us believe. In the third section we turn our attention to the role of the state as an animateur of the innovation process, and argue that traditional conceptions of the state fail to appreciate the devolved and interactive governance structures which are nowadays required to promote self-organised learning networks among firms, their associations and public agencies.

THE SOCIO-SPATIAL DYNAMICS OF INNOVATION[2]

The spatial dimension of innovation has received so little attention in the conventional economics literature that one could be forgiven for thinking that the process occurs on the head of a pin! With the advent of evolutionary political economy, however, this under-socialised, spaceless conception is being replaced by a richer, more realistic conception in which innovation is conceived as a socially embedded and spatially structured process (Lundvall 1992; Dosi *et al.* 1994; Cooke and Morgan 1994). The microeconomic foundations of the evolutionary approach are based on a theoretical critique of the neoclassical conception of the firm. The standard neoclassical theory has three key attributes: first, it assumes rational, maximising behaviour by agents with given and stable preferences; second, it focuses on equilibrium states; and third, it severely underestimates chronic information problems on the part of economic agents (Hodgson 1996).

From the evolutionary standpoint, the key assumptions of neoclassical theory are not merely unhelpful; they are positively dangerous if used as a guide to the way in which firms behave in the real world. To assume, for example, that firms possess near-perfect information, that they are objectively rational and that they optimise their utility means that neoclassical theory credits firms with a capacity for action which is as staggering as it is unrealistic. What this means is that neoclassical theory takes as resolved some of the largest questions in innovation and economic development, like how firms come to know what they know – that is, how they learn.

The contractual theory of the firm attempts to overcome some of the weaknesses of the standard neoclassical conception by relaxing some (but not all) of the more heroic behavioural assumptions (Williamson 1985). Like evolutionary theory, the contractual approach is partly predicated on the notion of bounded rationality, which accepts that there are limits to what agents can know. While the contractual approach opens up some interesting questions about alternative economic governance structures – principally between markets and hierarchies – it sees the firm as nothing more than a vehicle for reducing transaction costs under the assumption that inputs, outputs and technology are given. Hence one of the key weaknesses of the contractual approach is that dynamic evolution, learning and innovation are virtually ruled out in favour of an exercise in comparative statics (Foss 1993).

To appreciate the firm as a dynamic institution we must turn to theories which put learning, knowledge-creation and innovation at the centre of the analysis, which is precisely what evolutionary theories seek to do. As one of the pioneers of the evolutionary approach argues, understanding 'the ongoing, interrelated process of *change* in technology and organization is the central intellectual problem to be confronted by a theory of the firm' (Winter 1988). In evolutionary terms the firm is understood first and foremost as a repository of productive knowledge, a vehicle for continuous learning and knowledge-creation. Building on the notion of bounded rationality, the evolutionary approach stresses 'the inevitability of mistaken decisions in an uncertain world' (Winter 1988).

In standard neoclassical theory all agents are assumed to be equally capable of optimising because economic competence is assumed to be relatively abundant, when in fact it is scarce and uneven as between individuals and firms (Pelikan 1988). Evolutionary theory, on the other hand, is fully alive to the fact that there are significant variations in firms' knowledge bases and major differences in their capacity for creating knowledge from within and absorbing it from without. The uneven distribution of economic competence, which is firm-specific and partly tacit, helps to explain the wide variations in corporate performance and why apparently superior organisational forms diffuse slowly, if at all, within and between sectors, regions and countries. In other words, all capitalist firms share the same profit-seeking goals, but what differentiates them – in terms of competence, learning capacity, organisation, technology and culture – seems so much more striking (Nelson 1991; Coriat and Dosi 1994; Cooke and Morgan 1998).

With the accelerating pace of technological and institutional change it is perhaps no coincidence that economists and other social scientists are now suggesting that knowledge is the most important resource and learning the most important process (Lundvall 1994). Learning depends in no small way on *absorptive capacity*, which suggests that a firm's ability to recognise, assimilate and exploit knowledge, from within and without, is largely a function of the level of its prior knowledge (Cohen and Levinthal 1990). The concept of absorptive capacity refers to much more than technical skills; among other things it highlights the importance of a shared cognitive framework within the firm and the ability to transfer knowledge across functions throughout the firm. This concept also highlights the significance of *organizational* learning, which is more than the sum of individual learning.

The literature on 'learning organisations' frequently makes the distinction between first-order learning, which refers to the refinement of existing practices or doing things better, and second-order learning, which refers to the production of novel practices or doing better things (Nooteboom 1996). While first-order learning can be achieved through better use of codified (tradable) knowledge, second-order learning is more difficult for firms because novelty involves a greater element of tacit knowledge, which means 'we can know more than we can tell' (Polanyi 1966). Because tacit knowledge is personal and context-dependent, it is difficult if not impossible to communicate other than through personal interaction in a context of shared experiences. The ability to share knowledge is a key aspect of organisational learning and, as we argue later, this requires a good deal of trust among the participants.

The key point to emerge from this 'detour' into evolutionary theory is that knowledge is the most important resource in innovation and learning is the most important process, an interactive and socially embedded process which cannot be understood outside its cultural and institutional context. This helps us to understand why the linear model of innovation – which presented the innovation process as a series of sequential steps from basic research at one end to sales at the other – has proved to be such a fatally flawed model and why it has been supplanted by the interactive model. The two main flaws in the linear model are, first, that it fails to appreciate the need for continuous interaction and feedback and, second, that it invokes a spurious hierarchy of knowledge, in which pure science is king. Critics of the linear model have convincingly demonstrated that the primary sources of innovation often originate further downstream, including from blue-collar workers, without any initial dependence upon, or stimulus from, frontier scientific research (Aoki and Rosenberg 1987).

The interactive character of the innovation process suggests that, to be effective, firms, regions and countries need to develop organisational structures which promote continuous interaction and feedback. In particular, the interactive model 'underscores the importance of *cooperation* between firms and institutions and, thus, the role played by links and networks involving different organizations' (OECD 1992).

If the significance of interaction and feedback is now generally accepted in the innovation literature, what can we say about the spatial implications? With the advent of information and communication technologies (ICTs), which offer firms unprecedented opportunities to reduce the tyranny of distance, some writers have gone so far as to proclaim the death of geography because 'the digital planet will look and feel like the head of a pin' (Negroponte 1995).

We want to challenge this view by arguing that the death of geography has been greatly exaggerated. Indeed, there may be grounds for thinking that the regional dimension is becoming more, rather than less, important for our understanding of innovation and development. Contrary to fashionable notions about 'techno-globalism', the technological activities of large firms remain overwhelmingly biased towards their home countries. For example, a study of patenting data for the world's largest firms found that 89 per cent of their technological activities were performed in their home country in the second half of the 1980s, and this was construed as 'an important case of non-globalization' (Patel and Pavitt 1991). The fact that R&D and other innovation-related activities are so spatially concentrated, often in advanced regional agglomerations, suggests that there is something 'sticky' about these activities, something which sets a premium on physical, rather than virtual, proximity. The 'stickiness' comes from the fact that 'physical proximity facilitates the integration of multi-disciplinary knowledge that is tacit and therefore "person-embodied" rather than "information-embodied" and it also facilitates the rapid decision-making needed to cope with uncertainty' (Patel and Pavitt 1991).

In theoretical terms we might say that the greater the complexity, uncertainty and tacitness of transactions, the more sensitive they are to spatial distance, and the higher the premium attached to physical proximity (Storper and Scott 1995; Maskell *et al.* 1998). This theoretical point has been endorsed at the practical level by a senior technologist at Ford, who argued that 'the quality of face-to-face interaction is higher than the electronic variety, even between people who know each other well' (Lorenz 1995). In other words, if ICTs have alleviated the tyranny of distance with respect to standardised transactions, based on codified knowledge, they do not seem to have undermined the need for physical proximity when novelty, tacit knowledge and learning are involved.

If physical proximity was once valued as a means for reducing costs, today it is valued as a means for enhancing learning capacity; in a world where product life cycles are being rapidly abbreviated, the codification of existing knowledge is forever being tempered by the growth of new knowledge, and the latter always has a strong tacit dimension. Economic geographers are turning in this direction to explain the resurgence of technologically dynamic regional agglomerations. One of the first to do so was the American geographer Michael Storper, who argues that there is an important association between social learning and spatial agglomeration, which has two roots. The first and more limited case concerns localised input–output relations, or traded interdependencies, which constitute webs of user–producer relations essential to information exchange. The second and more general case concerns the role of *untraded* interdependencies (like labour markets, public institutions, norms of trust and reciprocity) which mediate the process of economic and organisational learning. As Storper argues:

> Where these input–output relations or untraded interdependencies are localized, and this is quite frequent in cases of technological or organizational dynamism, then we can say that the region is a key, necessary element in the 'supply architecture' for learning and innovation. It can now be seen that theoretical predictions that globalization means the end to economies of proximity have been exaggerated by many analysts because they have deduced them only from input–output analysis. (Storper 1995)

Storper's argument that regions (or, more accurately, core regions) occupy a pivotal role in the 'supply architecture' of the learning economy may seem provocative to the globalist school of thinking, which tends to the view that global forces, especially multinationals, are somehow impervious to spatial considerations. But we are beginning to appreciate that globalisation and localisation, far from being mutually exclusive processes, are actually much more interwoven than is generally recognised because foreign direct investment is often attracted to, and has a reinforcing effect upon, innovative clusters in the targeted country (de Vet 1993; Cantwell 1995).

If untraded interdependencies help to explain the resurgence of dynamic regional agglomerations, how do we explain the decline and fall of these agglomerations? Part of the answer lies in the concept of *lock-in*, which highlights the weakness of strong ties. That is to say, the networks which bind the agglomeration can inadvertently undermine it if they become ignorant of and impervious to more innovative trends elsewhere in the world, which is what happened to the coal and steel complex in the Ruhrgebiet, the minicomputer sector in Greater Boston, the mechanical watch industry in the Swiss Jura and, to a lesser extent, to the automotive cluster in Baden-Württemberg (Glasmeier 1991; Grabher 1992; Morgan 1994).

It is not difficult to accept that dynamic regional agglomerations enjoy strong untraded interdependencies, that their core 'upstream' activities, being sensitive to pockets of tacit knowledge, are not as spatially mobile as the less strategic 'downstream' activities which abound in other, more peripheral regions. What the conventional literature on innovation finds more difficult to accept, however, is that firms might be able to learn more than they often imagine from their 'downstream' activities, like branch-plants, most of which are located in less-favoured regions. But, as Erica Schoenberger reminds us, learning and knowledge-acquisition flow in more than one direction, hence they should not be seen as flowing merely from centre to periphery, from top to bottom, even if this is the dominant direction. In a series of corporate case studies she shows that large firms were imperilled by failing to appreciate that local innovations in their far-flung branches carried important lessons for the firm as a whole (Schoenberger 1994). To the extent that branch-plants are allowed to experiment within the factory, to interact with sophisticated users and to embed themselves in their regional milieu then, under these circumstances, they may be important learning laboratories for the firm as a whole. In other words, learning is not confined to the 'upstream' activities of the firm – research, design and development etc. – rather it is something that occurs, as the interactive model suggests, at all levels of the firm (Cooke and Morgan 1998).

The notion that multinationals can learn from their branch-plants in less favoured regions is slowly being appreciated, even if headquarters managers and scholars have been equally reluctant to acknowledge the fact. Perhaps the best illustration of this phenomenon – of what we might call reverse learning – comes from the German auto industry. Slow to adjust to the new paradigm of lean production at home, because of a combination of corporate inertia, labour market regulations and strong unions, the German auto firms are trying to make up for lost time by using their foreign branch-plants as learning laboratories for new methods of production which they hope, at a later stage, to import back into their core plants in Germany. One of the most conspicuous examples of reverse learning is VW's new Brazilian plant at Resende, 150 kilometres from Rio de Janeiro, where VW is experimenting with a radical version of modular production in which the plant is jointly managed by VW and its core suppliers, all of whom produce their components on site. Similarly, Daimler-Benz has entered an alliance with the Swiss watchmaking group SMH to produce the Smart minicar at Hambach in eastern France. This joint venture, known as Micro Compact Car (MCC), is said to be the most revolutionary experiment ever undertaken in modular production, not least because MCC and its on-site suppliers, dubbed 'system partners' to signal the co-makership philosophy, have abolished all distinctions between their respective employees in the 'Smart Ville' complex. Less dramatic forms of reverse learning are underway at Daimler's new US auto plant in Alabama, which has been designated a 'centre of competence' for the group as a whole (Morgan 1994; Simonian 1997).

The German auto firms are learning a number of things from these foreign experiences, like how to become a low-cost–high-quality producer; how to involve suppliers in a collaborative approach to design, development, procurement and assembly; how to become a system integrator in an era of modular production; and how to organize more flexible, team-based work systems, etc. In all these cases the firms are engaged in what we earlier referred to as second-order learning – that is, producing novel practices – and they are doing so *not* in their core plants at home, as we might expect from product life cycle theory but, rather, in branch-plants located in the less-favoured regions of foreign countries.

We emphasise these experiments to highlight two points: first, that learning and innovation can occur in prosaic 'downstream' activities and, second, that learning and innovation can occur in the lowly context of less-favoured regions. However, we now need to make a distinction between development *in* a region and development *of* a region, because otherwise we run the risk of assuming that (corporate) growth is always synonymous with (regional) development (Morgan and Sayer 1988). Multinationals like VW and Daimler have the scale, the resources and the power to get preferential treatment in their less-favoured regional locations. In addition to handsome state subsidies, they get the pick of the labour market along with a wide array of customised services from regional authorities which are prepared to move heaven and earth to ensure that these flagship firms get what they want, when they want it. Unencumbered by the constraints in their brownfield plants at home – traditional employee habits, unions, public regulations and the like – it is not surprising that foreign greenfield plants offer new learning opportunities or that they often deliver better results than their brownfield sister plants. However, unless the benefits ripple through to the wider regional economy – through the firm's engagement with local suppliers, training schools and technology transfer agencies for example – these flagship plants can easily become isolated islands of innovation in a sea of mediocrity, which is precisely what we mean by development in, rather than of, a region.

If LFRs are to contain more than just islands of innovation, and if they are to develop a more widespread capacity for innovation, then they will have to address the structural weaknesses of their regional economies as internal linkages in these regions – between firms in the same sector, between firms and the enterprise support system and between the public and private sectors – are either weak or non-existent. This in turn betrays a lack of social capital, that is the norms of trust and reciprocity which lubricate dynamic networks of collective action. Drawing on our earlier discussion, we might say that, in these circumstances, the lack of institutional innovation is perhaps the most important deficit; if so, what these regions need to do in the first instance is to create agreement-reaching and cooperation-enlisting mechanisms to promote the growth of more innovative linkages, more dynamic networks and more robust forms of voice.

It is not that LFRs lack networks *per se*, what they lack is dynamic networks which facilitate learning and innovation rather than networks which reflect and protect the *status quo* and thereby foreclose the possibilities for change and development. This highlights one of the problems with Putnam's use of the concept of social capital, which is that he assumes too readily that the capacity to engage in collective action is always commendable and always beneficial for political democracy, civil society and economic development (Putnam 1993). But certain forms of collective action – like the Mafia in Southern Italy, ETA in the Basque Country or the IRA in Northern Ireland for example – can have noxious effects which actually retard political and economic progress. In other words we have to make a distinction between social and unsocial capital, between networks which promote development, be it political or economic, and networks which manifestly do not (Levi 1996).

If this argument is correct it means that regional policy needs to treat intangible assets like social capital every bit as seriously as it treats tangible assets like physical investment. In practical terms this would involve creating a better framework for interaction in the LFRs, a framework in which firms, associations and cognate public agencies are encouraged to explore joint solutions to common problems and, where a dialogue has been established, to develop a more receptive attitude to information exchange and interactive learning – the building blocks of a commonly agreed strategy for regional development. This brings us to the role of the state as an animateur of innovation and regional development.

RETHINKING PUBLIC POLICY: THE STATE AS ANIMATEUR

As a bald generalisation we could say that the state is gradually being rehabilitated as a necessary and legitimate agent in economic development, after a period when it was denigrated, especially in the UK and the US, as a 'dead hand' on social and economic progress. That the state has a positive role to play in promoting innovation and economic development was recently affirmed by no less an institution than the World Bank, which in the past has been criticised for extolling the market over the state and for downplaying the institutional architecture of market-based economies. In its 1997 report, however, the Bank has finally come to terms with the fact that 'state capability' is a vitally important complement to effective markets; its president, James Wolfensohn, has gone so far as to say that the state must be 'a partner, catalyst and facilitator of economic development' (World Bank 1997). This new departure is part of a more general reassessment of the role of the state at both national and regional levels in OECD countries.

This reassessment has been fuelled by a growing disenchantment with the two dominant traditions of the state: the dirigiste tradition, which embodies a naive and exaggerated faith in the capacity of the state as an independent actor, and the neoliberal tradition, which seeks to substitute the market for the state wherever possible. As opposed as they seem in principle, these two traditions are paradoxically at one in regarding the *scale* of state intervention as the key issue, an index which tells us nothing about the efficacy of the state's interventions. An alternative conception of the state is beginning to emerge – the associational conception – in which the key issue is not the scale of intervention but its mode, not the boundary between state and market but the framework for effective interaction (Sabel 1994; Cooke and Morgan 1998). In this conception one of the key developmental tasks of the state is to create the conditions – the formal framework as well as the informal norms of trust and reciprocity that constitute social capital – in which firms, associations and public agencies can engage in a self-organised process of interactive learning. This is easier said than done of course, not least because it involves two institutional innovations which centralised political systems may be reluctant to sanction.

First, it involves the devolution of power within the state system from remote central ministries to local and regional tiers which are better placed to forge durable and interactive relations with firms and their business associations. Just as large firms are devolving authority to enable local business units to learn from and respond more rapidly to changing customer requirements, so the state needs to do likewise. Herein lies the significance of the principle of subsidiarity, which recommends the devolution of decision-making to the lowest competent level, a principle which promises more accountable and more effective governance.

Second, it may also involve delegating certain tasks, like enterprise support services for example, to accredited business associations because the latter have assets, like knowledge of and credibility with their members, which the state needs to harness to ensure the effectiveness of its enterprise support policies. The point to emphasise here is that a state which withdraws from direct provision to indirect animation need not be a weak or ineffective state; on the contrary, if its goals are more effectively met through regulated delegation then it can actually become stronger by doing less and enabling more.

If the state is expected to adapt to, and learn from, a rapidly changing environment it needs to function less like a machine and more like an open system. In other words it needs to be more responsive to the nuances of its environment, more interactive with its partners and more sensitive to feedback from the users of its services. Moreover, since the environment is regionally differentiated, public agencies need to be empowered to act on their unrivalled local knowledge (Murray 1991, 1992).

Devolving power to regional tiers of the state creates the opportunity for more meaningful discussions to take place within the regional arena and this is important because 'discussion is precisely the process by which parties come to reinterpret themselves and their relation to each other by elaborating a common understanding of the world' (Sabel 1994). In some ways this is a modern restatement of Hirschman's plea that voice be treated as seriously as exit in social, political and economic life (Hirschman 1970). This theme has been further elaborated in the hermeneutic perspective developed by Michael Piore, which contains two key ideas. First, he argues that political and economic processes are like 'conversations' whose evolution is governed by who talks to whom and what they talk about:

> The role of public policy and political leadership is to orchestrate those conversations, initiating discussions among previously isolated groups, guiding them through disagreements and misunderstandings that might otherwise lead conversation to break off, introducing new topics for discussion and debate. (Piore 1995)

The second idea concerns the significance of the narrative, a story which interprets a sequence of events, where the meaning is generated by the way certain events are accented in the telling:

> No single person can control a narrative; the stories that grab our attention are told too often by too many people. It is this constant repetition on all sides, in fact, that gives them their power... But a leader is a most prominent narrator. He or she gets to talk first, to tell the story most often, and it is the leader's voice that is heard above all others and by the most people. This makes the narrative the most powerful instrument in the direction of a hermeneutic process, the most selective political instrument in contemporary economic and political life. (Piore 1995)

This hermeneutic perspective helps us to understand that power lies not just in the ability to deploy material resources – like capital investment for example – but also in the capacity to influence who talks to whom, what they talk about and what meaning they attach to these conversations. Politicians have much more control over these immaterial sources of power and, in practical everyday life, they can accent what experiences are deemed to be salient in a whole series of ways, including the audiences to whom they speak, the individuals with whom they choose to associate, the events they commemorate, the firms they visit and the public programmes they use as exemplars. Through these seemingly prosaic activities political leaders are able to confer value at little or no cost to the public purse and this is one way to create what Piore calls 'communities of meaning'. These communities are not created through the mere aggregation of individuals, as in classical liberalism, but via a process of interaction in which individuals realise themselves through the community, in the tradition of civic republicanism.

Without devolved regional governance structures there is no political agent at the regional level to orchestrate these 'conversations', between the public and private sectors and between firms within the private sector for example.

In the absence of regional government this role could be performed by regional development agencies, chambers of commerce or even a large hegemonic firm, but none of these agents commands the political legitimacy or the moral authority of a democratically elected regional government. While the latter is not a panacea, regional government is an important ingredient in the recipe for regional development to the extent that it is able to help others to help themselves by animating communities of meaning, by building capacities for action and by crafting networks through which agents are able to collaborate for mutually beneficial ends. In other words it is not regional government *per se* that is important but *competent* regional government which appreciates the significance of enabling and orchestration.

The issue of political competence at the regional level is set to become a more important issue as more and more economic development responsibilities, such as enterprise support, innovation policy, education and training and the like, are devolved from central to regional tiers. The regional level is now perceived as an important arena in which to design and deliver policies to foster innovation. For example, in its Green Paper on innovation the European Commission says:

> The local or regional level is in fact the best level for contacting enterprises and providing them with the necessary support for the external skills they need (resources in terms of manpower, technology, management and finance). It is also the basic level at which there is a natural solidarity and where relations are easily forged. It is therefore the level at which small enterprises can be encouraged and helped to pool their strengths in partnerships in order to compete with bigger enterprises with greater resources or to make the most of the opportunities which these enterprises can offer. These issues are of special importance in the less favoured regions. (European Commission 1995)

While we concur with the main thrust of this argument we cannot accept the Commission's view that there is a 'natural solidarity' at the regional level or that 'relations are easily forged' there. The problem with this view is that it naively assumes that spatial proximity is a sufficient condition for forging collaborative networks, when all the evidence suggests that these have to be actively constructed (and sustained) through conscious and painstaking efforts on the part of firms and public agencies (Cooke and Morgan 1998).

That said, the regional level would seem to possess two potential assets which make it a suitable level at which to engage in the kind of support recommended by the Commission. First, it is able to act on local knowledge, part of which is tacit, concerning the calibre of firms, the formal and informal linkages between these firms, the quality of the labour force and the capacity of the institutions which are responsible for providing technical, commercial and training services. Second, the regional level is quite possibly the most appropriate level at which to build social capital because this is the level at which regular face-to-face interactions, one of the (necessary) conditions for

trust-building, can be sustained over time. The literature on trust and cooperation suggests that these are more likely to occur where there is a strong
possibility that the agents will meet again, in other words where the shadow
of the future looms large over the present (Axelrod 1984; Luhman 1979).

What needs to be emphasised, however, is that these two assets – local
knowledge and social capital – are *potential* assets which need to be mobilised
through conscious political action because, contrary to what the European
Commission seems to assume, they do not exist in some primordial form at
the regional level.

These assets need to be mobilised and exploited if public agencies are to
develop more effective enterprise support systems in LFRs. At the moment
these systems betray a number of weaknesses, the most important being that
some 80 per cent of SMEs are unable or unwilling to take advantage of these
support services (European Commission 1995). Low service take-up is not
unrelated to the fact that most services are delivered in a crude supply-side
fashion by an enterprise support industry that finds it easier to offer a standard
menu of services which has been designed for rather than with local firms. In
some cases the priorities of regional service providers are radically at odds with
the priorities of the firms in the region, a fatal mismatch which suggests that
the former are more interested in reproducing themselves than in providing a
service to SMEs in their region (Dankbaar and Cobbenhagen 1998).

We need to recognise that high-quality services are neither simply demand-
led nor supply-driven; rather, they are the product of constant interaction
between supply and demand, a process of interactive learning in which providers
receive regular feedback from users on the utility of the service (OECD 1993).
Once again, this is easier said than done. Even in the most celebrated service
centres – like the Steinbeis Stiftung in Baden-Württemberg and Citer in
Emilia-Romagna – we know too little about the real impact of their services.
If the truth be told, most state-sponsored service providers are reluctant to
sanction a genuinely independent evaluation of their activities and this makes it
much more difficult to enhance the quality of service provision (Morgan 1996).

The problems of supply-side bias and standard service menus reflect the
fact that enterprise support agencies in LFRs often lack the skills to engage in
interactive service provision, and this is perhaps the main reason why these
agencies have a credibility problem *vis-à-vis* the private sector. To overcome
this problem these public agencies will have to acquire more intimate knowledge of their key sectors, which implies the flexibility to recruit from the
business community. The challenge of interactive service provision, in which
the aim is to design services *with* rather than *for* corporate clients so as to
enhance the latter's absorptive capacity, cannot be met through traditional
supply-side regional policy; that is to say, technology centres and the like are
not likely to resolve the innovation deficit in LFR-based firms if the latter are
unable to exploit these services – the 'cathedrals in the desert' syndrome.
Hence one of the most important tasks in LFRs is to stimulate 'conversations'

between providers and users to ensure that enterprise support services are driven by the requirements of local firms rather than the administrative needs of the delivery agencies.

Many of the tasks we have identified thus far – like interactive service provision, communities of meaning, capacities for action and cooperation networks – can be addressed by regional agents within the LFRs. But it would be wrong and unjust to suppose that these regions have the capacity to regenerate themselves entirely through their own efforts. If LFRs are to be transformed into something other than what they are today, if they are to develop a more robust endogenous capacity for innovation and development in other words, this can be achieved only through more concerted action on the part of a multi-level governance system, which in Europe means the European Commission, the member states and the regions themselves.

Although the Commission had a regional policy budget of 170 billion ECU for the period 1994–99, this was equivalent to just 0.45 per cent of GDP in the EU, an extremely modest sum relative to the scale of the problems in the LFRs, a situation which will be exacerbated with the enlargement of the Union. What compounds the problem is the fact that the Commission is charged with promoting competition as well as cohesion, and the former goal leads it, often inadvertently, into actions which make the latter goal more difficult. Perhaps the best example of this dual vocation is the way the Commission allocates its Framework Programmes for research and technological development (RTD) with little or no reference to the needs of LFRs. This RTD budget is allocated to 'centres of excellence', most of which are to be found in the most prosperous core regions of the EU. Indeed, some 50 per cent of all RTD funds is concentrated in just twelve 'islands of innovation', the so-called 'Archipelago Europe', running from London to Milan and embracing Amsterdam–Rotterdam, the Île de France, the Ruhr, Frankfurt, Stuttgart, Munich, Lyon–Grenoble and Turin (European Commission 1996). If LFRs are to be better equipped to meet the challenge of innovation then the Fifth Framework Programme, which begins in 1999, should ensure that these RTD resources are not so spatially skewed to the core regions of 'Archipelago Europe'.

As for the member states, the Commission concedes frankly that 'solidarity in the Union begins at home', a reference to the continuing significance of national action in achieving spatial cohesion (Euopean Commission 1996). It also admits that national action is the most important instrument for promoting innovation, not least because the Fourth Framework Programme accounts for just 4 per cent of publicly funded RTD in the EU. This underlines the significance of the nation-state as an actor in social and economic renewal, a point often lost on over-zealous regionalists and supra-nationalists alike.

In other words the burden of promoting innovation and development in the LFRs should not be borne entirely by the regions themselves, otherwise the task will quite simply overwhelm them. We need to recognise the limits of unilateral action at any one spatial scale, be it regional, national or supra-national, because each has an important role to play and each is dependent, albeit in different ways, on the competence and resources of the others. This point is sometimes obfuscated by the more radical proponents of a 'Europe of the Regions', who seek to privilege the regional scale over all others. In contrast to such regional unilateralism, in which the threats outweigh the opportuni-ties for LFRs, we contend that there is no viable substitute to strategies based on a multi-level governance approach, and other authors have recognised this too (Jeffery 1996).

But if this approach is to pay dividends the most powerful agents – like the European Commission and the member states – need to appreciate that they can accomplish little without the active cooperation and involvement of their regional partners. As for the LFRs there is something tragi-comical about the servile stance they adopt with the European Commission, which they look upon with awe and assume, wrongly, that it holds the key to unlocking a more prosperous future. The truth is a good deal more prosaic: the Commission is only as powerful, and only as effective, as the regional partner with whom it is working and on whom it depends for a whole series of things, including local knowledge, reliable information, political commitment, competent administration and a capacity to forge networks of engagement within the region. In other words, robust multi-level partnerships are predicated on each level recognising and respecting the distinctive competences of the others. Sadly, however, the partnership arrangements in many LFRs leave much to be desired, so much so that the Regional Policy Commissioner was forced to say that 'the Commission is not and cannot be satisfied with the present situation' (Wulf-Mathies 1995).

These partnership arrangements – formalised in the monitoring committees in each LFR – need to be reformed to render them more inclusive, more demo-cratic and a good deal more innovative. With the advent of new-style regional policies – like RTP, RIS, RITTS and RISI – a radically different set of skills and expertise will be needed because innovation-related projects are as differ-ent from road-building projects as chalk is from cheese. In other words, the monitoring committees, schooled in the old regional policy, need to be refash-ioned to enable their regions to exploit the potential of the new regional policy.

To be effective, the new innovation-oriented regional policies require more robust multi-level partnerships within the LFRs, in which the regional actors are genuinely empowered to develop bottom-up initiatives that draw on their local knowledge, and these need to be prosecuted alongside more supportive top-down measures from the 'higher' levels of the member states and the Commission. Even where they work well, however, innovation-oriented poli-cies can never be more than an important ingredient in the recipe for regional development in the LFRs, and they are certainly not the recipe itself (Davies and Morgan 1998). This needs to be emphasised because job creation, one of the most urgent priorities in LFRs, is not necessarily one of the benefits of innovation. Indeed, if product innovation tends to be job-enhancing, process innovation is often job-displacing.

What this means is that the new innovation-oriented regional policies need to be flanked by, and complemented with, job-creating regional policies because, whatever its causes, unemployment remains the single most debilitating social problem in the LFRs. It is irresponsible nonsense to pretend that these two forms of regional policy are mutually exclusive: the stark reality is that LFRs need to be more cohesive *and* more innovative.

NOTES

1. This is not to endorse the crude voluntarism which characterises the neoliberal approach to development, like the notion that 'thinking makes it so' etc. The point Hirschman is trying to make here is that 'mental maps' are themselves an ingredient in the development process; for example, the sense that change and progress is both possible and desirable constitutes a potentially dynamic force.

2. The arguments here draw upon Cooke and Morgan (1998).

2 Developing Regional Innovation Strategies: The European Commission as Animateur

INTRODUCTION

During the last decade European policy-makers have acknowledged increasingly the need to improve the interaction between the demand and supply sides of the innovation process at regional level. From an early emphasis on supply-push policies based on the creation of new technological resources, the policy focus has gradually shifted to technology dissemination mechanisms and finally to means of galvanising 'non-innovative' firms to recognise and respond to their needs. The former were developed mainly through policies of the science and technology type, which were more concerned with the strengthening of the science base and the provision of research inputs, while the latter have been formulated recently within the realm of regional and industrial policies, and has been more concerned with economics-related issues dealing with the innovative capacity of firms and the diffusion of technology through technology transfer networks.

In the case of regional policy, the Commission has emphasised the significant contribution to economic development made by research and technology development (RTD) initiatives. However, the Structural Funds

> do not intervene in favour of RTD for its own sake, but as one important means of promoting economic development, higher productivity and competitiveness and thereby narrowing existing disparities ... funding for RTD related actions will have to demonstrate that the economic development impact in the regions is in keeping with the resources deployed. (European Commission 1993)

In addition, it has been recognised that the effectiveness of Structural Fund interventions aimed at technological innovation depends on the quality of the partnership between public authorities, the principal innovation support organisations and local firms. Indeed, technology cannot be expected to assist in resolving the problems of competitiveness unless it functions as part of a system which is institutionally and organisationally capable of adapting to changing demands on a continuous basis. (Landabaso, 1993)

It is precisely this issue of the development of an adequate level of 'social capital'[1] in the less-favoured regions, to complement the massive investments in infrastructure by the Structural Funds, that the Regional Innovation Strategy (RIS) approach funded under Article 10 of the ERDF (European Regional Development Fund) is intended to tackle.

The ERDF allocation to all Article 10 actions is only some 400 million ECU during 1995–99, or less than 0.6 per cent of the total ERDF funding of 70 billion ECU placed at the disposal of the member states for the period 1994–99. In contrast to the standard ERDF interventions (via programmes in the Objective regions of the EU or through the Community initiatives), Article 10 supports actions 'aimed mainly at exploring new approaches to economic and social development that encourage greater co-operation and the exchange of experience between actors in local and regional developments'. The article's distinctiveness is reinforced by the fact that the innovative actions are implemented through ERDF project financing *selected by the European Commission* (with the help of external independent experts). They are also managed very differently from the mainstream Structural Funds actions, which are run through operational programmes, not projects, and normally negotiated with the central administrations of the member states, rather than directly with the regional actors benefiting from them and/or responsible for their implementation.

The pilot projects funded under Article 10 of the ERDF have three key features:

- They are based on public–private partnership (the private sector and the key regional players should be closely associated in the formulation and implementation of pilot projects).

- They should have a demonstration character (the policy actions tested in a region should be amenable to being duplicated in other parts of the Union).

- They should exploit the European dimension through inter-regional cooperation networks across Europe (in order to avoid reinventing the wheel and efficiently diffuse the lessons learnt).

Thus, Article 10 provides a laboratory for developing new and improved management methods and forms of actions which may, at a later stage, be adopted in the more traditional programmes. In terms of the innovation promotion pilot actions (Regional Innovation Strategy and Regional Technology Transfer (RTT) projects), two general objectives can be discerned:

- on the one hand, to redefine the policy framework and instruments for supporting innovation-led economic development in less-favoured regions through, in particular, a greater emphasis on an a priori assessment of the needs of firms;

- on the other, a more 'implicit' aim, to initiate a learning process with respect to policy formulation at the regional level through the building of a consensus among all relevant actors on the types of mechanisms and measures required.

Although the thinking underlying the development of RIS began as far back as 1991, the approach fostered by the European Commission has been given a political impulse and legitimacy by main policy documents since 1994. First, the RIS are an attempt to give a practical content to the White Paper on 'Growth, Competitiveness and Employment', namely:

> ... stimulating the development of 'clusters' of competitive activities that draw on the regional diversity of the Community. The proliferation within the Community of 'clusters' that combine industrial, technological and geographical advantages may hold one of the keys to job creation. This requires the active involvement of all the actors concerned, something which can be greatly facilitated by structural measures taken at Community and national level. In this area, as in the preceding ones, the main emphasis should be on a horizontal, transectoral and multidisciplinary approach ... (European Commission 1992, p. 79)

> ... Steps must be taken to allow better application of the results of the research carried out in the Community, i.e. the establishment of operational mechanisms at national and European level for the transfer of technologies from university laboratories to companies, from one company to another ... One key aspect must be substantially to step up measures to improve the business environment, in the form of scientific and technical information, financial services, aid to protect innovations, training in new technologies, etc. (European Commission 1992, p. 103)

Second, an RIS translates into practice the proposals made in the 1993 Commission 'Communication on Cohesion and RTD Policy' namely:

> The Commission is therefore willing to provide technical assistance through the Structural Funds for developing regional research and technological development strategies in the context of the preparation of the next round of CSFs in partnership with the Member States ... (European Commission 1993, p. 11)

Third, the RIS can be regarded as a response to the suggestions to the Commission made by the Regional Policy Committee of the European Parliament about 'increasing awareness in SMEs [small and medium sized enterprises] from LFRs [less-favoured regions] about RTD [research and technological development] activities' (European Parliament 1995).

Finally, in 1995 the Green Paper on Innovation, in its twelfth action line to 'encourage innovation in enterprises, specially SMEs, and strengthen the regional dimension of innovation', clearly supported an action at Community level through

> developing support for regional innovation strategies and inter-regional technology transfer (joint action involving regional policies – Article 10 of the ERDF – and the innovation programme)... [recognising that] The local or regional level is in fact the best level for contacting enterprises and providing them with the necessary support for the external skills they need ... It is also the basic level at which there is natural solidarity and where relations are forged ... (European Commission 1995, p. 57)

In short:

- An RIS seeks to promote a new participative approach to policy-making with a particular view to enhancing networks of formal and informal relations among the key stakeholders in a regional economy.

- It should develop policy instruments or mechanisms for promoting innovation suited to the needs of SMEs (hence not solely technological innovation) rather than the development of a regional RTD infrastructure.

- An RIS also recognises that in the framework of subsidiarity, the regional level is the most appropriate for developing and delivering services to enterprises with a view to increasing the level of competitivity of the region in a global economy.

The rest of this chapter is in four sections:

- The first discusses briefly the theoretical underpinnings which to a greater or lesser extent have influenced the thinking behind the development of the regional innovation strategies action of the European Commission.

- The second provides a summary of the operational reasons which have influenced the decision of the Commission to fund and support pilot actions aimed at producing a more strategic and enterprise-oriented regional innovation policy.

- The third describes the development of the RIS type approach at European level since 1991 and describes the key methodological principles of the current pilot actions funded under Article 10 of the European Regional Development Fund (ERDF).

- In the fourth and final section, a series of building blocks towards a new regional policy better suited to the needs of the 'knowledge economy' are suggested.

FROM THEORY TO PRACTICE: WHY A REGIONAL INNOVATION STRATEGY?

Competitive advantage, innovative environments, industrial districts, clusters, innovation systems, networking – the last decade has seen these and other theoretical concepts appropriated by policy-makers when tackling the issue of how to promote economic development at regional level in an increasingly globalised economy, or what has been referred to as 'the local in the global'. However, it can be argued that all these theories, although based largely on empirical studies, pose as many questions as answers to the regional govern-ments or economic development agencies entrusted with the task of defining appropriate instruments and selecting delivery mechanisms for aiding small and medium-sized enterprises to innovate and grow.

Most are based on the analysis of success stories, like the well-known cases of the Third Italy or Baden-Württemberg, and offer few hints on how to translate the factors (often intangible) underlying the success of specific regions to other less fortunate regions lagging in terms of economic develop-ment or undergoing a structural decline in their industrial structures. Often the recommendations made are of a tautological or nebulous nature, provid-ing only broad guidelines on what not to do or what type of broad approach should be favoured. Suffice it to say that such recommendations rarely offer a blueprint to policy-makers and operators for the formulation of concrete mea-sures or projects.

Lagendijk (1996)[2] offers an excellent review of the various theories alluded to above and attempts to identify both the main messages of each of the approaches and their policy recommendations. He concludes that while there are major differences in terms of the starting points of each of these approaches of conceptualising regional innovation potential, they

> seem to converge on the fact that economic action is somehow *embedded* in the
> local socio-cultural and institutional context; and that this embedding is crucial
> to understanding the role of agency in the creation of innovative capacity.

In a similar manner, Amin and Thrift (1994) note that research into the 'growth regions'[3] leads to the conclusion that success in generating self-repro-ducing growth cannot be reduced to a set of economic factors.

To a certain degree, the RIS approach aims to translate the 'innovative milieu (Aydalot 1986) theory into an operational concept. That is, it should establish the foundations of a regional innovation system by improving the structural competitiveness[4] of indigenous firms, SMEs in particular. If, as such theories suggest, the innovation capacity of a region is the result of an accu-mulative learning process, then actions such as an RIS are based on the premise that this process can be organised and facilitated through the promo-tion of networks and partnerships among the key regional actors in order to arrive at a 'learning economy'. In this sense, the RIS approach acknowledges that 'the lack of social capital helps to explain one of the EU's key problems, namely its poor record of converting scientific and technological knowledge into commercially successful products and services' (Morgan 1996a) – that is, the inability to transfer technology from laboratory to industry, from one company to another and from region to region (European Commission 1993). Hence, the underlying issues are not technological but are embedded in sociological and cultural parameters influencing the effectiveness of organisational patterns of networking among regional stakeholders.

In parallel, or even slightly preceding, the theoretical developments concerning the territorial networking dimensions of innovation, an equally significant change has occurred in the innovation process *per se*. Whether due to technology-push or market-pull factors, the introduction of new innovations into the economy was, to simplify, considered to be a linear process where innovation was arrived at via a series of sequential and largely independent steps: from the basic research laboratory to diffusion. Increasingly, however, the deficiencies of this model and, in particular, its lack of attention to feedback loops and the interactions between numerous actors in a wider process of innovation led to the adoption of a new interactive model of innovation. In short, 'the accent has shifted from the single act philosophy of technological innovation to the social process underlying economically oriented technical novelty' (OECD 1992, p. 24).

A second aspect of this change is a reduction in the perceived importance of science and a greater emphasis on the learning aspects of 'simpler' everyday acts in the innovation process. As Lundvall has argued,

> not all important inputs to the process of innovation emanate from science and R&D efforts... learning takes places in connection with routine activities in production, distribution and consumption, and produces important inputs to the process of innovation. (Lundvall 1992, p. 9)

In short, the innovative capacity of a nation or a region must be considered to be dependent not only on the RTD infrastructure available but also on the various internal and external networks of relationships which engender a collective process of learning. In terms of a regional approach, this view has been summed up by Cooke and Morgan (1994), who argue that

> innovation is first and foremost a collective social endeavour, a collaborative process in which the firm, especially the small firm, depends on the expertise of a wider social constituency than is often imagined (workforce, suppliers, customers, technical institutes, training bodies, etc.).

Alongside the development of this theoretical framework, a gradual realisation has occurred that assessing the innovative potential of a region must be extended beyond the traditional type of 'input–output' indicators.[5] These are largely concerned with measuring and describing RTD capacity (focusing on university laboratories, research centres and R&D units of larger firms) and need to be complemented by 'process indicators' measuring the broader linkages between the different actors involved in the innovation process in a particular region, which can be just as significant a factor in determining the capacity of the regional economic fabric to regenerate and adapt to techno-logical and organisational change.[6]

To sum up, recent theoretical and empirical developments suggest a number of reasons which justify the development of a regional innovation strategy based on a process of analysis and discussion among the principal regional stakeholders; these include the following:

- When the innovative potential of a region is considered to be dependent not only on the R&D resources or competitive pressures to adapt, but also on the density and quality of networks of cooperation between regional actors (and indeed extra-regional linkages with stimuli or sources of innovation), then unless we accept a fatalistic historically determinist view of the world, these collective learning and diffusion mechanisms based on social–cultural factors can be developed.

- When innovation is considered as a learning process dependent not only on technological competence but also on what Dankbaar *et al.* (1994) have termed entrepreneurial and learning competence, a better balance needs to be developed between policies supporting industrial competitiveness on the supply side (supporting R&D) and those doing so on the demand side (supporting innovation and diffusion). A new balance is also needed between measures supporting infrastructure and measures supporting absorptive capacity, i.e. the resources available inside the enterprise.

Such an approach demands a constant sounding of the needs of firms, espe-cially the 'technologically dependent' smaller firms whose demands remain largely latent and often untouched by the standard programme of activities of regional technology transfer or diffusion agencies.

However, the shifts in policy objectives over the last five to ten years, while influenced strongly by such applied theoretical thinking, are also in large part due to a learning process engendered by the success and failures of regional and innovation policies at all levels of the 'subsidiarity chain' of European governance.

STRUCTURAL FUNDS AND INNOVATION: THE POLICY CONTEXT

RIS and its predecessors drew heavily on the experience and lessons from past policy experiences in the field of RTD promotion.[7] In particular, a number of 'first-generation' responses to the increasing 'technology gap' between core regions (the so-called 'islands of innovation') and the less-favoured regions, notably the Objective 1 regions,[8] were undertaken in the period up to 1994.

These policy responses were essentially of two types:

- a specific Community Initiative (STRIDE – Science and Technology for Regional Development in Europe) aimed at upgrading the RTD potential of the regions supported by the Structural Funds under Objectives 1 and 2;

- an increasing pressure on national and regional authorities to include RTD subprogrammes in the Community Support Frameworks.

STRIDE was a Community Initiative for the promotion of innovation and RTD efforts in the less-favoured regions of the European Union. It had a budget of 400 million ECU (grant aid up to three-quarters of eligible costs in Objective 1 regions) and it ran for four years starting in 1990. However, if the pattern of expenditure under STRIDE, and under other RTD-related programmes financed under the Structural Funds, is compared with the 'technological profile' of the less-developed regions there is a clear contradiction between the policy response and the factors which lead to low levels of innovative activity in these regions.

On the one hand, the less-favoured regions are characterised by:

- an imbalance in the science and technology system in favour of the public sector, and the academic part in particular, with very low levels of innovation in the private sector;

- low levels of technology transfer between public R&D centres, universities and the private sector (little cooperation and lack of 'intermediaries') and among those firms themselves (lack of coherence and integration of the scientific subsystem into the productive context;

- mismatch of the regional supply of innovation with demand;

- lack of links between the various stages of the process of innovation in the region);

- weak or non-existent links between firms and regional innovation centres and international networks offering access to the new sources and technological partners required to provide the fresh contacts and knowledge which will facilitate incorporation of technologies into the productive structure of the region.

On the other hand, the standard response of the authorities in these regions to the opportunity to invest in the promotion of innovation through a flexible grant-based programme like STRIDE was to adopt an implicit approach (in most cases no clear strategy is set out within the operational programmes) based on the following:

FIGURE 2.1: PROMOTE REGIONAL INNOVATION
SYSTEMS TO INCREASE REGIONAL COMPETITIVENESS

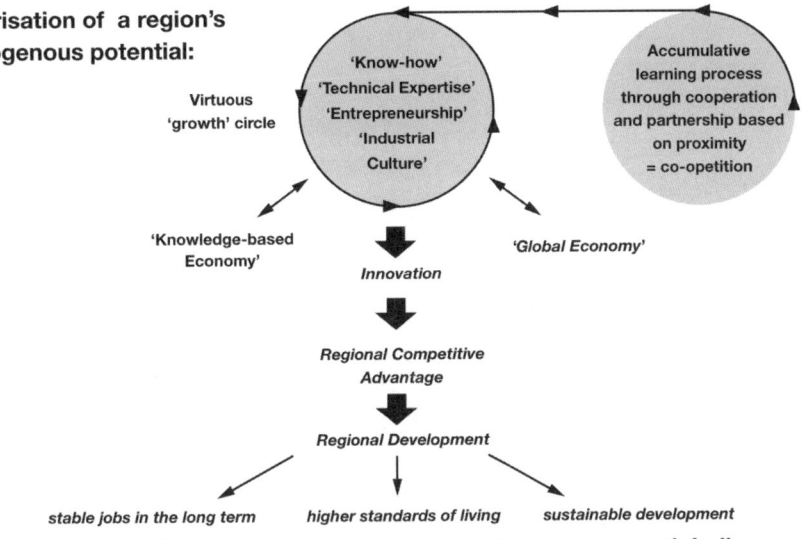

The 'intelligent region': cooperate locally to compete globally

- low participation by the private sector and little attention to technology transfer projects;

- infrastructure measures designed to boost public centres, usually academic ones, not closely involved with the structure of production in the region;

- little participation in measures intended to foster links between innovation centres and firms within international programmes and cooperation networks;

- little attention to training of the workforce and retraining for human resources (which constitute a strategic resource and one of the main hindrances to a permanent adjustment of the regional economic structure to technological change).

In our view, the basic reasons for this contradiction are two-fold. First, in the absence of an analysis of the specific features of supply of and demand for innovation in the region, those responsible for regional planning tend to use the 'linear' model of the process of regional innovation as a point of reference for preparing RTD operational programmes. That is, they assume that investment in the 'upper layers' (or the injection of science into the regional innovation system) will automatically mean that the new R&D effort will have an economic effect on the market.

The limitations of the linear model have been clearly exposed in the work of Soete and Arundel (1992) by comparing it with their own 'systemic' model of the innovation process. These limitations are shown in the lack of inter-relation between the different stages and the retroactive nature of the innovation process within the linear model, which is fundamentally based on science-and-technology push. It is only by focusing on the demand of firms and the economic nature of the innovation process that policy approaches can deal successfully with the promotion of innovation. Recognising the importance of the economic-pull factors (demand by firms) in the innovation process is critically important in the design of policy.

Second, some regional planning administrations have little experience of the key strategic approaches in this field (which inevitably require a multidisciplinary approach which links the public sector to the RTD community and the private sector). In general, these administrations tend to favour large (infrastructure) RTD-related projects which are easier to manage than innovation promotion projects, normally less easy to pin down and more indirect in nature and which must be adapted to differing socio-economic situations and count on a large number of those involved in the economy. That is, these are projects which require among other things a high degree of decentralisation in their design, management, implementation and monitoring as well as a certain degree of consensus and cooperation with key regional players.

This suggests that an increase in the innovative capacity of the regional structure inevitably requires new forms of organisation and institutional cooperation to help improve the 'structural competitiveness' of firms in the less-favoured regions, which is precisely one of the main objectives of RIS.

The problem of absorption of RTD and innovation-related Structural Fund measures in the Objective 1 regions brings to the fore a number of structural problems and institutional deficiencies in the context of the less-developed regions. Before 1988, less than 200 million ECU were devoted to RTD-related activities through the Structural Funds (less than 1 per cent of the total for Objective 1 regions). After the 1989 reform of the Structural Funds, for the period running from 1989 to 1993, the total intervention of the Structural Funds as regards RTD and innovation, including telecommunications, amounted to over 3.5 billion ECU (1989 prices) of a total sum of approximately 60 billion ECU. Within Objective 1 regions there were large differences in the allocation to RTD programmes, ranging from approximately 1.5 per cent of the total in Greece to nearly 5 per cent in Ireland and Italy. The Commission has also promoted the Business and Innovation Centres initiative, which has raised a lot of interest on the part of regional and local authorities in LFRs.

This intervention included programmes such as CIENCIA in Portugal, the Science and Technology Plan for Greece, the Scientific Infrastructure Programme for Spain, the Science and Technology subprogramme within the Irish Industrial Development Programme and the RTD National Programme for Italy called RICERCA, etc.

For the current planning period 1994–99 the resources dedicated to RTD related actions in Objective 1 regions have increased considerably to over 4.5 per cent of a much larger budgetary envelope than in the previous period. It is important to point out that recent studies show that the Structural Fund contribution to gross expenditure on R&D is now around a fifth in the case of Ireland and a third in the case of Portugal, with Greece in between the two. This gives an idea of the extent to which the national science and technology systems in these countries are supported by Community Assistance.

On average, Objective 2 regions have used structural assistance for RTD about three times as much as Objective 1 regions, largely because of their more developed industrial structure and the greater availability of RTD facilities. In these regions, an explicit aim of Structural Fund interventions has been to use innovation as a means of reconverting and replacing declining industries. As a number of previous studies have shown,[9] the technology gap of these regions is due more to the limited capabilities of private firms to undertake and invest in innovative activities than it is to insufficient innovation support infrastructure (university/public research laboratories, transfer organisations, etc.).

Despite such a change of emphasis in policy guidelines, many regions continue to find it difficult to mobilise resources or identify mechanisms which can serve to further the innovation potential of local firms, particularly SMEs. This leads to a continued emphasis on the supply side of the regional innovation system in terms of the measures adopted within the operational programmes of the Structural Funds.

According to a recent synthesis analysis of Objective 2 programmes (Bachtler *et al.* 1995) for the period 1994–96, research, innovation and development measures account for some 13.4 per cent (784 million ECU) of the Structural Funds allocation,[10] if relevant training measures, business development measures and actions promoting environmental technology are included in the total. However, the same study found that 'unfortunately, there is relatively little precision in the development of research and development measures in most Objective 2 programmes – in what they are to achieve and why, who they are required by, etc.' (Bachtler *et al.* 1995).

Hence, there remains a clear need for greater attention to be paid to the impact of innovation-related measures on the business environment, particularly its pertinence to the needs of SMEs. The choice faced by regional planners is to give a balanced weight to the supply-side and demand-side measures of operational programmes aimed at improving the adaptation of the local economy to technological change. The real challenge is to ensure a *broader view of the innovation process* in considering the types of measures appropriate for each particular regional industrial fabric. In this context, innovation goes beyond research and technological development (RTD) activities and spans a diverse series of activities covering, among others, technology transfer, design, quality assurance or testing, organisational management, training, finance and business services. Hence, innovation promotion in the

Structural Funds often concerns measures and subprogrammes other than those specifically labelled as having RTD- or innovation-related objectives.

For instance, given the key role of human resources in this broad view of innovation, the Structural Fund interventions need increasingly to find synergies between ERDF and European Social Fund measures in order to maximise the benefits for the technological adaptation of local firms. In addition, in certain regions the organisational aspects of innovation mentioned above may require the identification or definition of new forms of delivery mechanisms combining the skills and know-how of private and public actors.

To summarise, we believe that in the absence of a regional strategy to promote innovation which is based on the identified needs of firms and help to a stronger and better integrated regional innovation system, an injection of public funding into the system will be inefficient in terms of the return for regional economic development.

THE GENESIS OF REGIONAL INNOVATION STRATEGY IN THE EUROPEAN COMMISSION

A reflection along these lines had begun as early as 1991 at European level as it became clear that the initial reorientation of Structural Fund expenditure was likely to be hindered by both the continued use of the outdated linear model as a theoretical reference for policy-making and the weak strategic policy making know-how in most less-favoured regions. On 28 June 1991, the Directorate General for Regional Policies (DG XVI) organised a workshop in Brussels to discuss a concept entitled 'Regional Technology Strategies' (RETAS) with a number of international experts and other Commission services in order to test and develop further the initial idea of a pilot action in the field of innovation promotion at regional level.[11]

The experts and the services' representatives were invited to comment on the proposed objectives and basic features of the pilot action explained below. The initial objectives of a Regional Technology Strategy were:

- to improve the regional capabilities for RTD and economic development planning;

- to enhance the endogenous RTD resource utilisation;

- to promote awareness of the need for innovation by local firms;

- to augment the capability of SMEs to absorb and apply technology;

- improve cooperation and networking of local actors in the area of RTD and creating international linkages;

- to widen training opportunities in RTD;

- to provide a framework for cost-efficient choices in policy planning and implementation, and developing alternatives in the area of RTD.

At the outset, it was proposed that the pilot action should be:

- Strategic: the projects should adopt a strategic planning concept to regional development in the particular context of technological development and innovation. The plan should incorporate short-term and medium-term actions within a long-term framework.

- Bottom-up: the priorities for action and the areas and sectors for intervention should be chosen on the basis of the expressed needs of the main participants in the process of innovation: firms and the RTD community in the region. Such a process provides a framework for these regional actors to produce a more informed opinion about possible ways for action.

- Endogenous: the reference point should be the actual economic circumstances and RTD capabilities of the region.

- Regional: it should take account of the specific territorial dimension, within a national and an international context. Regional administrations should play the leading role in the design, implementation, monitoring and follow-up of the exercise.

- Integrated: an effort should be made to link efforts and actions from the public sector (EU, national, regional, local) and the private sector towards a common goal. It should also integrate all financial resources available in the form of aid programmes into different parts of the strategy, thus alleviating the need for regional authorities to react on an individual basis to different EU initiatives in the RTD area. It should try to maximise the economic impact of EU RTD actions.

- Applied: it works from and for the market with a strong developmental approach in terms of its impact on productivity, employment, rate of technological upgrading, etc.

- International and cooperative: an international perspective should be adopted in terms of the analysis of global economic and technological trends as well as on the need to cooperate internationally for being effective in the area of R&D, technology transfer and innovation.

- Incremental and cyclical: the exercise is dynamic in the form of a plan for action that has to be reviewed in the light of previous experience and an ongoing evaluation.

- Innovative: the exercise should bring together two previously distinct communities within the framework of an open debate: economic development experts and technology and R&D personnel.

The general reaction to the above principles was highly positive from all participants in the workshop and many interesting suggestions were made which substantially enriched the initial idea, not only with respect to methodology, objectives and content but also regarding its proposed target recipients, implementation and management. Moreover, there was a high degree of consensus on the necessity to place innovation promotion at the top of the regional policy agenda. Following this workshop, the Commission continued to work on the administrative and budgetary procedures for the launching of the action as well as in further developing its content and methodology (Landabaso 1992).

In March 1992 the Regional Policies Commissioner met with the head of the Welsh Development Agency who explained that they had been working on the idea of producing a framework for regional technology which seemed to fit in well with DG XVI's RETAS ideas. One month later the Commission received a proposal from two Welsh academics, Philip Cooke and Kevin Morgan, *A Regional Innovation Strategy for Wales* (Cooke and Morgan 1994b).

In view of the increasing interest in the RETAS concept, the policy orientations being discussed in the Commission and the recommendations of the European Parliament, Bruce Millan, Commissioner for Regional Policies, at the suggestion of Eneko Landaburu,[12] Director General of DG XVI, decided to invite four member states with mainly Objective 2 regions (regions in industrial decline) to propose the name of a region undergoing industrial restructuring to test the RETAS concept through a pre-pilot action. Accordingly, by the end of 1993, Wales, Lorraine, Limburg and Saxony had launched what was renamed by then as a Regional Technology Plan (RTP). In 1994 it was decided to test the same concept in four pre-pilot Objective 1 regions in order to widen the trial to less-developed peripheral regions. Four RTPs were started in Norte, Castilla y León, Central Macedonia and Abruzzo by the end of that year.

By the spring of 1997, six out of eight projects had completed the process of establishing an RTP to varying degrees of success. Norte and Abruzzo are starting the exercise again with different management teams and newly appointed steering committees. Neither project had proceeded under the RTP phase due mainly to budgetary and institutional problems in the regions concerned.

The RTP pilot projects created a great deal of interest from other regions and this led the European Commission to publish an open call for proposals, in September 1995, to initiate pilot schemes for the implementation of Regional Innovation Strategies (RIS) under Article 10 of the ERDF. In parallel with this action, DG XIII launched a Regional Innovation and Technology Transfer Strategies and Infrastructures (RITTS) exercise which follows the same objectives and has a very similar methodology.[13]

Regional Innovation Strategies are designed

to respond to the question of how to improve the innovative capacity of regional firms through the strengthening of the regional innovation system [and] aimed at promoting public/private co-operation and creating the institutional conditions for a more efficient use of public and private resources for the promotion of innovation, especially in the less favoured regions. (European Commission 1994a)

The new (and definitive) acronym RIS was adopted with a view to encouraging the regional managers of these pilot actions to adopt a broad definition of innovation

> embracing managerial, commercial, technical and financial factors which enable a new, or an improved product or process to be introduced into the market place; or which enable a public or private organisation to introduce or improve service delivery to regional firms.

Following an independent evaluation of the 43 proposals received following the call for proposals, 19 projects were selected. To these, two more were added (Norte and Abruzzo), which restarted the exercise. In addition, Saxony-Anshalt has decided to continue the process on the basis of their own funds. In all, today over 1,000 key regional actors are involved in the strategic planning of innovation promotion at regional level (representatives from the planning, industrial and RTD departments of regional governments, presidents and managers of RTD centres, universities and technology parks, leading businessmen, union representatives, etc.) through partnerships in the steering committees of RIS in nearly 72 regions.[14]

What can be said at this stage in terms of the success of the RTP/RIS initiative? Within the Commission services the projects deemed to have produced a valid RTP based on a reasonably broad regional consensus included two of the four Objective 1 regions. In terms of the concept of social capital, it is possible to state that in all RTP regions a changing perception of the role of innovation in economic development has occurred among the actors involved in the exercise. Indeed, this process has been likened to an

> ongoing cultural revolution based on a new vision of the innovation process, less technically oriented, taking into better account the global support to SMEs in their innovative activities and based on co-operation rather than isolation. (Nauwelaers *et al.* 1996)

Moreover, it should be stressed that the relative success in designing an RIS in, say, an LFR cannot be assessed *only* against a benchmark of what is considered to be best practice in Europe in designing and developing regional innovation action plans. This would be to ignore the question of what is good project management in a specific institutional environment and the applicability of certain methodologies given the state of knowledge/and/or know-how and existing partnerships at the beginning of the project.

Equally, important lessons have been learned by the Commission side in terms of its role in assisting and providing a methodological framework within

which the RIS projects in regions with extremely diverse economic and institutional structure can operate. On a purely administrative level, the running
of Article 10 raises the challenge of applying and adapting rules designed for
the traditional programme approach of the mainstream Structural Fund programmes. This requires a process of constant consultation with colleagues in
other Commission services and is a stimulus to the development of new rules
better suited to the realities faced by project leaders while respecting the
requirements of the European institutions to manage efficiently and effectively the disbursement of the limited funds available.

In addition, the experience of the first eight exercises has underlined the
need for the Commission services to strike a delicate balance between an over-
directive approach and the inevitable need to guide certain regions where
levels of understanding of the concepts involved are lower among the key
stakeholders at the outset of an RIS.

CONCLUSIONS: TOWARDS A NEW REGIONAL POLICY FOR THE PROMOTION OF INNOVATION

With the recent launch of Agenda 2000, the European Union has begun a
process of reflection on new policy orientations. In the field of regional policy,
the principal objective remains to create the conditions throughout the Union
for balanced and sustainable economic growth. Given the limited budgetary
resources available in a 'Europe of twenty-one', the Commission, the member
states and the regions must ensure an increased effectiveness of regional policy
as an instrument of economic development in the less-developed regions.
Many of the current Objective 1 regions have undertaken a massive upgrading of infrastructure, while the level of infrastructure development in the five
main candidates for early accession is probably better than that of Greece,
Spain or Portugal at the time of their accession. Hence, the key challenge for
both the current less-favoured regions and the new entrants to the EU will be
to improve their social capital through developing new innovative policy measures in partnership with the business sector.

Instead of building comparative advantage on the basis of low-cost–low-
salary production, European regions should be helped to develop competitive
advantage based on innovation. That is to help firms, SMEs in particular, in
less-favoured regions to produce better and/or different products and services
through regional policy.

As Porter (1990) has observed, 'Competitive advantage based on factor
costs… is rapidly undone… A low-wage country today is quickly replaced by
another tomorrow.' Hence, the only viable strategy for LFRs in the medium
and long term is to try to modernise and diversify their regional economies
towards higher-value-added economic activities. In short, they need a regional
policy for the promotion of innovation whose main aim is to raise regional
competitiveness through the modernisation and diversification of the productive structure of the region by making permanent adjustments to take account

of accelerated technical change in an increasingly globalised economy. This, in turn, requires the design of new ways of introducing the promotion of innovation in the regional economic development agenda of the less-favoured regions. We would argue that such a redefinition of regional policy will need to take account of the following features.

From RTD to Innovation Promotion

Innovation promotion policies at the regional level are much more closely related to economic development policies than to science, technology or R&D. Although regional innovation policies should consider science and technology aspects, they should focus on the economic aspects of the innovation process.

This has two main implications. On the one hand, it means that such a policy should support all steps – not only in technology and research – but also managerial, organisational, financial, training, etc. – necessary for regional firms to remain competitive in international markets. On the other hand, it should change the emphasis from a technology push approach into one of demand-pull, which aims primarily at the identification and understanding of the demand for innovation, expressed or latent, in firms within the less-favoured regions.

From Physical Infrastructure Development to Institutional Support for the Creation of Innovative Environments

Such a policy would progressively evolve from supporting RTD physical infrastructure and equipment (in public RTD centres and university laboratories) towards strengthening the organisational base of the regional productive tissue by encouraging cooperation among local actors in the field of innovation. That means strengthening the various internal and external networks of relationships which engender a collective process of learning which fosters innovation at regional level.

Indigenous Research Versus Technology Transfer: Access to Technology Resources in the Periphery

A policy of this kind would not only focus on the generation and development of the weaker region's indigenous RTD activities but also facilitate the identification, adaptation and adoption of technological developments elsewhere in a specific regional setting. That is, it would facilitate technology transfer and the flow of knowledge, be it tacit or codified, across regions, it would exploit and maximise the benefit of the European dimension by facilitating access from LFRs to international networks of 'excellence' in the field of RTD, technology sources and RTD partners. Such a policy would also be aimed at facilitating the diffusion of the fruits of RTD developments in a balanced way throughout the European territory to those areas and enterprises which may be in a position to exploit them in the market.

A Leading Role for Regions in the Promotion of Innovation in Line with Subsidiarity and for Reasons of Economic Efficiency

A policy of this kind would be adapted to the particular features of the innovation process in each region and concentrate on the creation of the appropriate conditions, in particular those of an institutional and organisational kind, which enable these regions to develop their own more efficient policies for the promotion of innovation. Thus the regions themselves (and their regional governments in partnership with other key socio-economic actors), on the basis of the subsidiarity principle, would play the key role in the definition of priorities and instruments.

A Coordinated and Multi-disciplinary Approach

Such a policy would be able to link up with and integrate into the other industrial, technological and regional measures and policies within a medium- to long-term planning horizon. This also means that such a policy should avoid being exclusively sectoral and 'top-down' in order to adopt a multidisciplinary and 'bottom-up' approach.

'Co-opetition' as a Response

Cooperation and competition are increasingly becoming two sides of the same coin ('co-opetition') in the field of innovation in a progressively global economy, in particular with regard to SMEs, as recent theoretical research and empirical evidence is showing. This implies, in turn, that there is room for new innovative public policies to support and help organise the right institutional framework and cooperation networks within which these co-opetition links take place, in order to increase the competitiveness of a regional economy.

In this sense some of the recent theoretical work on cooperation and competition among SMEs tends to confirm this view. Oughton and Whittman (1997) examine inter-firm cooperation (between SMEs) and external economies through the concept of collective economies of scale and 'show that the successful realisation of collective external economies lowers entry barriers and increases the survival prospects of participating firms, thus resulting in market structures characterised by larger numbers of small firms ... ', which leads them to 'point to the importance of institutional factors in determining firm behaviour and economic performance ...'

A recent study by COTEC (1997)15 concluded that

> the key success factors in innovative activity in SMEs are a pro-active strategy, a management team committed to innovation and willing to take risks, a high qualification of the workforce, the interaction of firms in technology networks and the existence of a dynamic firm environment.

Arnold and Thuriaux (1997) in another recent review of technological capabilities conclude that

> industrial procurement orthodoxy has been shifting from adversarial to 'partnership' models over the last twenty years or so, especially in industries where co-development is desirable [and they indicate that] if contemporary writers are correct that networking is central to the innovation process, then the ability to network must itself be a crucial capability. This means, then, making use of external knowledge, using partners to access complementary assets and managing the producer/user relations which have consistently been identified in the innovation literature as key to innovative success.

Other recent empirical evidence also points in the same direction. Based on a recent firm survey, Spielkamp (1997) concludes that

> in the cases of successful implementation of research results, the social interweaving of the academic and business communities is a crucial factor. When direct contacts and informal networks form the primary channels for transmitting scientific findings and technical knowledge from the academic to the business community, a flexible, decentralised and deregulated practice of technology transfer promotion can most effectively contribute to establishing and stabilising these informal networks ...

From an analysis of seven industrial sectors in the USA's Appalachian region, Rosenfeld *et al.*(1997) argue that

> successful clusters arise from dynamic activities and resources, such as access to specialised information and assistance, means and tendencies to associate and learn from one another, reliance on local suppliers, availability of skilled and experienced labor, tough competition, entrepreneurial energy, and shared vision ... [and he concludes that] trust is a major factor in the strength of a cluster, increasing the opportunities for firms to take advantage of their collective capabilities and knowledge ...

which is derived to a large extent from the availability of a region's social infrastructure (the associations and organisations that bring business people together where they can get to know and trust each other).

Rosenfeld goes on to recommend a policy which encourages networking, recognising that

> while many of these firms do compete with each other in regional markets to supply larger customers, a large number have differentiated themselves with their special capabilities over the past few years, thus increasing the likelihood of cooperating on mutually beneficial issues. Thus they may find there is now less direct competition and more opportunities for cooperation.

In short, such evidence underpins the view that one of the main objectives of future European regional policy should be to support the efforts of institutional actors in less-favoured regions to cooperate regionally in order to compete globally.

The current phase of RIS projects may provide further support for a significant realignment of the objectives of EU Structural Fund assistance to less-favoured regions. However, to do so they will need to prove that the strategies and pilot projects developed can produce tangible results in terms of improving employment and growth prospects. While theoretically one may argue that social capital is a necessary condition of economic development, in practice the success of policy measures must be judged against concrete and verifiable outputs.

NOTES

1. Social capital has been defined as '...features of social organisation, such as networks, norms and trust, that facilitate coordination and cooperation for mutual benefit' (Putnam 1993). For an interesting reflection on the regional economic relevance of this concept see Morgan (1997).

2. He examines five main theoretical approaches: new industrial spaces; industrial districts; innovative milieux; 'Porter's diamond (competitive advantage and clustering); and national systems of innovation. His analysis both provides an objective critique of the various theories and highlights the deficiencies of each when drawing policy conclusions.

   For instance, he notes that: in the 'industrial district' approach, 'the prime factor behind regional economic success is the institutional capability to create the competencies and "weak ties"... [hence] ... regional agencies need to play a continuous and creative "positioning" game in which the unique nexus between the regions and the wider global economy is constantly reshaped.' This leads to the perturbing conclusion when shaping policy that the approach is founded on a concept of lock-in 'residing in some fortuitous combination of social and cultural factors ... [so that] although the theory suggests active regional policy can improve the competitiveness of local economies, it also stresses that policies will only be effective if the right socio-cultural background exists.'

   Similarly, the 'innovative environment' approach argues that such mileux 'derive their success from the capacity to engage in processes of collective learning ... born out of a common cultural background which binds local agents and institutions in synergetic networks'.

   However, this leads essentially to a circular form of reasoning: 'innovation occurs because of a milieu, and a milieu is what exists in regions where there is innovation'.

3. For instance, the research on innovative mileux of the GREMI group (Camagni 1991) or that of Cooke and Morgan (1994) on the 'intelligent region'.

4. 'The competitiveness of a firm certainly depends on its own forces, but to no less an extent on the quality of its environment, sometimes referred to as "structural competitiveness"' (Chabbal 1992).

5. For instance, gross or business expenditure on R&D as a proportion of GDP. As Lundvall (1992) notes, there are two obvious problems with such an indicator: 'First, it reflects only an input effort and does not say anything about what comes out of the effort. Second, R&D expenditure is only one kind of relevant input to the process of innovation – learning in connection with routine activities may be more important than R&D.'

6. For a fuller discussion of these issues see Nauwelaers and Reid (1995a and 1995b).

7. A more detailed explanation of this section can be found in Landabaso (1997).

8. This 'technology gap', which in keeping with the arguments of this chapter should be undoubtedly rebaptised 'innovation gap', is by now well documented, at least in terms of the more traditional RTD 'input–output' indicators such as Business Expenditure on R&D (BERD). See for instance European Commission (1992), European Commission (1994a, pp. 95–104), European Commission (1994b).

9. Not only access to material, financial and human resources but the management of innovation within firms or groups of firms.

10. Actions supported under the heading of general R&D measures include the promotion of increased cooperation between business and existing R&D facilities and the reorientation of existing facilities to serve better the innovation requirements of business. This reflects the fact that R&D infrastructure is usually already in place in higher and further educational institutes in Objective 2 regions or in leading firms.

11. Seven international experts from six different countries were invited, including the directors of a Greek technology park, a Spanish technology institute and five international consultants from Germany, France, Ireland, Italy and Spain. On the Commission side, representatives from the Directorate-General for Science, Research and Development (DG-XII), including a director from the joint research centre, and the Directorate-General for Telecommunications, Internal market and the valorisation of research (DG-XIII), including a manager from the ESPRIT Programme and the person responsible for the SPRINT programme, together with representatives from the Directorate-General for Regional Policy (DG-XVI) participated in the workshop. Previous to this workshop, several informal discussions on RETAS had taken place inside DG-XVI services and with a number of international experts, notably Richard Binfield from SRI (Stanford Research International), Roy Rothwell from SPRU (Science Policy Research Unit) and Christopher Hull from the European network TII (Technology, Innovation, Information).

12. Landaburu's speech to the Conference, 'L'Innovation, instrument de développement économique régional: considérations dans l'optique de la politique régionale', Brussels, Palais des Congrès, 22 June 1992, set the policy framework for the launching of RTPs and the promotion of RTD-related actions under the mainstream Structural Funds programmes.

13. For a full outline of the current methodological approach see European Commission (1997), *Guide to Regional Innovation Strategies*. In order to maximise synergies and ensure a multidisciplinary approach, which is inbuilt in the innovation notion of RIS, Directorate-General XVI (Regional Policy and Cohesion) and DG XIII (Innovation Programme) have joined forces to carry out the joint management and follow-up of all RIS and RITTS projects. In so doing, the services of the Commission are seeking to combine an economic development logic with a technology-oriented perspective, both of which are of paramount importance when working in the field of innovation promotion.

14. Approximately 43 new RIS/RITTS projects are underway following a first generation of 22 RITTS and 8 RTPs.

15. COTEC is a private foundation, chaired by the King of Spain, whose objective is to contribute to Spain's economic development through the promotion of technological innovation in the firm and in society.

3   Towards a Knowledge-Intensive Regional Economy: The RTP Process in Limburg

THE LIMBURG REGION

Limburg is one of the twelve provinces of the Netherlands; it is the most southern province and covers an area of about 2,200 square kilometres, with a population of about 1.1 million. Limburg borders the German Land of North Rhine-Westphalia to the east, the Flandrian province of Limburg to the west and the Walloon province of Liège to the south. Until the 1960s South Limburg was a peripheral mining region, and with the closure of the mines the region faced high unemployment rates. In the ten years from 1965 to 1975, more than 44,000 miners lost their jobs and 30,000 jobs were lost in related industries. Large programmes initiated a long and successful restructuring of the Limburg economy. Since the late 1970s, Limburg has seen a strong economic revival, with unemployment falling since 1984, to the point where the unemployment rate was 8 per cent in 1997.

Limburg's strength lies in its industry. The industrial tissue of Limburg is dominated by four industrial sectors, each with one or two large companies at the centre of activities: the chemical and plastic industry (DSM), metalworking and mechanical engineering (NedCar/Volvo), the manufacture of building materials (Sphinx and Mosa) and the production of office equipment and copying machines (Océ and Rank Xerox). Industrial employment is proportionally greater in this region than in the rest of the Netherlands and is still increasing, while in the rest of the country it has remained stable. Employment in Limburg is on the rise in the other sectors of the economy as well. As a result, the unemployment figure in Limburg scarcely differs from the national figure, although there are still (major) differences within Limburg. Despite these generally favourable trends, the gross regional product per inhabitant in Limburg still lags behind that of neighbouring regions, both in the Netherlands and in the EU.

The industrial sectors expected to see the biggest growth, such as the transport equipment industry and the rubber and plastics processing industry, may be over-represented in Limburg compared with the rest of the Netherlands, but they are under-represented compared with the average in Europe. An additional threat is the sharp rise of industrial nations in regions such as South-East Asia and Central and Eastern Europe.

Limburg, or more precisely the southern part of the Netherlands, is an industrial region par excellence. Partly this is due to policy decisions in the past which were aimed at improving the socio-economic structure of the region by reinforcing the position held by industry. Knowledge intensification within the existing industrial activities is a key element. From this perspective, the RTP is, first and foremost, aimed at industry, but it does not lose sight of the importance of other sectors such as the (commercial) services sector.

The Province's Innovation 'Territory'

The province is autonomous with respect to regional economic policy and hence regional innovation policy. It has its own funds for stimulating economic development and a high degree of freedom in its choices. Nevertheless, it is obvious that the province determines and executes its technology policy in close communication with the national government. In recent years, the province has become increasingly important in enacting improvements in the economic, technological and innovative position of companies. It has done so through many different projects aimed, for example, at providing support to companies who wish to participate in the Framework Programme of the EC, and promote cross-border technology transfer in cooperation with universities in the Euregio Maas-Rein (which encompasses five regions from three countries – Dutch South Limburg, Belgian Limburg, the Province of Liege, Aachen and the German-speaking community of Belgium). Furthermore, the province of Limburg has played an active leading role in the STRIDE programme since 1991. These and many other projects and programmes always had the full support of the provincial government. In fact Limburg has been (and still is) an example for many other provinces in the Netherlands. The main improvement that the RTP brought regarding provincial innovation policy has been the recognition of the need to focus even more than in the past on the process of achieving a consensus between all the participants with regard to the building and implementation of strategy based on investigation that is both broad and thorough.

In the Netherlands, most policy instruments of direct support for R&D are the domain of the national government, whereas the indirect forms of support are more often the domain of regional authorities. In terms of volume, the national government also provides the most important source of funding for technology. Limburg businesses make generous use of these funds. In 1993 they received approximately 15 million ECU from the national technology funds – approximately 20 per cent of the resources made available that year. In cooperation with the province, the national government has a clearly defined task with regard to European Regional Development Fund (ERDF) and Interreg funds, which are the main financial resources for funding tech-nology-related projects.

The second stream of funds (in size) is provided through the participation of Limburg companies in European technology programmes: in 1993, Limburg companies received about 5.8 million ECU from the EU and some 75 per cent of these funds went to small and medium-sized enterprises. The third financial stream is channelled through the province's office. At the start of the RTP, the province's own annual budget for innovation policy amounted to 2.5 million ECU. Nevertheless, an RTP process has to take into account more administrative levels than just the regional one. The RTP has therefore been realised in close communication with representatives of the EC (DG XIII and DG XVI) and the Ministry of Economic Affairs of the national gov-ernment.

Provinces are relatively free, in policy terms, to use European and national regional stimulation funds for innovation-related activities and projects. The province's main goal is to act on trends and developments which will improve Limburg's prospects. A core concern within the province's policy is to achieve sustainable economic development in Limburg. This concern manifests itself in two different goals:

- to encourage employment by reinforcing Limburg's business community;

- to stimulate sustainable economic growth by reinforcing the envi-ronmental component of production and by reducing negative impacts on the environment.

In order to achieve these goals, the province has selected a number of spear-head sectors: industry and business services (including the environmental production sector), transport and logistics, tourism and recreation, agro-busi-ness and horticulture. The province's economic policy is aimed primarily at these sectors, with the emphasis on sustaining and expanding employment. Its main elements of innovation policy are achieved through either stimulating collaboration in the region or co-funding projects. These projects are mainly within EU programmes (Stride, Interreg, ERDF, etc.) or are technology pro-jects initiated by regional development bodies. Up until the RTP, the province had a less coherent and a fairly reactive innovation policy. To this extent, the province works closely with other authorities, intermediary organisations and the business community in implementing its policy on stimulating the knowl-edge intensity of industry. The province pursues the policy, initiates and directs activities and provides financial support. The responsibility for imple-mentation usually lies with third parties (intermediary organisations, consultants, other companies and institutions).

Another core point of the province's economic policy is to strengthen the position of Limburg as an industrial region. In the eyes of the provincial authorities, industry is the foundation upon which other economic activities (such as transport, services and trade) can build, and as such it forms the basis for employment. An important element within the industrial policy is to raise the level of knowledge within existing companies and to expand knowledge-intensive industry. Knowledge intensification and innovation are the key when it comes to reinforcing the competitive position of companies. The basic task is to increase the number of innovations within companies. That requires reinforcing the level of knowledge within companies, specifically SMEs, but it also means initiating activities which will make the knowledge infrastructure more accessible to companies, and ensure a better match with their knowledge requirements. After all, the knowledge companies apply is derived largely outside their own business.

Regional Context for Innovation

Limburg has a relatively well-developed research infrastructure. If not directly available at a regional level, surrounding regions across the border can provide a very complete research infrastructure. Limburg is located in the centre of an area with a very high knowledge intensity: within a radius of around 100 kilometres, there are seven universities (RWTH Aachen, Université de Liège, Universitaire Campus Diepenbeek, Katholieke Universiteit Leuven, Universiteit Maastricht, Technische Universiteit Eindhoven and Open University Heerlen) and several major research laboratories (Julich, VITO, Philips, DAF, DSM, Océ, etc.). However, the national borders appear to be major barriers in any search for technological assistance. The vast potential of knowledge available to SMEs is far from being fully utilised.

A comparison of the knowledge and R&D intensity of Limburg's industrial sector with that in the rest of the Netherlands shows a diverse picture. As table 3.1 shows, a number of above-average knowledge-intensive sectors are under-represented in Limburg, while a number of below-average knowledge-intensive sectors are over-represented. There appear to be opportunities for Limburg to expand its innovation potential on just this point.

Limburg's industry is particularly strong in medium- and low-tech sectors, and these are generally not regarded as the high-growth sectors for the future, as table 3.2 shows. None of the sectors over-represented in Limburg compared with the European average is expected to show strong growth (> 3 per cent). It is specifically those sectors that are expected to grow moderately (1-3 per cent) which are well represented in Limburg.

These outlines show that there is a great need to reinforce the position of industry in Limburg, specifically in terms of technology and innovation. That holds in particular for regional SMEs, although large industrial complexes are more dominant in Limburg than in the Netherlands as a whole. For example, the share of industrial employment contributed by companies in Limburg with 500 or more employees comes to 40 per cent, as opposed to 29 per cent nationally. Nevertheless, the SME sector remains an important factor, in terms of both employment and innovation potential.

TABLE 3.1: RELATIVE REPRESENTATION OF INDUSTRIAL SECTORS BY KNOWLEDGE INTENSITY

		Relative size of the sector in Limburg vs. the Netherlands		
		under-represented	*about equal in size*	*over-represented*
knowledge intensity	*above average*	– printing and publishing – basic metal – instruments and optical devices	– electrical engineering	– chemicals and fibres – machines – transport equipment
	below average	– food and beverages – wood and furniture	– textiles, clothing, leather – metal products	– paper and paper goods – rubber and plastics processing – building materials, earthenware/ceramics and glass

Source: ERAC analysis based on TBO-INRO/CBS (SWP) data

TABLE 3.2: HIGH-, MEDIUM- AND LOW-TECH INDUSTRIAL SECTORS IN LIMBURG

		Relative size by sector in Limburg vs. the Netherlands		
		under-represented	*about equal in size*	*over-represented*
R&D intensity by sector	*high*	– aircraft – pharmaceuticals – electricals – instrument engineering		
	medium		– other chemicals	– automobile – electrical machinery – other machinery – rubber and plastics – other transport equipment
	low	– basic metal – oil – food – wood and furniture	– metal products – textiles, etc.	– glass, stone, clay – other industry – paper and printing

Source: ERAC analysis based on information by MERIT (Stemming 2/CBS[SWP])

GENESIS AND OBJECTIVES OF THE RTP

When the European Union launched a set of proposals for drafting a Regional Technology Plan (RTP) which would involve systematically charting the economic and technological development of a region, the province of Limburg responded to this development at quite an early stage, and it was selected as one of the pilot regions. The province was looking for ways to integrate regional economic policy and technology policy and saw a great opportunity to achieve that within the framework of the Regional Technology Plan scheme of the European Commission. Limburg's intention in drawing up an RTP was therefore not the lack of a technology policy, but the desire to achieve more effective coordination between existing resources for regional economic development (Objective 2 and Objective 5b programmes), grants obtained from the European technology funds and provincial resources.

The combination of a regional economic and technology policy offers many advantages. The main objectives of the RTP Limburg were stated at the outset as:

> Developing a broader basis of support for technology and regional economic policy and the encouragement of cooperation between all the various parties in the field (business community, government, knowledge and education institutes and intermediary organisations), with the view to reinforcing the innovativeness of companies in the region (especially the SMEs) and fostering Limburg as an attractive location for knowledge-intensive enterprises.

What was important in this respect was the policy choice to aim at increasing the knowledge base of the SMEs, and not of a particular type of SME. In general, Dutch firms have to compete on the basis of knowledge and not on low labour costs. But technology policy cannot be customised to the specific needs of each firm. For that reason, within the frame of the RTP the province has adopted a general view on increasing the knowledge in SMEs which is based on a broad range of needs and not just focused on the new (high-tech) needs of firms. Translations to the real needs of a particular firm can then be made by the knowledge providers or intermediaries.

The expectations of the province at the start of the RTP project were very much in line with the points mentioned above, namely continuing to improve innovation within companies.

THE RTP PROCESS

The RTP Limburg was an initiative of the EC, adopted by the Economic Department of the province of Limburg (the regional authority). Coordination and process guidance were shared between the province of Limburg and a Dutch consulting firm. A steering committee with representatives from all the main actors involved in and concerned with the development of innovation in the region was set up to monitor and support the RTP process.

A schematic overview of the Limburg RTP process is presented in figure 3.1. Right from its start in June 1994, the steering committee reached a consensus on the structure and content of the RTP process. This early agreement was considered a key for the later success of the RTP. The next step was to take full stock of Limburg's technological and economic position and of its policy on technology. The project started with an extensive review of available information on the region. Main players in the technological infrastructure (the regional development bank and the innovation centres) were asked to provide the province with information about the innovative performance of SMEs in the region. A number of experts from within the region were also called into

FIGURE 3.1: A SCHEMATIC REPRESENTATION OF THE LIMBURG RTP PROCESS

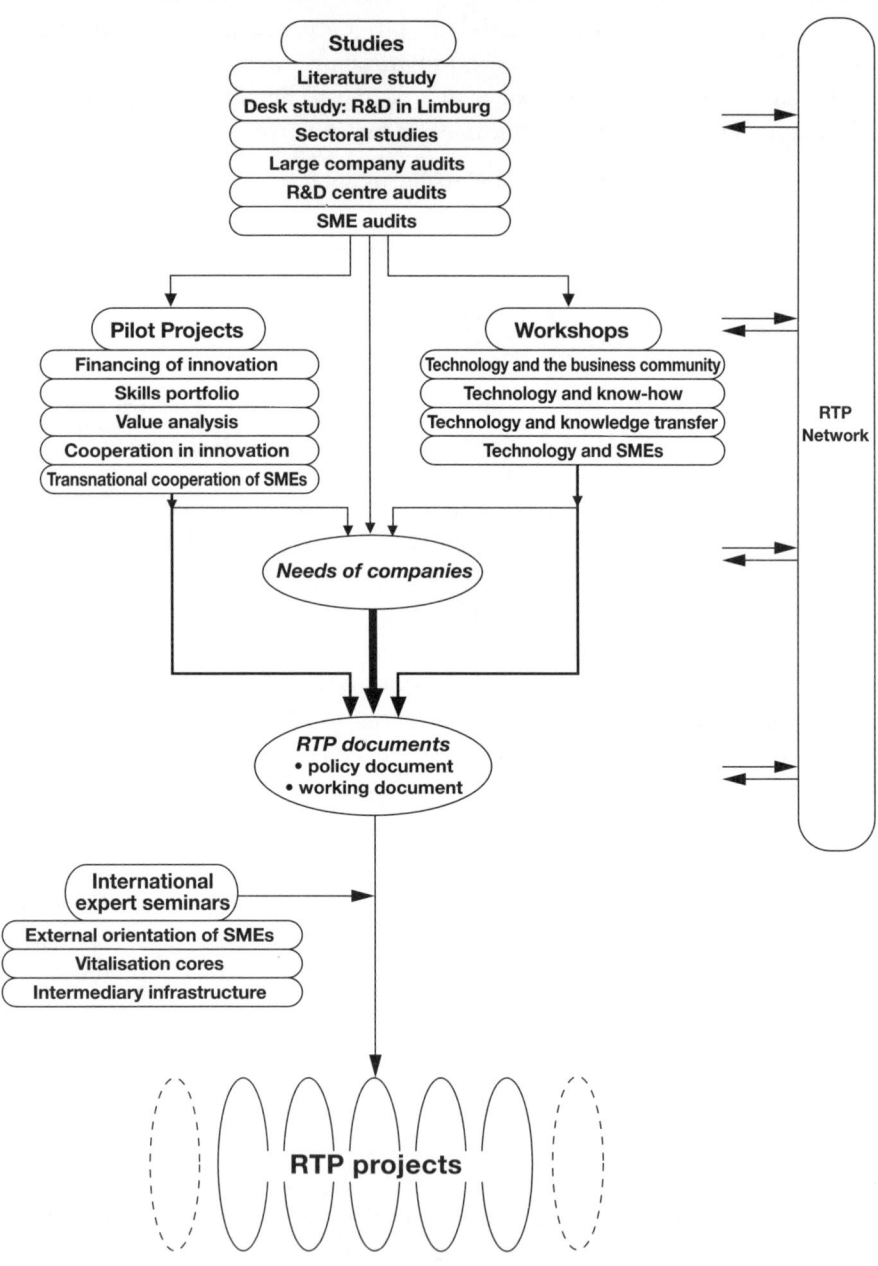

the process in order to conduct various studies (analysis of the knowledge infrastructure, analysis of technical education sector and branch analyses). In addition, specific audits (17 technology audits within large companies and 72 short audits among SMEs) were carried out. These audits focused on the bottlenecks and opportunities the companies had experienced or were experiencing in the area of innovation. Use of earlier information and enquiries was also favoured during the RTP, and the knowledge of intermediary organisations was exploited whenever pertinent. In this way, a precise picture of the strengths and weaknesses of the region with regard to innovation was obtained. The most important challenge to be overcome in assessing SME needs was to get the firms to the point at which they were willing to look into a mirror. Only then could they realise that they themselves were part of the problem, and could therefore also form part of the solution. Not everything could be solved by subsidising their plans.

Simultaneously with the RTP study – and this is an original feature of the Limburg RTP – a number of pilot projects have been carried out during the RTP, with the twin aims of developing information and testing the feasibility of:

- the development of clusters;

- the application of value analyses in companies;

- the development of methods for occupational qualification;

- instruments for financing innovation;

- international cooperation on technology for SMEs.

These projects were launched in the course of 1995 and have been completed. The results have been set out in separate reports, and were included in the RTP policy recommendations. What is interesting to note is that some of these pilot projects were undertaken in collaboration with other RTP regions in Europe.

During the second half of 1995 all studies regarding the innovation infrastructure situation were analysed and conclusions were drawn with respect to knowledge development, demand and supply of knowledge, knowledge transfer, intermediary services and the application of knowledge. These conclusions as well as the information previously obtained were discussed at various meetings in penetrating detail by the representatives of the province of Limburg, the regional development bank (LIOF), the Limburg innovation centres, MERIT and the two participating consulting agencies (MHP and ERAC). In so far as the information was sector-specific, there were also consultations with the relevant sector organisations, which allowed them to monitor the available information and contribute new elements to it.

An important contribution to the study itself, as well as laying the groundwork for support for the RTP, were the workshops that took place near the end of the RTP process (December 1995). These workshops involved representatives from Limburg's business community, knowledge institutes and intermediary organisations. The conclusions of the RTP study were examined during the workshops and suggestions made about possible activities aimed at solving the bottlenecks which had been indicated. The most revealing thoughts, frustrations and ideas came up when groups were confronted with perceptions of other actors. An instance was the confrontation of subcontractors with statements from their customers: as it was no longer a policy-maker who was trying to change their attitude, but their own customers who spoke, they had to take action. This created a clear awareness about their own shortcomings.

The final (provisional) stage with respect to the RTP was the rendering of the January 1996 interim report into concrete policy recommendations and a strategy for technology and innovation in Limburg as the core elements of the RTP. The policy recommendations and innovation strategy were subsequently described in terms of concrete projects, an implementation framework and the resources required. It is specifically these aspects that are the subject of the final RTP policy document, which was presented (together with an action plan) at a major event in July 1996 in which some 200 organisations (companies, intermediaries, suppliers, etc.) participated. The main goals of this event were to raise awareness in the region regarding the RTP document and to mobilise companies and intermediary organisations to implement the innovation strategy which the province of Limburg is promoting in its RTP.

From the Finish Onwards

In the week after this awareness-raising event, three international expert seminars were organised. The main goal of these seminars was to provide the regional authority with suggestions for possible approaches for the implementation of the main priorities of the RTP. Three to four foreign experts were called in per seminar with the assignment to provide critical (and possibly controversial) comments and suggestions on the different parts of the RTP Limburg. They gave advice on the role of the regional authority in each field; this was based on their expertise, and presented relevant experiences from other European regions. Each of the three meetings had a different focus: external orientation of SMEs, specialisation cores and the intermediary infrastructure.

Monitoring the RTP Effects

To measure the overall impact of the RTP policy (including the support of the Structural – and other – Funds), a two-stream monitoring system is currently being implemented, as follows:

- A 'process monitoring' system: this system indicates the impact of the RTP on the regional economy. The main data sources are statistics and surveys. This monitoring system can provide only rough indications and directions, since the regional economic situation is clearly influenced by more factors than the RTP policy.

- A 'policy monitoring' system: this system registers the effects of the individual projects in quantitative and in qualitative terms. The relevant information will be provided by the participants in the projects (mostly companies), by the project managers (consultants, intermediaries and others) and by the (EU) programme managers (ERDF, Interreg, etc.). The information collected through this monitoring system enables the provincial RTP project team to draw conclusions on the effects of individual projects. This can then become valuable input for further policy decisions to be made by the province.

The Role of Large Companies

In Limburg there are many multinationals (e.g. Philips, DSM, Rank Xerox, Océ and NedCar), and their importance to the Limburg economy is one of the reasons why they became involved in the RTP process. Along with the in-depth technology audits, most of them also participated in the various workshops, pilot projects and study groups. In fact, they proved to be a major contributor to the analysis of the business and technological needs of the Limburg business community.

However, it is not just their size and employment impact that make the involvement of these companies in the RTP useful. Another main reason to involve them in the process is their relations with SMEs in the region, where the contractor–subcontractor relation proved to be important. Many SMEs proved to be in close contact or close cooperation with large companies in the field of innovation and technology. So it is obvious that, in the process of thinking about a future regional innovation policy for Limburg, large companies have to be involved in this strategic planning process.

Almost all large companies were audited during the RTP process. These technology audits produced a vast amount of information not only about their own needs in terms of knowledge and skilled people but also about the needs of their SME-sized suppliers. In addition, by stressing the importance they attribute to high value-added linkages with regional suppliers, they proved to be important in stimulating the awareness regarding increasing the knowledge intensity among SMEs. So, one can say that as well as being an 'object of study', the large firms also played a role as a 'tool' in the study and actions.

Furthermore, large companies were involved in the management of the RTP process through their involvement in the RTP steering committee. Moreover, after the RTP document was written, several large companies took the initiative in launching new projects (in the field of clustering, co-engineering education/training and opening the research departments to SMEs in the region).

Because of their deep knowledge of the business and technology needs of the Limburg economy, representatives of large companies were asked to become members of a so-called expert pool. This is a group of business representatives formed to provide the province with a second opinion on the quality of project proposals coming from intermediaries, consultants and others, which one can regard as a customer panel with an important advisory role in distributing public money to intermediary organisations in the innovation infrastructure. Thus, regarding the implementation of the RTP findings, we see that in Limburg large companies play an important role at the strategic (RTP Steering Committee), tactical (expert pool) and implementation (project) levels within the RTP process.

Looking Back

The throughput time of the RTP Limburg was quite long. Practice is inevitably much more recalcitrant than theory. The methods for setting up the RTP were sound, but it took longer than anticipated to reach consensus on conducting research and drawing up conclusions. Furthermore, the long throughput time can also be attributed to the fact that, in this process, three objectives had to be tackled simultaneously: doing research, implementing the findings and achieving a consensus. It was a two-steps-forward-one-step-back kind of process. Once the parties involved in the RTP finally reached agreement, however, it took only a short time to generate regional consensus on Limburg's innovation strategy. The advantage, however, is that the province is now at a stage where the RTP exercise has delivered much more than just a report.

The RTP process turned out to be much more difficult and complicated than was expected. Performing studies, analysing the regional infrastructure, reaching commitment and implementing the findings at the same time with more than 150 people involved was a great experience. It is difficult to foresee all the elements at the beginning of the process. The guidebook provided by the EC was very useful and allowed for flexibility in setting one's own course.

THE INTERNATIONAL DIMENSION

In general, we could state that the added value of the international dimension of the RTP exercise was appreciated by the province of Limburg mainly in relation to specific topics of the RTP (rather than to the overall process of strategy-building), through bilateral contacts (rather than through multilateral relations), and towards the end of the process (rather than at the beginning of it).

Cross-National Cooperation

Despite Limburg's relative openness towards cross-national relations and networking, it had no natural tendency towards international exchanges of experiences in the field of policy-building related to the areas of technology and innovation. Compared with the business or academic sectors, the public administration sector is certainly the least open to international exchanges.

There is however a recognition that, in principle, ideas from elsewhere may be a valuable input to public policy, giving new insights or suggesting new practices. Moreover, this recognition has grown significantly during the course of the RTP. The province now believes that externalisation on the part of companies should be matched with a similar practice on the part of the regional authority. A crucial added-value is expected from the RTP exercise here, i.e. to favour learning processes in regional policy-making through a greater openness to outside experiences and ideas, as discussions with policy-makers from other regions may lead to a better understanding and (sometimes) appreciation of their own situation. Limburg, having identified the need for increasing cross-national cooperation at the policy level, included a cross-border orientation from the beginning of the RTP exercise.

Cross-border cooperation was sought and found with respect to the pilot projects. The 'Skills Portfolio' pilot project, which was set up to extend the instruments intended to develop software which employers could use to compile and update individual employee portfolios, was executed in collaboration with a company from Wales. And the RTP regions of Lorraine and Saxony were involved in the pilot project 'Transnational Cooperation in the SME Sector'.

However, despite the clear intention and willingness, it must be said that only now, after the RTP studies have been completed and the policy document has been written, are there concrete possibilities of learning from each other. Because of the inherent differences in starting points of the various RTP regions, cross-national exchanges on the RTP process proved to be rather difficult. Experiences of other RTP regions concerning procedural issues were therefore not a major input in the Limburg RTP. Exchanges with other regions on content issues were however much more interesting, but more in the broader sense of gaining a deeper insight into the subject than in having much influence on the content itself. It appears that at the onset of an RTP process a region has too little knowledge about the subject to really gauge the value of experiences elsewhere for its own needs. It also seems that, after the completion of the RTP, when the regional authorities have gained a much better understanding of their own innovative potentials (and difficulties and experiences from other RTPs can be better appreciated), ways for cross-national cooperation can be initiated much more effectively. One can only have a good discussion when all parties have done their homework. It is vital to know the context before one learns from other experiences. By doing the RTP exercise, one learns to see what is relevant in that context and what is not. The province of Limburg expects that the most important learning effects from other regions will therefore be diffused after the RTP projects are officially finished. A question one might ask in this respect is whether instead of withdrawing from the exercise, the Commission should stimulate and facilitate networking more, because networking, in our view, is especially important *after* the RTP policy document is written.

The RTP Network

As regards the role of the RTP network, the main functions of this network were appreciated as providing a benchmarking function and a learning function, in the sense of the development of concrete policy actions at the implementation stage. The network has also enhanced the relationship with the European Commission in this area and has made a genuine contribution to improving the Limburg region's reputation within Europe. The network also serves as the basis for further cooperation between companies and intermediary organisations from the various European RTP regions, in this way allowing them to reap the harvest of a well-aimed stimulation policy. Limburg sees it therefore as an objective to remain an active member of the European network of RTP (RIS and RITTS) regions. The province feels it can play a prominent role within the network, as it has had a head-start over the other regions in this field.

Use of Foreign Experts

There were no foreign experts engaged in the earlier stages of the RTP process, but rather local experts with international experience. This method was considered a success, since it combined the 'outsider view' with the knowledge of the local situation. At the earlier stages of the RTP this was regarded as most beneficial for the process. Limburg gradually evolved towards more integration of the international dimension in the policy-building practice as foreign experts were called in to discuss possible ways to realise the three main RTP priorities. To this extent, small workshops, involving field operators from the region as well as the province, were organised around several crucial themes in order to examine more deeply the options available and their feasibility. The applicability to the Limburg situation of lessons from other regions was discussed among foreign experts and representatives from the region.

MAIN RESULTS AND MAIN LESSONS FROM THE RTP
LIMBURG

If we had to single out the most important result, it might very well be the *increased cooperation* within the region and with other regions that resulted from the RTP process. This result goes far beyond the reports written and studies done. Nevertheless, the RTP has produced a treasure trove of valuable information. It has not only provided an accurate picture of the way business and, in particular, industry function in Limburg and the various aspects related to technology and innovation, but has also elicited suggestions and ideas from various corners regarding a policy aimed at technology and economic development. Another important benefit from the RTP experience in the middle and long run is that the province will become a 'sparring partner' for the firms in the region. Firms will acknowledge the clear (neutral) role a province can play in building the technological infrastructure and increasing the knowledge base of firms. Firms will no longer play such a waiting game, but will turn to the province early with their questions and desires. They have become aware of the importance of articulating their problems to intermediates and the province.

As the province has been engaged with technology policy for some time already, the analysis hardly revealed unknown facts about the general needs of industry on the highest aggregation level in terms of innovation. Consequently, no totally new insights came out of the RTP. However, the RTP led to a lot of sector-specific suggestions for improvement. The policy document, for instance, included a list of 67 conclusions; most notably, the RTP:

- demonstrated more clearly the need for more external orientation of the SMEs;

- confirmed the broad vision of innovation prevailing, well beyond the technological aspect;

- showed more clearly the tensions between subcontracting firms and their suppliers;

- confirmed the need to support moves by SMEs towards benchmarking approaches;

- made the province aware of the diversity of the problems that firms face, many of which are fairly straightforward but need attention.

Next to these more specific points for improvement, the overall innovation strategy aimed to 'reinforce the level of knowledge within industrial companies in Limburg, especially SMEs, and improve their access to the knowledge and educational infrastructure and the extent to which this infrastructure meets their needs' (RTP Limburg 1996).

In addition, ten priorities have been selected for the implementation of the RTP, as a short-term elaboration of the strategy: for each of the priorities described below, concrete projects are proposed and the collaboration of regional actors is already secured:

1. External orientation of the companies: improve companies' external orientation, and make better use of research efforts of others. Help companies to look beyond their borders.

2. Internal orientation of companies: intensify projects aiming at promoting an integrated approach to innovation within companies; augment them by introducing value analyses, management techniques, strategic research for the business community and specific innovation projects.

3. Cooperation: increase the level of cooperation between suppliers and purchasers, and between suppliers as a group; develop cluster activities.

4. Knowledge transfer and knowledge activity: increase the level of knowledge within strong industrial sectors that are over-represented in Limburg and whose knowledge and/or R&D intensity is average or above average; develop awareness-raising tools and consultative platforms, and open-door policies in knowledge and research institutions.

5. Demand for knowledge: develop supply management tools, such as value analysis and skills portfolio, for encouraging companies to focus on the future, and to assign a key role to such elements as personnel, technology and market.

6. Education and training: develop better labour market information (about the demand for training and education); bring about more effective cooperation between the suppliers of education; improve the reputation of technical programmes and increase the number of students entering.

7. Supply of knowledge: increase the transparency of the supply of knowledge in the cross-border region; support the identification of the needs of individual companies by knowledge institutions, increase the cooperation between those institutions in the regions.

8. Intermediary structure: develop a more integrated functioning between intermediary structures, in order to serve the market better; inspect various options for cooperation and coordination, or for moving towards more organisational concentration.

9. Innovative start-up companies: create a friendly climate for start-up companies, specifically aimed at technostarters; develop the offer of start-up capital, support and professional supervision in the knowledge institutions.

10. Follow-up of RTP: put in place a structure that will make it possible to monitor RTP-related activities and give a new impetus to a combination of technological and regional policy that will satisfy the wishes of the business community.

Looking more specifically at the innovation policy of the province itself, we can state that one of the main changes in the regional debate around technology policy as a result of the RTP is that the technology policy of the province will focus on more industrial sectors than the two (high-tech) sectors focused on up until now – medical technologies and telecoms. It is recognised that 'technology' is not just something for high-tech sectors. Furthermore, in addition to 'town and spatial planning', technology policy is becoming an integral part of the industrial policy of the province. At the moment, both policy fields are still two separate chapters in the industrial policy, but this will change in the future because more attention will be paid to the interlinkages between the two.

The Limburg RTP also became a means for lobbying for more autonomy and responsibilities of the regional authorities. Finishing the Limburg RTP had an important impact on the discussions in other provinces in the Netherlands on whether they should become involved in the RTP/RIS schemes as well. Other provinces became more and more enthusiastic about this and, as a result, it became an important issue in the communication between the provinces and the Ministry of Economic Affairs. The ministry appreciates and supports the various attempts the provinces are making in building their own regional innovation strategies. A permanent communication between the provinces and the ministry is one of the results of this process.

Linking the RTP to Structural Funds

As Limburg has Objective 2 and 5b areas and borders with two other countries, the region is receiving money through Structural Funds and Interreg measures. Within these and other programmes, innovation and technology (transfer) are key issues. One of the province's objectives at the start of the RTP was therefore that it expected the RTP to provide a direction and framework for innovation-related projects. This way, the RTP could play a pivotal role in synergising the innovation-related financial sources from European (Structural Funds, Framework Programme, Interreg), national and provincial authorities.

Through close contacts and agreements with the programme managers, the innovation-related elements of these programmes were brought into harmony with the ten priority lines of the RTP Limburg. On the implementation level, this means that every innovative project proposal will be discussed between the RTP team and the programme managers of the specific programmes, thereby attuning the financial sources to the RTP policy and giving a clear message to those who ask for provincial funding. The message to these intermediary organisations is that every innovation-related project they submit has to be in line with the RTP philosophy and strategy. It is this kind of anticipation that has a positive impact on the regional consensus in the end.

The Challenges Ahead

The main political challenges for the RTP management in the coming years are updating the RTP, keeping it on the political agenda and intensifying cooperation even more.

As writing an RTP is an evolutionary process, attention should be paid to updating the RTP as well. This implies financial efforts, not least from the Commission. It should give clear signals to the regional authorities (in words and actions) that it shares the responsibility it also asks from them. In order to show their concern with regional technology plans, DG XVI might want to consider earmarking certain budgets for innovation (e.g. earmarking part of the Structural Funds budget as being money for implementing RTPs or RISs). This also helps to keep the RTP on the agenda of the local and regional authorities. We believe that if DG XVI presumes that everyone in the region backs the RTP then it should show its own commitment as well.

Although the RTP documents are written and the EU funding has come to an end, the region clearly realises that it has only just begun improving its innovative capacity and knowledge intensity. The RTP process has contributed to a large extent towards knowing where to go and how to get there. The process of promoting innovation in the business community, specifically among small and medium-sized enterprises, has got underway. The discussion has only begun. At the moment, the majority of parties involved agree on the main points, but now the implementation will start. The present task is to get the Limburg business community and all the various parties that play a role in the innovation process to take action and to continue doing so. It is now vital that all the parties involved acknowledge the importance of a joint innovation strategy, and it is very important to keep the companies involved. It is a challenge to get the firms to accept the regional authority as a cooperative partner.

CLAIRE NAUWELAERS[1]

4   Creating a Regional Innovation Policy in Lorraine

THE LORRAINE REGION

The Lorraine region, with 2.3 million inhabitants on 23,500 square kilometres in the north-east of France, is one of the regions in the core of Europe that suffered most from the decline of its traditional industries, namely coal, steel and textiles. Severely hit by the closure of the mines and the drastic reduction of activities in traditional industries – steel and coal in the north, textiles in the south – the region has been involved in twenty years of profound restructuring and reconversion, striving to escape the trap of mono-industries. During the 1980s, the region lost around 10,000 jobs per year, and 14,000 inhabitants between 1982 and 1990 (INSEE 1997).

The legacy of the past is still acutely visible in Lorraine, with industrial wastelands and unemployment (more than 11 per cent of the active population and 21 per cent among the younger people in 1996; INSEE 1997) as prominent signs of the important challenges faced by this region. As a direct consequence of the economic and social situation of the region, Lorraine has experienced a high rate of outmigration of its population, mainly of its qualified young people, which is of course an alarming factor for its development. The concentration of activities and population is growing within the metropolitan axis (Nancy–Metz), at the expense of the rural areas and old industrial basins in the region. Concentrated in metalworking (40 per cent of industrial employment), agrifood (12 per cent), wood and paper (10 per cent), and textiles – clothing (7 per cent), the industrial activity of the region has to evolve towards more value-added production and to production linked with endogenous resources, with less dependence on captive markets or larger firms. The development of industrial services is also a major challenge, because this sector is severely under-represented in the region.

Lorraine is not without assets, however. The region benefits from a good geographical position, at the crossroads between France, Germany and Belgium. It hosts many universities and higher-education establishments, with high standards at both national and European levels, and has a number of technical lyceums and vocational training organisations that together constitute an extensive support for the education and training of the population. It benefits from the availability of good-quality technical centres, covering the main technical needs of the regional sectors. Signs of renewal of the industrial tissue are now apparent, with a number of new activities flourishing in the territory, mainly in the vicinity of its two main centres, Metz in the north and Nancy in the south. A number of new SMEs with a high content of information and knowledge are developing in sectors such as information technologies and biomedical supplies. Moreover, the reconversion policies of the 1980s are beginning to produce their effects: the cleaning of a part of the wasteland and a remarkable increase in the number of enterprises applying for the first time to the innovation support schemes available, showing that enterprises are catching up on the modernisation of their production systems.

The industrial fabric of the Lorraine region is characterised by an important presence of large and multinational enterprises, and a weak presence of SMEs. Large groups account for 70 per cent of the region's employment and 80 per cent of its turnover (INSEE 1997), with a high (by French standards) rate of employment in foreign, European-controlled companies – 27 per cent in 1993 (Ministère de l'Industrie 1996).[2] This foreign presence represents an asset, because of the direct and indirect effects of the activities and competencies of these companies in the region, but at the same time also a threat, in as much as the decision centres of these companies are located outside the region.

Lorraine is thus a region in the middle of its reconversion process, with a number of assets but also with a heavy legacy from the past, which puts its enterprises and citizens at threat in a new globalising, knowledge-based world. The requirements of increased competitiveness leave little time for the region to adjust to change.

Institutional Context

Despite a recent move towards more devolution of powers to its 24 regional entities, France is still a highly centralised state: while the decentralisation laws of 1982 assigned new responsibilities to the regions in the field of economic development, higher education and transport, the prevailing institutional context is not yet conducive to much autonomy in the hands of the regional level of authority.

In practically every field under its competence, the region needs to conclude agreements with the state – the so-called 'Contrats de Plans État-Region', which define the financial resources allocated to the region by the state. This process ends up very often with a situation where the region implements policy instruments developed at the central level, with little room for adaptation to the specific regional context. Apart from state contributions, the region also has direct resources, but their size is not to be compared to the importance of the means that would be needed to adequately cover their powers.

The land-planning policy – the main policy area concerned with reducing regional disparities in the country and, therefore, directly addressing the regional development issue – is characterised by a tension between two contrasting viewpoints. On the one hand, the view of the state representatives tends to be that leaving too much responsibility to the local and regional levels would lead to difficulties in running a coherent land-planning policy that takes full account of the general interest. On the other hand, the view of the newly empowered regional authorities advances the belief that more autonomy and freedom would generate new resources and energy for generating successful development paths, with more reliance on endogenous resources. Until now, the first view has clearly dominated the institutional landscape in France, even though the latter is gaining audience.

In another area, namely that of the industrial and restructuring policies, which have a particular importance in such an old industrialised region as Lorraine, the presence of the state is ubiquitous: within the European countries, France has one of the highest proportions of economic activity controlled by the public sector, which acts not only as a regulator but also as a banker and an industrialist. At the end of the Second World War, a wave of nationalisations occurred, under the conviction that only the central state would be able to generate the resources needed at that time for the rebuilding of the economy. From then, successive 'plans' have been decided as the expression of the will of the state about the direction of the economy. The main instruments of the state for influencing the economy consisted, and still consist today, of the public enterprises. While the efficiency of the indicative planning policy has been increasingly put in question, the tendency of a 'hands-on' policy by the national government towards the economy remains conspicuous today.

The specific restructuring policies put in place in the regions most affected by industrial decline in France (with Nord-Pas de Calais and Lorraine as the main target regions) followed the same line: failing sectors and depressed territories were supported through the relocation of new industries settled by the state, such as the automobile industry in Nord-Pas de Calais or the telecoms industry in Brittany. Little confidence was placed in the potential role of local and regional actors to take their faith in hands and support their development by their own forces. Although the new guidelines for restructuring policies in the 1990s acknowledge the potential role of localised industrial systems and provide (in theory) for more responsibility on local actors, their application still remains to be seen, after decades of state assistance. Only quite recently have regional authorities, with their new competencies, tended to envisage their role as a more creative and more responsible one than of 'just' implementing within their own territory decisions already taken in Paris.

This institutional context should not be forgotten when analysing the process and the results of an initiative such as the RTP, which has a built-in prerequisite that regions are both willing and able to define their own policy. In the case of a French region, the RTP process is inevitably a subtle negotiation process between the regional authority and the central one.

REGIONAL CONTEXT FOR INNOVATION

The history of Lorraine explains why it lacks industries with a high knowledge content: its past prosperity and its very identity had been constructed on the exploitation of its natural resources (coal, steel and wood) in mass production. Also, because of its particular position close to Northern Europe, the region has not been favoured in terms of the localisation of publicly supported high-tech enterprises or research centres.

In 1990, the region contained only 1.1 per cent of French industrial employment in high-tech industries, while 5.8 per cent of the employment in low-tech industries was found there (OST 1994). In other words, industries with low technology and low R&D content were over-represented in the region (even if the concentration of high-tech industries in Île-de-France is accounted for). In terms of industrial R&D, Lorraine is one of the weakest French regions, with around 1 per cent of private R&D carried out there in 1992, and a concentration of engineers and researchers in the active population of 3.7 per cent as compared with 11.5 per cent in France as a whole in 1992 (OST 1996).

The dependence of the industrial tissue on large groups means that the majority of smaller firms have developed a subcontractor culture, with a relative lack of entrepreneurship and innovation. The management of enterprises is still very much dictated by technological imperatives, while marketing, commercial and innovation efforts are marginalised in too many traditional enterprises. As a whole, the region suffers also from a deficit in industrial services, on the one hand because the large groups do not locate their strategic functions in Lorraine, which is perceived as a region executing orders, and on the other hand because SMEs have not developed a sufficient demand for those functions. This subcontractor culture also has its effects in terms of enterprise creation, since Lorraine has a rather low rate of new enterprise births, and this is even more marked for the creation of business-related service enterprises.

The Lorraine region has also to catch up with the rest of the country in terms of qualifications: in 1994, for example, 33 per cent of the population did not have a degree (compared with 29 per cent for the country), and only 8 per cent held a high-level degree (compared with 11 per cent for France as a whole) (Cordelier and Poisson 1996).

A lack of 'attitude' towards innovation is clearly at the heart of the development problem in Lorraine.

The Support for Innovation

The Lorraine region is one of the best-endowed French regions in terms of academic research laboratories (if one excepts Île-de-France, which still has a high share of fundamental research). In terms of applied research, however, the region ranks much lower.

Public R&D contracts and grants awarded to enterprises are traditional means used in France to stimulate R&D in the private sector. It is not exceptional to find around 30 per cent of private R&D financed by the state through 'large technology programmes' or innovation credits to enterprises, which aim to orient private R&D in directions that are judged important for the future. In 1990, Lorraine has benefited from just 0.1 per cent of the French public funds (which are heavily concentrated in the capital region: 58 per cent in 1990), which means that those funds contributed only to 2 per cent of its industrial R&D funding (OST 1994).

The private support for innovation is a weak element of the system, although very little is known in terms of the availability and quality of the services by private actors. The public technology transfer support infrastructure has been the subject of major initiatives from the state and the region. Their main elements are described below.

The Lorraine region hosts a number of technical centres and technology transfer centres, covering adequately the various fields of activities pertinent to the region's activity. A deficit in some sectors (the agrifood and mechanical industry) has however been confirmed by the RTP analyses.

The 'Regional Network for Diffusion and Transfer of Technology' (hereafter simply 'the network') includes some thirty members (regional technology transfer centres or CRITTs, technical centres, and chambers of commerce) who commit themselves to a three-fold mission: raising technological awareness within 'defensive' enterprises, providing technological advice and guidance to 'offensive' enterprises, and building an information base on the evolution of techniques that is of use to the members of the network. The members of the network are the technological advisers within the participating structures, and they are responsible for finding the best answer to the needs of the companies within the supply available in the region. The technological advisers attend regular meetings, where they exchange methods and information, and participate to training sessions for updating the practices and competencies.

When the 'Lorraine Technologie' policy was debated in the region, and finally endorsed by the national and regional authorities in 1994, it became clear that one of the main underlying ideas behind it was that the Regional Advisory Centres would be asked to respond to enterprises' demands as well as to sell their services. Their financing had to become dependent on their results, rather than be granted automatically. Under this policy, the regional technological advisory centres are committed to an innovation awareness programme carried out via a concerted visits programme to enterprises. The Association for Technology Transfer in Lorraine (ATTELOR) is in charge of coordinating the actions and ensuring that a sufficient number of enterprises are visited and serviced by the members of the network. The members adhere to a charter of objectives, which contains an obligation to refer customer enterprises to other members of the network in case they express demands falling into those members' competencies.

The main weaknesses of the system, as it was functioning at the start of the RTP, were identified (through the first study phase) as follows :

- The system is mainly servicing the 'offensive' enterprises, i.e. the enterprises that are spontaneously innovative.

- The system is geared towards the support of technical adaptation within existing units, rather than towards the creation of new enterprises or the support of 'softer' adaptation in existing units (change in management methods, human resources development, commercial innovations).

This perception of the weaknesses of the innovation support system evolved out of the RTP process, as is shown below.

GENESIS AND OBJECTIVES OF THE RTP

The RTP initiative came when the industrial restructuring of the Lorraine region was underway but certainly not achieved, and where new threats to its development, linked to an increased globalisation, called for strengthened regional responses. With a clear consensus on the industrial vocation of the region, the main challenge was identified as the modernisation of SMEs and the creation of new activities with more value added. Therefore, innovation, which in this region is understood mainly as technological innovation, was acknowledged as the key factor for restoring competitiveness to enterprises, and to the regional industrial fabric as a whole. With the experience gained through earlier regional technology policies, the region was ready to make a step further towards boosting its development.

On the institutional and policy side, this political will in favour of the support to technological development in SMEs had already been expressed in the region through several joint state–region initiatives: the creation of ATTELOR in 1984, the creation of the network in 1989, and the development of the 'Lorraine Technologie' policy in 1994.

ATTELOR, created by the region and the state, and involving universities, high schools and enterprises, aims to provide a forum for debating the development of technologies in the regional industrial tissue. The network began as a base of technology advisers, and was then formally accepted as a pilot network supported by the Ministry of Research and Industry, with the specific aim of fostering the relations between regional SMEs and regional technology transfer centres. Subsequently, the 'Lorraine Technologie' policy has been launched within the 'Contrat de Plan État-Region, with the aim of promoting awareness of technological development in enterprises not yet familiar with the technology transfer process in partnership with technology resource centres. In other words, this policy reinforced the action of the network towards new customers, the firms with a weaker or latent demand for technology transfer.

Thus the Lorraine region already had a long and solid history of technology policy, being one of the first regions in France to put in place a network of technology advisers. The creators of this network were rightly proud of this new form of organisation, which finds its counterpart now in the majority of French regions. However, at the same time, this achievement introduced a certain degree of inertia in the system, as any tendency to reflect on the system could be perceived as a potential threat to the main pillar of technology transfer in the region, namely ATTELOR.

Nevertheless, the RTP initiative was welcome in the region, as the authorities (the region and the state delegates there) saw it as an excellent occasion to give a new impetus to regional technological innovation policy, which was recognised implicitly as running out of steam after the considerable achievements of the past. The expectations from the RTP were not clearly stated at the start, although the development of a less technologically oriented support system to innovation, the association of new actors such as the Business and Innovation Centres (BICs) or the technopoles, and the development of new instruments to stimulate less innovative SMEs, were certainly three objectives present on the hidden agendas of the persons and organisations supporting the RTP in the region.

At the beginning of the RTP in 1994, ATTELOR had a rather ambiguous position with regard to this initiative, being both its natural promoter *and* on the defensive in case the RTP would end up dismantling the network, which had taken so much time and effort to set up.

Other established actors, such as the BICs, which were not well integrated into the system, had of course different expectations from this initiative: it represented a unique opportunity for them to open doors and connect to the dominant nucleus of actors and schemes geared towards the support of enterprise development in the region. A number of minor actors saw the RTP as the occasion to have their activities more widely recognised, or their causes defended – examples being a very proactive organisation striving to develop clusters of enterprises in a small zone of the region, or an unfortunate inventor seeking finance for his project.

As is shown in the final section of this chapter, this apparent contradiction at the start of the exercise, which threatened to make for a difficult game where one party would necessarily gain at the expense of another, has been transformed into a win-win situation, where a new direction for the evolution of the system has been embarked upon without any major conflict, and, even more, has achieved a convergence of interests between most of the regional actors.

THE RTP PROCESS

The first step in the RTP process was the consensus between the members of the directing committee, a nucleus composed of the traditional four actors in charge of the policy in the region (the region, the state delegate for research, the state delegate for industry, and the state organisation for support to research and innovation in industry – ANVAR), augmented by the ATTELOR association. The importance of state agents in a regional initiative can be seen clearly through the composition of this committee. The directing committee was composed of individuals used to working together, notably for periodically elaborating the 'Contrat de Plan Etat-Région'. A formal agreement on the RTP exercise was reached by mid-1994 by the members of this committee, conferring full legitimacy to the exercise and providing the guarantee that the achievements of the exercise would be properly relayed by the adequate authorities.

Regarding the RTP coordinator (a member of the regional administration within the Research and Education Department), it is noteworthy that although the necessity of appointing a permanent coordinator had repeatedly been discussed, that decision was never taken, and the actual coordinator had to do the job mostly 'after hours'. While this situation was far from ideal, given the complexity and the importance of the job, it has to be explained in political terms: it was considered essential that the main figure of the RTP was someone from one of the public institutions, and with a sufficiently high level within the hierarchy. Giving this responsibility to, for example, a university professor, or a specialist in a technology transfer or business support institution, would have risked transforming the whole exercise into mere intellectual discussions without any clear link with the policy circles. The stakeholders of the RTP, on the other hand, showed their eagerness to locate the RTP right from the start at the core of the decision centre in the region. In this sense, legitimacy and credibility have taken precedence over efficiency in the management of the RTP. This situation played its role in the relative slowness of the RTP process in Lorraine, as well as in its other features, such as the weak attention to the study part.

The second building block of the RTP in Lorraine was the constitution of a steering committee. This process was pursued rather informally, the inclusion of members in this group being decided by the directing committee without any formal registration or any participation procedures being erected. The composition of the steering committee evolved over time: at first, it was a rather restricted circle of actors, a fact which raised concerns among actors not involved; in a later period, fears and curiosity were raised when it became apparent that policy and the use of funds could be reshaped by this body. Only after these steps could this committee become a wider discussion forum, as stipulated in the commission's framework. The participation of enterprises in this committee, whether large or small, had always been very weak: the tradition of public–private collaboration is not very strong in France, and enterprises are not used to taking part in a policy elaboration process. The main role announced for the steering committee was one of validating the approach followed, notably through commenting on the studies' methods and results, stimulating new directions for the strategy, and diffusing information on the RTP work to the regional actors. In reality however it also acted in some respect as the 'guardian' of the established order, a role which is not much in line with the RTP objective but which reflects the attitude of some of its members towards change and the possible redistribution of power induced by the RTP.

Along with the three elements of the management structure of the RTP mentioned above (directing committee, coordinator, steering committee), the region appointed external referees, on a suggestion from the European Commission. Academic experts from RIDER – University of Louvain (Belgium) – and MERIT – University of Maastricht (Netherlands) – were hired, with the remit of checking out the validity of the process followed in Lorraine with respect to the community requirements, providing comments and advice on the methods and results of the work undertaken under the RTP, taking charge of some parts of the exercise, and, last but not least, helping to confer an international dimension on the regional exercise.

The RTP Activities

In terms of a working plan, the RTP in Lorraine started with a very loose schedule and an unclear picture of activities to be carried out. In retrospect, this difficulty of building an organised and rational plan of activities from the start is probably due to the 'traditionalist' attitude of a number of actors in the region. As an example, the need to conduct an assessment of the support infrastructure which was more than a catalogue of centres with their list of activities was not understood (or not accepted, as we argue below).

After the constitution phase described above, the process went on, in the first half of 1995, with the 'analysis of demand' phase of the RTP, which in Lorraine turned out to be an analysis of existing data on SMEs' technological needs. During the years preceding the RTP, the network had produced standardised data from the enterprise visits made by technology advisers of the network, since one of the components of the Lorraine technology policy was an obligation for all advisers to analyse and report on the needs of the companies they visited. Through the RTP, this source of information, which had never been exploited, was analysed for the first time. Although this analysis can be judged lengthy and descriptive rather than interpretative (it ended up merely with the production of a list of tables, summarising the existing data), it had the merit of giving flesh to the RTP process: something new and tangible was produced. After some hesitations regarding the diffusion of the results of the analysis, the data were finally presented, first to the directing committee then to the steering committee.

The study detailed the technological needs of the enterprises visited, by sector, size and geographical zone, with a distinction between needs in terms of new process, new products, organisation and technological information. Some insights were also present into the relations between the enterprises and the competence centres which were supposed to answer their needs. Whatever the limits of this analysis (notably the fact that the only enterprises surveyed were the clients of the network), it nevertheless gave a global vision of the needs of the productive tissue in the region, and a general picture of the action of the network, two things which were hardly ever available in the past. Some lessons emerging from the data whetted the appetite for a better understanding of the situation with regard to innovation in the region, within policy-making circles. Notwithstanding all the precautions necessary regarding the incompleteness of the analysis, the conclusions reached were sufficient to start new discussions and put crucial questions on the RTP table.

The main conclusions of the 'demand analysis' were as follows:

- SMEs had an important demand in terms of organisation, production management and quality management, and therefore the necessity of a 'non-technical' form of support was essential.

- SMEs, and notably the very small enterprises, revealed a need for training and recruitment, so initial and continued training had to be coupled with the work of the network.

- Needs in terms of scientific and technical information were important, thus the need to connect the network to sources of scientific information was patent.

- The profile of needs was very different between very small, small and medium-sized enterprises, and hence it was necessary to segment the target customer group of the policy and to pay particular attention to very small enterprises showing a real potential for the renewing of the industrial fabric.

- 40 per cent of enterprises visited did not express any need for support, and therefore the capacity of the network to raise awareness and help the revelation of latent needs of enterprises should be further explored.

- Service enterprises were not covered by the work of the network; nevertheless, they play a role in the innovation process.

- The rate of penetration and response of the network towards enterprises' demands varied according to the sectors; hence the necessity to understand the different rate of performance of the network and to redefine plans accordingly.

- From a policy standpoint, the most challenging comment stemming from this analysis was the following one: very few demands directed to one member of the network were transferred to another member; as a consequence, the rate of 'autoprescription' (members consulted by an enterprise deciding that the service had to be provided by themselves) of the network was very high. This raised the explosive question of whether the network was really functioning as a network, with mutual knowledge of the competencies and cooperation to better service the enterprises.

In parallel with the demand analysis, the external consultants held a number of face-to-face interviews with key actors and produced a note on the 'Regional innovation system in Lorraine', signalling the strengths and weaknesses of the region in terms of innovation and innovation support. In addition to winning the confidence of a number of key actors of the RTP, this operation helped them to introduce a number of ideas to be discussed subsequently in the frame of the RTP, such as the weakness of a purely technological definition of innovation, the role of the services, the necessary openness of the support structure, and the possibilities for linking knowledge centres (in terms of R&D as well as training activities) with the industrial tissue. The main value of this step was not so much the content of the note but rather the possibility it gave to the external experts of winning their place at the heart of the RTP process, rather than being confined to the writing of particular studies at the periphery of the RTP social engineering process. Their disturbing questions were heard by the actors in the RTP, and remained in the debate in the follow-up to the process.

The next step of the process, in the second half of 1995, consisted of setting up a number of working groups, around four themes decided by the steering committee on a proposal from the external consultants. Those themes were vast enough to cover adequately the whole problem of innovation in the region, and to offer the possibility to any interested actor of participating in at least one group. Membership of the groups was open, and the chairmanship was devolved to people chosen for their competence rather than status, at the suggestion of the external consultants. This last provision allowed 'non-traditional' organisations to gain a voice; these organisations included for example the technical lycea for the 'training group', a formation that would normally have been led by a university. The four themes were:

- enhancing the visibility of the network;
- extending the innovation-financing possibilities;
- supporting innovation management in SMEs;
- the role of training and education in innovation.

It may not be apparent to an external observer how sensitive some of these subjects were in the region. The fact that the regional actors were able to start an open debate, based on a clear discussion note, stating in a straightforward manner the problems and the challenges under each subject, is a great achievement of the RTP for this region. The aim of those groups was, under each theme, to define more precisely the problems and refine the diagnosis, and to develop recommendations on what actions to take to improve the situation.

To start the exercise with a fresh view, experts from other EU countries and other French regions were invited to study the discussion paper for the group, and to participate in its first meeting, bringing in their own experience with regard to the questions at hand.

Overall, the work of the groups, which met two or three times each, was well appreciated and delivered a number of new directions and concrete proposals, which all went along the lines of a more global, less technical support of innovative projects.

At that point of the exercise, no real analysis of the 'supply side' of innovation was available. Indeed, this compulsory element of the Commission's RTP work programme had led to intense debate within the directing committee of the RTP. For more than a year, the prevailing conception was that the supply side was well known and well labelled (through state or network recognition) and that no analysis was needed. It was apparent that 'analysis' was understood as 'inventory' and that most people were trying to avoid an 'evaluation' type of analysis.[3] The fact that the French state was also conducting a procedure of certification of transfer organisations, which might be considered as fulfilling the needs at regional level (although they were by no means real evaluations of their effectiveness), contributed to freezing the situation for months.

However, when the analysis of demand and the working groups started to produce challenging results, a growing strand of opinion emerged to advocate a real analysis of the global support infrastructure for innovation, extending beyond universities and transfer centres, and taking on board the needs of the users rather than the views of the providers. Therefore, very late in the process (at the end of 1995) the decision was taken to hire a French consultant, who was not involved in regional activities, to undertake this critical analysis in a short period of time.

The long preparation time was probably needed to open the minds of regional actors and to have them accept such an exercise. Although it would have seemed more rational to start the exercise with a knowledge-building phase and then use this knowledge to define strategy, this would have been difficult in Lorraine because of the resistance of the main actors, who were not open to critical reflection on their own functioning.

With this new activity starting, the RTP was thus gaining real momentum, and was on the ascendant at the very moment when it should have come to an end, according to the Commission's schedule. This time-frame was obviously too tight for the Lorraine region, and the authorities of the RTP had to ask for a six-month extension until mid-1996.

The elaboration of the mandate for the supply analysis was made easier through the availability of the results of the first phase of the RTP: it was given the objective of analysing the coherence, efficiency, adaptability and visibility of the support structure, with specific attention being given to 'less-visible actors' such as technical lycea and private sources of expertise. The analysis, conducted mainly through interviews and panels of the main actors concerned, confirmed the weaknesses of the support system already touched upon, i.e. its too-limited orientation to the technological dimension and the lack of visibility and availability of support for the other dimensions of the innovation process, its exclusive focus on industry (as opposed to services), the weakness of the 'networking' element between transfer operators, and the existence of unexploited potential outside the system, namely within technical lycea and private suppliers. The need for more economic or technico-economic information sources has also been put in evidence through this study.

In addition, another study contract was granted to a consulting company in Paris, in order to examine the possibility of finding development programmes of interest to the regional industrial fabric, and particularly to SMEs, from the existing resources in the research laboratories of the region. The results of the analysis confirmed the expectation: the regional laboratories could not work directly with SMEs because of the distance between the two cultures and a number of practical problems. Therefore, it was not possible to put them at the forefront of a system aiming at supporting innovation in SMEs, notably the defensive ones.

Lastly, the state delegate for industry in the region contributed to the exercise with two studies, one on the innovative firms in the region and the other on the evolution of the main sectors of the region. The first study confirmed that a focus on the high-tech enterprises as a vector of innovation for Lorraine was too short a view, and that innovation in existing firms had to be supported, notably in the areas of financing, training and market information and through favouring inter-firm partnerships.

This last point, the need for more partnership and cooperation between enterprises as a vector of innovation – since it is true that 'enterprises learn most, and most quickly from other enterprises' (Dankbaar 1993) – has also emerged as a finding in all other activities of the RTP. As minds were unclear on how to deal with this question, however, and because little information was available on existing experiences inside the region and elsewhere, it was decided to organise a workshop on the subject in early 1996. This gathered 90 persons, among them a number of enterprises managers, and provided a forum for the presentation of experiences in the region and from Belgium, the Netherlands and the UK. Besides a better knowledge of existing clusters and networks functioning in the region, the conference provided a real stimulus to develop pilot actions in this field, and a number of concrete projects have flowed to the RTP coordinator as a direct result of the conference.

In the first months of 1996, the RTP had thus produced a number of results, from various sources and involving a large set of regional actors, which were all converging in the same direction and pointing to new inflexion for the regional innovation policy. Those conclusions have been gathered by the external consultant, in a consultative document approved by the directing committee. The strategy was expressed under three axes: reinforcing the absorptive capacity of SMEs for technology and their innovation management capacities; reinforcing and reorienting the innovation support system; and developing the tools for designing, monitoring and following up policies in the region. In total, 35 propositions for actions, emerging from all the previous phases, were suggested under the three axes.

The consultative document was disseminated by mail to 300 regional actors, including 200 enterprises, which were asked to react on the document, define priorities between the actions, and propose concrete projects to implement the action lines. A meeting was then organised to publicise the results of the consultation, and the last steering committee meeting of the RTP ratified the amended strategy and action plan, as the final step of the RTP, in June 1996.

The consultation did not change fundamentally the strategy as it was drafted, but clarified the following priorities from the regional actors: a strong interest had been expressed for the first axis (reinforcing the absorption and management capacities of enterprises), including the inter-firm networking dimension, a wish for more interaction among the members of the network, a necessary effort in terms of the financing of innovation, the openness of the network to other actors and to exchanges outside the region, and the coordination of the various aid mechanisms existing in the region. In addition, a number of actors showed their commitment by launching or participating in projects related to those priorities.

The Output of the RTP

In brief, the innovation strategy for Lorraine, as it appears at the final step of the RTP, stands as follows:

- Reinforcing technology absorption capacity and the innovation management process within SMEs through:

  - creating teams around the enterprise managers in order to ensure the follow-up of innovative projects;

  - supporting the creation of networks between small and large enterprises;

  - coordinating the available tools for supporting the hiring of qualified people and the retraining of employees;

  - creating training courses for management of innovation for SMEs managers;

  - introducing the innovation management and SME dimensions in the engineers' courses;

- integrating industrialists' experiences in the initial and continued training courses.

- Reinforcing and reorienting the support structure for innovation in SMEs through:

  - reinforcing the availability of finance for innovative projects, via the creation of a network of innovation financiers, complementing the national system of advances, creating a regional fund of participation, supporting risk-capital organisations, etc.;

  - developing a non-technical support offer;

  - improving the support to 'basic' innovations, via the organisation of the transfer activity in technical lycea;

  - articulating the offer from technical lycea and private sources with the network activities;

  - reinforcing the action of the network, through reinforcing its communication policy, favouring multi-interventions involving several members of the network, fostering the awareness of the technology advisers on the managerial dimension of innovation, increasing the openness of the network outside Lorraine, reinforcing cooperation within the network, and measuring this evolution with concrete indicators, etc.;

  - improving the professionalism of intermediaries and transfer actors;

  - developing the scientific, technical and commercial information services available to enterprises.

- Improving the design, monitoring and evaluation of the policies, through:

  - a better coordination of existing aid mechanisms;

  - developing tools for the information of regional authorities (creation of an observatory);

  - creating a permanent committee as a continuation of the RTP steering committee, a 'network of networks' in Lorraine.

Eleven projects have been budgeted under this strategy at the end of the RTP.
  With regard to the existing policy, the RTP encouraged innovation in several respects:

- putting priority on 'day-to-day' innovation, as opposed to technological ruptures in high-tech firms;

- recognising that the non-technical side of innovation has to be supported too;

- pointing to the necessity to open the network to other actors and other competencies than the ones involved currently;

- linking the financing problem to the innovation management question;

- acknowledging the crucial role of inter-firm networking as a vector for innovation.

The question of the role of training and education, which was repeatedly touched upon, appears as the weakest part of the RTP : even if a general recognition of the importance of this factor was prevailing, no really consistent strategic directions for action could emerge from the RTP work in this respect. More time and effort would certainly be needed to achieve progress on this question.

The RTP Process

Constructing a consensus among the regional actors is not exactly the way policy is traditionally built up in Lorraine: the power is concentrated within the hands of the organisations in the directing committee, and no mechanisms exist to ensure the bottom-up character of the policy. Thus, with the settlement of a steering committee and the holding of a number of open meetings and discussion groups as described above, this region has experienced, thanks to the RTP, a more open and democratic way of discussing strategies and actions under technology and innovation policy. For the first time, a number of actors who were previously at the margin of the decision centres have found ways to open doors and make their voices heard in the hope of influencing the system. This is, in itself, a direct result of the RTP model as it was conceived by the European Commission.

The long history of technology policy in Lorraine and, accordingly, the extended experience of regional actors in the field, make the construction of a consensus on new priorities a lengthy and difficult process: a lot of acquired positions may be endangered by the new policy lines, more actors might enter the system and possibly call on the same customers as the actors already within the system, requirements for more efficiency might single out less-capable members of the system, and so on. It is highly probable that, without the EU impulse, it would not have been possible to overcome the inertia in the system, in the way it has been possible with the RTP programme.

Maintaining cohesion and ensuring ownership of the RTP by all members of the directing committee was, in a sense, the main task for the RTP coordinator throughout the exercise. The French institutional context, whereby the region has in fact little power in the face of the central state, made it necessary that any orientations decided by actors in the region were thoroughly backed up by the state delegates – or, the other way round, that any directions suggested by the state in the particular context of the region were debated, amended and agreed by the regional actors concerned. Managing this complex alchemy, which meant in fact that both national and regional partners would end up with the impression that they were the real initiators of the new directions (rather than having had them imposed by the other partner), was the main task for the RTP coordinator. In the French situation, this implies that an RTP has to be discussed in the capital city as much as within the regional borders. Otherwise, the risk is large that it will result merely in a catalogue of wishes from below, with little chance of these being turned into a real action plan with adequate means.

Evaluating the real impact of the RTP in terms of the balance of power between the state and the region of Lorraine is very difficult at this stage, even if it seems that, in the debates around some subjects closely related to the RTP, such as the financing of innovation, the region might have gained more voice in the national arena than it had before this operation.

THE INTERNATIONAL DIMENSION

Although the international dimension, in terms of exchanges of practices and lessons with other regions involved in similar exercises, is certainly not the main result of the RTP of Lorraine, the fact that this exercise originated at the European level, rather than in the region itself or at the national level, has been crucial to the success of the whole exercise.

There are two reasons for this. The first is that the EU brought a new conceptual framework with the RTP initiative, as explained in detail in chapter 2. The confrontation of the principles of the RTP (a demand-led, integrative and strategic approach, based on regional consensus and international experiences) with the practices in the region provided food for thought and a ground for rethinking the policies in a rather fundamental sense. But this framework alone, imposed as it was 'from above', would not have produced its effects if the region was left to itself to apply the abstract ideas to its specific context. Indeed, no 'RTP methodology', except some very general steps to be respected, was proposed at that stage by the EC, and the regions were left to invent the practical steps to take in order to achieve the ambitious goals of the initiative. This situation was partly the product of a deliberate wish of the Commission to leave room for subsidiarity, but also a result of the fact that, at that moment, no one was able to give precise advice on how to conduct such exercises. It seems probable that such a loose framework, proposed for this region without any methodological support, would not have helped much in reaching the results it had finally been able to gather from it. The 'interpretation' of the RTP model by external consultants who had access to experiences in other regions and to expertise throughout Europe was a necessary intermediary for the region.

The second channel through which the international dimension was new for the RTP in Lorraine was the direct connection with advisers, operators and policy-makers in other European regions. Although the participation in RTP network meetings (including the workshop organised in Lorraine by the network) was judged rather negatively within the region, direct contacts were appreciated, notably on the occasion of working groups. It was felt that the inter-regional activities could have been based on a fine observation of methods used in the various RTPs, so that the timing and the selection of topics would have been more appropriate.

It cannot be said at this stage, however, that the evolution of the regional innovation policy in Lorraine owes much to ideas and practices borrowed from other regions involved in similar exercises in the EU. It has been clear throughout the exercise that the internal work has been given top priority. Nevertheless, the RTP has promoted the idea of benchmarking in Lorraine, with a positive expectation that it might bring inputs in the region. The existence of a network of regions involved in RTP-like exercises is an important element in helping to keep this stimulus awake, since the actors in Lorraine are probably more receptive than before to such inter-regional activities. Current perspectives point to the possibility of developing joint projects with other regions, at the implementation stage rather than at that of policy design.

MAIN RESULTS AND MAIN LESSONS FROM THE RTP

The RTP operation in Lorraine succeeded in putting on the policy agenda a new conception of innovation, extending beyond the technological dimension. The studies and debates within the RTP have demonstrated that the main barrier to innovation within the regional enterprises was linked not so much to their technological competence, as to their ability to manage such change. This result represents an important change of mentality in the region, and carries with it the germs of a complete rethinking of the whole innovation support system.

This story illustrates a clear case of evolution from a linear model of innovation towards an interactive one. The statement that 'more technology' is not sufficient to ensure competitiveness of enterprises is indeed a recognition of the fact that innovation does not necessarily flow from the R&D sector, but is the product of a much more complex dynamic involving the different parts of the firm itself, the enterprises' partners (suppliers, customers, firms in collaboration, capital providers, technology resource centres, etc.). The EU initiative acted as a catalyser to speed up the recognition of the necessity of a change in approach.

Besides the change of content of the policy, the RTP also introduced a change in method of policy design, in three senses. To begin with, it was the first time that an open discussion had been organised on policy orientation, with a large representation of the actors concerned, and, as we have seen, a more democratic way of building policy was thus initiated through the RTP.

A number of actors who were previously hidden within the system have come to light thanks to the RTP. Second, a more knowledge-based approach evolved through the RTP, since the new orientations were founded partly on a new understanding of the reality of the innovation process in the region (through the studies). One key actor in the region once reported that the main result of the RTP for him was that it forced him to think. Third, the openness to external experiences, which was not a natural move before the start of the RTP, has been somewhat increased as described in the preceding section. Here too one may say that the design of the RTP at EU level helped a lot to achieve this change of policy-building method.

What is also striking with the Lorraine experience of building an RTP is the complexity and, sometimes, the difficulty of managing the three levels of authority involved in the process: the European, the national and the regional. As stated in the beginning of this chapter, France is still a highly centralised country, despite the fact that the regions have been allocated competencies in a number of areas, notably in economic development. The thinking of the RTP scheme in European circles has obviously been guided by the situation in member states, with much more devolution of power to the regions: here, the subtle mix between top-down considerations stemming out from the centre and bottom-up initiatives from the region had to be managed with much care in order to avoid one or the other level taking too important a lead. Had the national government come up too abruptly with solutions from Paris then it would have put at risk the possibility of a constructive regional dialogue. However, had the region played the game of strong leadership then it would have run the risk of hurting the state by giving a signal that it did not intend to respect its partnership relations with Paris. This situation implies that in France the role of the regional institution as a promoter of the dialogue among the main regional actors has, as argued in the Introduction of this book, to be understood in a larger sense, so that it includes the dialogue with the national level.

Life After RTP in Lorraine

The result of the RTP work materialised in a strategy and action plan, which was later used in the preparation of a 'Convention Régionale de l'Innovation et du Transfert de Technologie', which would bind the state and the region to support innovation in industrial enterprises, in particular SMEs. This was an interesting move, since it allowed the region to design an innovation policy, tailored to local specificities, without the need to go through a reorganisation at the level of the state. While all regional actors could agree rather rapidly on the new approach, the process was slowed down somewhat by the fact that at least three ministers had to sign the text for the national part.

Within this convention, the institutional instruments put in place by the RTP to renew the method of policy-building in the region were perpetuated after the official end of the EU operation. The convention set up a 'Comité d'Orientation pour la Politique d'Innovation en Lorraine', which was to be the successor of the RTP steering committee, and to act as a consultative body for the innovation policy, with a mission of analysis, follow-up and orientation, and a function of 'Observatoire' of the demand and supply side of innovation and its impact on growth and competitiveness. The orientation committee is composed of representatives of SMEs (10 managers), public authorities (10 representatives), interface structures (11 representatives) and competence centres (12 representatives from universities, resources centres, technology transfer centres, big enterprises, financing institutions, training organisations, etc.). The members of the orientation committee commit themselves to put the resources of their organisations at the service of the policy and action plan decided. One representative of the European Commission is also a member of this committee which establishes working groups to carry out its analysis, orientation and follow-up missions, and is responsible for the systematic evaluation of the policy. The successor of the directing committee (with an identical membership) is established as the 'Technical Secretariat' of this orientation committee.

As to the content of the policy, the 'Convention Régionale de l'Innovation et du Transfert de Technologie' recognises that innovation is a collective process, implying good relationships between the firms and their environment, and declares that the barriers to innovation come from within the enterprise as well as from an insufficient coordination between the enterprises and their partners. Acknowledging the crucial importance of SMEs for the renewal of the productive tissue and for employment, but also their fragility, the public authorities in Lorraine agree to reinforce the innovation and technology transfer policy in the region, in the following directions:

- strengthen the innovative capacity of SMEs: help enterprises to develop their capacities to exchange with partners;

- adapt support to the needs of enterprises: reinforce diffusion and valorising of technological endowments of the region and bridge a link between enterprises and technological partners;

- reinforce the interface between enterprises' demand and technological supply: increase the professionalisation, the coherence and the proximity to enterprises of interface structures;

- improve transparency of the support structure for enterprises.

A number of actions are mentioned in the convention, to give flesh to the above orientations. They encompass the use or strengthening of existing instruments, such as:

- maintaining systematic visits to enterprises by the network and reinforcing coordination between the plans of the various organisations;

- reinforcing the circulation of information between the interface structures;

- increasing the number of 'first' technological services from the members of the network;

- extending the professionalisation instruments developed in the technology diffusion network to other interface structures;

- facilitating the access of SMEs to an existing server distributing information about key technologies;

- the confirmation of the 'Réseau de Financement de l'Innovation' with the reinforcement of own funds; the development of information on the possibilities offered by European programmes for the financing of innovation.

New instruments are also mentioned, such as:

- the creation of long-term placements of engineers in SMEs;

- the favouring of technology transfer actions between SMEs in particular and resource centres;

- the setting up of networks between large enterprises and SMEs;

- the certification of technology resource centres (which indicates their capacity to undertake projects with SMEs in mixed teams);

- the connection between the network and other sources of support, namely private consultants and technical lycea;

- the setting up of an 'Observatoire Régional des Technologies' which will gather information on the needs of enterprises, the support available in Lorraine and the key technologies;

- the setting up of a technological watch function in SMEs;

- the installation of a specific system of support for the instruction and follow-up of smaller innovative projects in view of their financing;

- the setting up of a support system for the management of innovative projects in firms (training of managers);

- the involvement of industrialists in existing training courses.

In addition, a study on harmonisation of the various support schemes for innovation is announced under this policy, as well as on the integration of training.

One year after the end of the RTP, concrete actions had been taken with regard to the following measures: creation of development teams within

SMEs, support to networks between SMEs and between large firms and SMEs, long-term placement schemes, innovation management training courses in universities, and the creation of a regional grant system for students in their last year wishing to work on a spin-off project.

On the whole, the result of the RTP, as it is stated in this convention, may appear relatively slight: the new ideas emerging during the RTP work have somehow been included in the convention, but in a rather timid manner, and the RTP has lost strength in the transformation process into a state–region convention. The supply-side and technological orientation of the innovation policy approach are still very much present in the document. Since the budgetary implications of the orientations and measures are not available, and some actions are labelled in rather vague terms, it is not easy to predict, at the start of the 'post-RTP era', whether the touches of progress put on paper will evolve into real achievements for a better support to innovation in the regional industry, or whether they will be diluted into supply-side measures and actions.

Nevertheless, the inertia of the system cannot be forgotten in giving an opinion on the new regional innovation policy in Lorraine: it may be that the compromise achieved between static and progressive tendencies in the region represents real progress by regional standards: having a regional convention on innovation and technology transfer signed by the region and the state is quite a big achievement. The institutional context, the history of the region in terms of economic development and previous policies, the existing complex set of actors and power distribution between them – none of these can be overlooked in judging the added value of an EU initiative such as the RTP in Lorraine.

There is, on the one hand, the *desirable* situation, stemming notably from theoretical and empirical knowledge of the innovation system, and, on the other, the *feasible* situation, which depends crucially on the understanding and the willingness of regional actors (firms themselves, but also support organisations and public authorities) to evolve in that direction, according to their own perceived interest. In our view the RTP in Lorraine has helped to shift the set of feasible policies a bit closer to the desirable ones, but also it has demonstrated that an 'optimal' model for regional innovation policy is an empty concept: it is so heavily contingent on the context, notably on the prevailing innovation culture, that any disembodied approach, not taking full account of the attitudes and willingness of regional actors to move in the required directions, is doomed to fail.

NOTES

1. The author was process consultant for the RTP in Lorraine. The chapter has benefited from the collaboration of Jean-Claude Moretti, from the Regional Council in Lorraine, who was the RTP coordinator. The views expressed represent those of the author alone.

2.   A company is defined as a foreign-owned company when at least 20 per cent of its capital is controlled by a foreign company.

3.   Indeed, some RTP funds have been allocated to the realisation, by the members of the network, of a set of standard information on the scientific and technological competencies of the laboratories and transfer centres, with no insights into their relation to the demand.

5 Learning Through Strategy-Making: The RTP in Wales

INTRODUCTION

Regional policy has been a prominent feature of the economic and social land-scape of Wales in the post-war period. In response to the gradual decline of Wales's traditional industries – coal and steel – regional authorities have pursued a range of development strategies based on a combination of physical infrastructure provision and inward investment promotion. In recent years, however, it has become increasingly evident that the substantial transfer payments required to sustain such a strategy cannot be relied upon. At the national level, for example, UK regional policy expenditure has been reduced by some 75 per cent in real terms since 1979 (Morgan and Henderson 1997). Similarly, the envisaged future expansion of the European Union to embrace the poorer countries of Central and Eastern Europe is also likely to leave fewer resources for the peripheral regions of the present EU, such as Wales.

It is in this wider context, then, that new forms of regional policy which emphasise building innovation and learning capacities have begun to emerge. This chapter outlines the development of one such initiative in Wales – the RTP. It begins by outlining the nature of Wales's economic and institutional structures, before moving on to explore the origins of the RTP in Wales, and the strategy development process adopted. It concludes with a preliminary assessment of the impact of the RTP in Wales. Throughout we argue that although many of the potential outcomes of the RTP exercise are likely to be seen in the medium to long term, the actual strategy development process has already represented an important break from past regional strategies by encouraging a collaborative and inclusive form of 'learning through strategy-making'.

THE ECONOMIC AND INSTITUTIONAL CONTEXT IN WALES

Innovation, defined as 'the successful exploitation of new ideas' (CBI/NatWest 1997), has long been a feature of economic development in Wales. From the late 18th century until recent decades, key activities such as tinplate, steel and coal production were made possible and profitable through the exploitation of new ideas in technology, transport and the organisation of production. In recent decades, however, the region's industrial base has undergone a significant transformation with the decline of its traditional industries and the emergence of a more diversified economy based on services and manufacturing.

An important feature of this period of restructuring has been the arrival of significant levels of foreign inward investment in the consumer-electronics and automotive electronics sectors. The most recent figures available here suggest that between 1982 and 1992 Wales headed the UK regional league table, in terms of both capital investment and new products (Hill and Munday 1994). The true impact of this influx in inward investment, however, stretches wider than direct investment and employment. It has also led to growing demands for component supplies and services, as well as quality and productivity increases from regional firms. This, in part, explains why between 1981 and 1993 gross value added per employee in manufacturing in Wales grew from 94 per cent of the UK average to 107 per cent, taking Wales to second in the regional league table (Office for National Statistics 1996).

Yet despite optimistic talk of an 'economic renaissance' (see, for example, Alden 1996), it is clear that the Welsh economy continues to suffer from major structural problems, lagging behind the UK average on many indicators such as GDP per head, economic activity rates and personal disposable income per head (see table 5.1). This period of restructuring in the 1980s has also revealed that Wales's SME base is typically characterised by a large number of second- or third-tier suppliers to inward investors and other large firms. These SMEs have little incentive to carry out R&D activities and often feel powerless to improve performance without the support or, more often, the threat from their end customer. In fact one of the few readily available data sources on inputs into the technological innovation process – expenditure on R&D by business – indicates that, as a percentage of regional GDP, Wales ranks among the lowest in the UK at 0.3, compared with the UK average of 1.3 (Office for National Statistics 1997).

TABLE 5.1: SUMMARY STATISTICS OF THE WELSH ECONOMY (1994)

	Wales	**% of the UK**
GDP per head (£)	8,173	83.7
Personal disposable income/£ head	7,245	89.4
Economic activity rate (%)	57.3	91.8

Source: ONS 1996

At the heart of the regional institutional framework in Wales is the Welsh Office. As a department of UK central government, the Welsh Office's responsibilities have grown since its formation in 1964 to include a wide range of functions and programmes, including health, education, training, industry, agriculture, environment, transport, etc. In practice, however, the scope for the Welsh Office to design and deliver specific Welsh 'regional policies' is limited to making small adjustments to national policies. In terms of innovation policy, for example, the Welsh Office is committed to delivering the programmes of the UK Department of Trade and Industry (DTI). Since the early 1990s the DTI has had an Innovation Unit to promote the subject among UK industry, but in general its activities have been devised by, and for, large firms rather than SMEs. The effect of this in Wales has been to make 'innovation' a distant concept for SME owners and managers as well as for intermediary organisations. While most of the work of the Welsh Office is of a policy nature, the actual delivery of services is the responsibility of local authorities, health authorities and various executive non-departmental public bodies (NDPBs).

One of the key NDPBs in the field of economic development is the multi-functional Welsh Development Agency (WDA). Established in 1975, the WDA aims to 'promote industrial efficiency and international competitiveness'. For much of its early life, however, the WDA focused on land reclamation, property development and direct investment in firms. It was only in the mid-1980s that it became fully responsible for inward investment, and only since 1990 has it developed a role in innovation and technology support among the SME base.

For most of the 1980s and early 1990s, UK government policy has been generally non-interventionist regarding public support of SMEs. Each WDA activity targeted towards indigenous SMEs has therefore been rigorously examined by the Welsh Office in order to satisfy itself that the activity is justified. At a time of rapid change for SMEs the role of the WDA in promoting innovation and being innovative itself has not always been fully accepted by the Welsh Office. Despite these pressures the WDA did, during the early 1990s, devise and introduce a number of innovative programmes to support SMEs, to deal with the needs of supply chains, technology development and the internationalisation of their marketplaces.

In the key area of skills training and management development the responsibility for providing funds for training and enterprise support in the UK rests with the Training and Enterprise Councils (TECs). These were first created in England in the late 1980s, and in Wales in 1990 (Scotland has a different system). The six TECs have budgets of typically £30 million each, but despite an apparent emphasis on local design and delivery of schemes approximately 80 to 90 per cent of their budgets must be used in support of programmes specified by central government. There is little opportunity for the TECs to contribute to either policy debate or funding support for more innovative schemes in the region.

The fact that the policies of many of Wales's key regional actors – Welsh Office, WDA and TECs – have been determined largely outside the region has prevented the development of a more coherent and strategic approach to the economic development needs of regional firms. While regional actors and their political leaders have talked confidently of a 'Team Wales' approach (a loose partnership of regional development organisations) to inward investment, there has been little attempt to achieve a consensus regarding the major issues faced by SMEs. This was demonstrated clearly at a meeting between regional actors held in the early 1990s to discuss participation in the launch of an 'Innovation Handbook'. This lasted for some three hours, during which time two hours was spent debating the definition of innovation, with the final hour taken up by most organisations deciding that this was a topic which did not fit into their agendas and which they would not wish to participate in.

In 1990 the WDA began to construct a series of new initiatives aimed at providing support services of greater relevance to the bulk of SMEs in Wales. In a positive sense, the WDA had recognised that much of its previous indigenous business support activity was too basic and low in value added for those SMEs in Wales faced with the challenge of being up to world-class standard in their manufacturing and management techniques. This challenge was posed by the looming Single European Market as well as by the demands of inward investors in the region. At the other extreme the WDA was forced, in 1990–92, to pass responsibility for its successful business start-up programmes to the new TECs. This was largely a political decision, taken to give the TECs some relevant activities to fulfil the 'enterprise' part of their remits.

The pressure from the Welsh Office for the WDA to justify its activities in the area of indigenous firm development meant that a radical rethinking of the WDA's programmes in this area was necessary. In response the WDA sought to learn from the experiences of other European development agencies, regional authorities and the European Commission, and develop a more strategic approach to the Welsh economy and indigenous firm development. One of the most immediate outputs from this period of reflection was the broadening of political collaborations with the four motor regions of Europe (Baden Württemberg, Rhône Alpes, Lombardy and Catalonia) to the economic sphere. Here the WDA secured Welsh Office approval to assist Welsh SMEs to establish joint ventures or trade opportunities in these regions through collaborations with key institutions such as the Steinbeis Stiftung in Baden-Württemberg.

THE GENESIS OF THE RTP IN WALES

The strategy rethinking taking place at the WDA during the early 1990s drew useful support from a number of sources. These included the early analysis leading to the DTI's White Papers dealing with issues surrounding the competitiveness of UK industry (DTI 1993). In addition, influential work was also undertaken at the Department of City and Regional Planning (Cooke and Morgan 1992) and Cardiff Business School (Hill and Munday 1994) at University of Wales, Cardiff, into the development of the Welsh economy and experiences of other European regions undergoing similar structural changes and facing competing priorities between inward investment and indigenous business support.

The WDA's efforts in transforming these new insights into programmes was, however, hampered by the lack of new government funding available. This meant that indigenous SME development programmes, with medium- to long-term impacts, found it increasingly difficult to compete for funds against capital programmes such as physical infrastructure provision or inward investment activities which, by their very nature, have short-term and highly tangible outputs.

The decision taken in 1992 to allow certain regional organisations to access European Structural Funds provided the WDA with its first opportunity to pursue new approaches to business development. This, however, was compli- cated by the fact that the then existing ERDF programmes in both Objective 2 (Industrial South Wales) and Objective 5b (Rural Wales) areas of Wales had been drafted in light of the traditional economic development priorities of capital-expenditure-led infrastructure provision rather than the more revenue- expenditure-intensive activities inherent in SME development. Thus, for the WDA to take advantage of the ERDF programmes to help its SME develop- ment activities, there was a clear need for some revision in the main programme priority areas.

The ERDF drafting process in Wales is based on a partnership approach centred on the Welsh Office, including local authorities, training organisa- tions and, in later years, the development agencies, universities and private sector representatives. Therefore the redrafting of the programmes could be achieved only if the wide range of 'partners' fully supported any revisions pro- posed. A consensual approach was therefore necessary.

The realisation that ERDF funding was vital to the future development activities of the WDA, and that any changes to the programmes could come about only through the support of regional 'partners' was an important moti- vation underpinning the discussions which took place between a number of organisations in Wales and the European Commission during 1992 and 1993, and which ultimately led to the RTP. Key 'theoretical' inputs to this process were provided by academics at UWC's City and Regional Planning Department who were exploring the possibilities of tackling the problems of less-favoured regions through programmes to support regional innovation. There was, however, a realisation that maintaining a practical outlook on what could be achieved was vital if the plan was to achieve widespread support of regional actors.

The period from the first discussion of the concept of the Wales RTP (orig- inally known as RETAS – Regional Technology Strategy) to the eventual commencement of the project took over two years, between 1992 and 1994.

Most of this time was spent in a series of bilateral discussions between the WDA and DG XVI of the European Commission regarding the scope, organisation and likely outputs of the RTP. Additional support was provided by the City and Regional Planning Department at the University of Wales, Cardiff.

The development of the RTP proposal for Wales was therefore driven at essentially three levels – the theoretical, the strategic and the practical:

- At the theoretical level: a group of academics at the University of Wales Cardiff, supported by the Institute of Welsh Affairs Report, established a broad set of objectives which helped to define the extent of the process and the regional actors required to achieve consensus.

- At the strategic level: the WDA and the University together began to define the main areas of activity which would be included in the exercise and the likely scope and content of the research.

- At the practical level: the WDA expressed the rationale required to justify the expenditure of time, energy and resources required to successfully deliver the Wales RTP.

Despite these supporting 'factors' the final few months of negotiations were fraught with difficulty. The European Commission demanded a letter of support for the project from the then Secretary of State for Wales, John Redwood MP – a renowned Eurosceptic. The requests for the letter of support went between the WDA and the Welsh Office on at least three occasions and it was evident that there was a reluctance among some in the Welsh Office to recommend that the Secretary of State for Wales give the support requested. It is said that the European Commissioner for Regional Development – Bruce Millan – was within two hours of approving an alternative UK bid for the European Commission support for the RTP before the required letter was reluctantly provided.[1] Yet despite these early difficulties the long process of strategy development was eventually able to commence in April 1994.

RTP STRATEGY DEVELOPMENT IN WALES

The RTP, as discussed in previous sections, was developed in a context in which innovation and technology had already begun to permeate the activities of a number of regional organisations. It also reflected a growing trend towards a more strategic outlook on regional development activities, indicated by initiatives such as Wales 2010, the Programme for the Valleys and the sub-regional Technopoles developed in South and North-West Wales.[2,3] Whatever their merits, these programmes provided a number of lessons (both positive and negative) which were subsequently incorporated into the RTP process. Of these, the most important was probably the recognition that the principles of partnership and inclusiveness were vital ingredients in any strategy. In many other respects, however, the RTP in Wales represented a significant break from the past in terms of regional policy-making, and it is this theme which we explore below.

The RTP exercise in Wales centred on a two-year period of research and consultation leading to the publication of an Action Plan (Welsh Development Agency 1996b) detailing priority areas with associated projects. Behind this process lay two guiding principles. The first of these was that the process should build on the substantial volume of information and expertise which already existed. This was motivated not only by the practical require-ments of working within a relatively small budget, but also by the perceived need to avoid antagonising the very organisations which had produced research and whose support would be vital to the success of the strategy. Second, considerable emphasis should be placed on developing and imple-menting priorities through partnership. Aside from these general orientations, however, the lack of specific guidelines meant that the overall objective of 'develop[ing] a consensus on a strategy to improve the innovation and tech-nology performance of the Welsh economy' (Welsh Development Agency 1996a,[4] p. 1) was one which had to be approached through a process of 'learning-by-doing'.

Organisation and Structure of the RTP in Wales

Without a regional government structure in Wales the task of coordinating and managing the RTP process was taken up by the WDA, which had been intimately involved in shaping the early RETAS proposals. To a large extent the resources, expertise and all-Wales remit of the WDA meant that it was probably the only regional organisation capable of mobilising and leading such as process. Yet, despite the WDA's prominent role in the RTP, strenuous efforts were made throughout the process to ensure that a 'horizontal' form of partnership was maintained.[5] This was reflected in all areas of the process, not least the management group, which was made up of individuals from the WDA's Technology Transfer Division as well as a project manager and princi-pal researcher from the University of Wales, Cardiff.

One of the first tasks of the management group, in consultation with the Welsh Office, was to select a steering group and chairman. Given the Welsh Office's reluctance to proceed with the RTP it was perhaps unsurprising that they rejected the management group's original intention to select an industry chairman, in preference to a Welsh Office representative. Indeed, the Secretary of State made this a precondition for Wales's participation in the RTP pro-gramme. We can only speculate why this stance was adopted, but it seems likely that in light of the Welsh Office's reluctance to allow the RTP to go ahead, they were keen to exert as much control over process *outcomes* as pos-sible.[6] In retrospect we believe that this decision may, in some ways, have helped the RTP exercise in Wales, because it ensured valuable, if tentative, involvement from a key regional actor during and after the process. By main-taining an 'insider' role in the RTP process the Welsh Office, it seems, had very little option but to support the priorities put forward and agreed by the steering group, and without which the possibilities for the successful implementation would have been highly uncertain.

The actual composition of the steering group was further complicated by the delicate task of ensuring a broad spectrum of representation from all aspects of Welsh economic life. The clear danger in such an exercise is that it can easily become top-heavy with public organisations at the expense of other actors with important knowledge such as firms, local government, social partners and academia. Similar difficulties were encountered with need to balance steering group representation between the various subregions of Wales (north, south, mid and west). Such problems are faced by most all-Wales initiatives, owing to the predominance of the south and the time taken to travel between parts of the region. For the RTP exercise this meant that the composition of the steering group tended to comprise mainly South Wales-based organisations.[7] The steering group, however, has never been a static entity. Instead it has continued to evolve, particularly during the implementation phase of the RTP which has seen the eventual appointment of an industry chairman and further representation from North, Mid and West Wales organisations.

In many respects the steering and management groups of the Wales RTP provided only a small portion of the total inputs into the various stages of the RTP process. Outside these groupings, the RTP process was further supported by important inputs from consultants and other regional or national experts. In addition, the guidance of the European Commission through their programme of formal visits, as well as more informal contacts, provided a significant impetus to the RTP process. The European Commission's support was also felt through their efforts to foster cross-regional exchanges of experience. This took place mainly through the RTP network, a body charged with disseminating information about RTP best practices, facilitating mutual learning between regions and the initiation and support of inter-regional projects (CEC 1994). From the management group's perspective, the main benefit of the network were the informal contacts and the benchmarking opportunities it afforded, rather than the formal 'content' of the meetings as such. It was disappointing, however, that the 'inter-regional projects' envisaged by the European Commission failed to be developed. Such projects may well emerge in future years, but is seems clear from Wales's experience that the significant effort required to mobilise the *intra*-regional strategy process during the lifetime of the RTP makes it difficult for time to be devoted to building more concrete forms of *inter*-regional collaboration.

The RTP Process in Wales

As noted earlier, the process of strategy development in Wales was very much one of learning-by-doing and tailoring perceived best practice to the Welsh context. This process was evident in all aspects of the RTP, not least in the evolution in the focus from a *technology plan* towards a more broad-based conception of an *innovation strategy*, as a result of the main issues expressed by firms during the consultation stage.

Figure 5.1 provides a summary outline of the various aspects of the RTP process in Wales. In short, the early stages of the RTP centred on three main research activities: desk research, bringing together various reports and papers on the Welsh economy, its innovative capacity and so on; 350 technology audits;[8] and a survey of innovation and technology support infrastructure. Together these elements helped contribute, incrementally, towards an emerging 'picture' of the main innovation issues facing Wales. An important part of the process, however, was the verification of all findings with the regional firms and organisations as a means of providing real-life examples of trends. The key issues to emerge from this process are summarised in Figure 5.2.

FIGURE 5.1: RTP WALES STRATEGY PROCESS

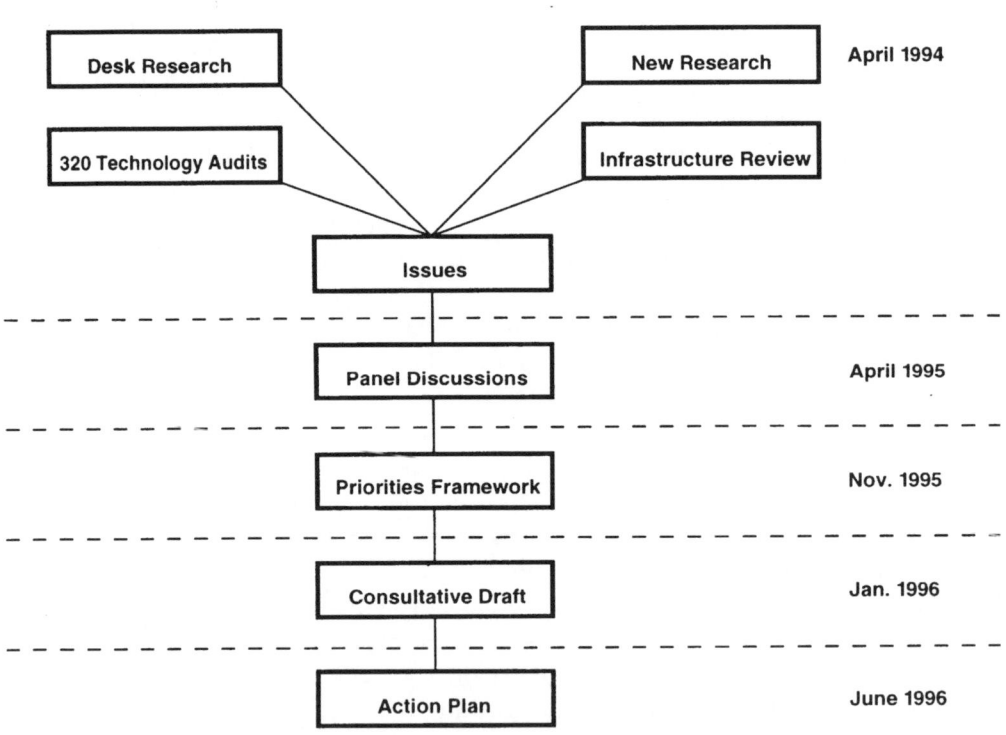

The RTP process in Wales was very much a product of what was possible within the existing economic and institutional regional context. It was quickly realised, for example, that without a broad-based support for the strategy, implementation would be extremely problematic.[9] Indeed, without the legislative power to ensure that regional organisations adopted the plan's recommendations it was reliant on achieving a broad base of support throughout the region. This goes some way towards explaining why 'consensus-building' was placed at centre stage in Wales, despite the limited attention given to such activities in the original *Guide Book* (CEC 1994). The practical result of this was one of the largest consultation exercises ever undertaken in Wales where firms were asked to comment on emerging results and issues and suggest ways of addressing them. More specifically the consultation exercise in Wales consisted of two main aspects, each designed to encompass as many regional organis-ations as possible.

FIGURE 5.2: INNOVATION ISSUES FACING COMPANIES IN WALES

- Many companies in Wales regard development work or innovation as a short-term response to customer demand and do not view innovation as part of their long-term business strategy (even if they have such a strategy).

- The most frequent barrier to innovation mentioned by companies was a lack of finance.

- Most companies get their innovations (and R&D) from other companies in their 'supply chains'.

- The need for better and more innovative interfaces between industry and academia is important in supporting innovative companies.

- Graduate employment in Welsh companies is low and may be closely related to companies' innovation abilities.

- Welsh companies need simple, transparent advice but also require high quality specialist support from business and innovation support agencies.

- Incubator facilities have proved successful in Wales and need to be developed further.

- Companies in Wales have reported that they expect future skills shortages and that there are training weaknesses in important technology areas.

- Wales appears to have the lowest level of R&D investments of any of the mainland UK regions, although the comparative figures for Higher Education R&D investments are more favourable.

- Patenting, or protection of intellectual property, arising from innovation is not seen as a means of improving competitive advantage by most companies in Wales.

Source: (WDA 1996b, pp. 4, 6, 7)

First, more than 30 panel discussions were held between February and November 1995 with representatives from industry, local government, higher and further education, schools, enterprise agencies, development bodies, trade unions and government. Panels were organised in consultation with regional support providers and brought together existing networks. Accordingly, meetings varied in terms of size and sectoral focus, but the majority featured a short presentation by a member of the management group, followed by discussion of the issues identified and potential actions.

In addition to the regional panels a special 'one-off' international panel meeting was held to consider and review the RTP process, analysis and conclusions. This was seen as an important mechanism to guard against parochialism by seeking an 'outside' perspective on the RTP. Many of the experts present at this meeting were themselves also involved in RTP/RIS or RITTS exercises elsewhere in Europe. For this reason the value of the panel meeting helped support the informal networking among regions, allowing the possibility for all involved to benchmark progress and exchange experiences and lessons emerging from the exercises. In short, the experience of the international panel was judged to be a positive one in Wales, providing further support for the process and findings. The value of this type of exercise has also been highlighted by the fact that several of the regional experts present at the meeting subsequently used international panels in their own RTPs.

The second aspect of the consultation exercise in Wales was the production, distribution and presentation of a Consultative Report (Welsh Development Agency 1996b). This outlined, in some detail, the main innovation issues, possible priorities and projects which were identified in the research and panel meetings. It was launched by the Secretary of State for Wales in January 1996 and circulated widely to firms, organisations and key individuals across Wales, requesting comments. In response, well over 100 organisations provided feedback.[10]

Action Plan and Implementation

The culmination of the relatively exhaustive consultation process discussed above was the launch of an action plan (Welsh Development Agency 1996a) in June 1996 by the Secretary of State for Wales. This set out details of six priority areas and some 60 projects where support had been committed. Of these projects the plan designated six 'flagship projects', each associated with particular priority areas (see figure 5.3).[11] These were to be implemented in the immediate period after the launch.

In the period following the launch of the action plan a certain amount of refocusing of the organisational structure and objectives of the RTP has taken place. This has generally been in line with the European Commission's guidelines which anticipated that regional steering groups would remain in place to monitor the progress of action plan implementation (CEC 1994, p. 31). In Wales, however, it was also felt that the differing challenges presented by the implementation phase required the group to expand and move towards a more strategic, monitoring role.

FIGURE 5.3: PRIORITIES AND FLAGSHIP PROJECTS FOR THE WALES RTP

- **A culture of innovation is vital for personal and economic success**

  The Welsh Innovation Challenge: a project to integrate existing innovation award competitions, providing a national profile with improved promotion, publicity and assistance with commercialisation.

- **Wales must profit from global innovation and technology**

  The Welsh Optoelectronics Forum: a project to help expand the networking activities of the region's optoelectronics sectoral group.

- **Companies learn best from each other, therefore supply chains and networks are crucial**

  Innovative Teaching Company Schemes: an extension of the successful Teaching Company Scheme (technology transfer from the university sector to industry via a two-year graduate placement) to enable companies in particular supply chains address a common innovation need.

- **Finance for innovation must be readily available in Wales**

  Technology Implementation Funding Programme: a project to identify technology and innovation needs in SMEs and provide part funding for the acquisition of new technology and consultancy for technical problem solving.

- **High quality business and innovation support is essential for Welsh companies**

  Support Centres for Information Technology and Multimedia: establishment of centres to provide demonstrations of and access to information technology.

- **Education and Training for innovation and technology are vital for the Welsh economy**

  Bargaining for Skills: a project to assist employers and trade unions in working towards goals training goals.

Source: WDA 1996a

The steering group now meet on a twice-yearly basis, one of which will coincide with an annual RTP conference to discuss progress made in implementing the action plan. A second, more focused, edition of the action plan is also likely to be produced to take into account the development of implementation. Little consideration, however, has been given to the question of monitoring and evaluating the RTP in Wales. This, we feel, is partly a result of the efforts required in implementing the plan, but also a tacit acknowledgement of the difficulties involved in measuring the region's innovative capacity. Bearing this latter point in mind, the remainder of this chapter offers a preliminary assessment of the strengths and weaknesses of the RTP *process*, drawing out potential lessons for current and future RIS regions.

Assessing the RTP Process in Wales

With ambitious objectives such as the generation of an innovative culture in Wales it seems clear that many of the outcomes of the RTP exercise will be long term in nature. In this respect, then, it is perhaps only possible to assess the RTP in terms of the strategy development *process*; for example, to what extent has the process mobilised support behind the proposals contained in the action plan? Is there evidence of a better understanding of the role of innovation in regional development activities among support organisations in Wales? And, if so, is this reflected in the most recent Objective 2 Plan and the activities and interactions of regional stakeholders? Finally, are there any lessons that can be learned for future strategy exercises?

To begin with, it is difficult to assess fully whether the initial objective of building a consensus on a strategy to improve the innovation and technology performance of the Welsh economy has been met. Yet, despite the rather slippery notion of a regional consensus, it does seem to be the case that the RTP has generated a greater awareness and understanding of the importance of innovation and technology in facilitating regional development, particularly among the regional development policy and support communities. This is, perhaps, most clearly demonstrated by the substantial numbers of organisations which participated in the consultation phase and attended a subsequent RTP conference held in March 1997 to discuss progress and future priorities. It could, however, be argued that the consensus reached in Wales was a relatively low-level one given the uncontroversial nature of many of the priorities. This may well be true, but in many respects it was a clear, stated, objective of the steering and management groups to ensure that the ideas contained within the action plan would be able to achieve a broad level of support. The question, then, is how can we explain this largely pragmatic approach in Wales?

In answering this question three interrelated factors touched upon earlier in this chapter appear to be important. First, as noted above, the experiences of previous strategy efforts in the region had failed largely because of their limitations in regional support. Second, the original desire to change the region's ERDF programmes in favour of support for innovation and technology activities required the support of the 'regional partnership', and third, the lack of direct political involvement in the process meant that it was never possible for the RTP to shape policy in the region because there was,[12] and isn't, a distinct *Welsh* policy. Together these factors explain why the RTP is able to act only as a 'framework for decision-making' which regional actors were able to subscribe to if they chose. As regional actors have no legislative requirement to implement the priorities contained in the action plan, the success of implementing the strategy rests heavily on the support of regional organisations.

As for the extent to which the RTP has begun to shape the activities of regional organisations, the priorities set out in the action plan have been incorporated into the latest Objective 2 programme for Wales (1997–99). Moreover, it is envisaged that approximately 20 per cent of the total programme will be devoted to RTP priorities. In light of the original motivations of actors such as the WDA towards redrafting Objective 2 plan priorities, this must be viewed as an important development, opening up a range of new funding possibilities for innovation and technology-related activities. In addition to these changes, a number of regional organisations have shown commitment (both individual and collaborative) towards the RTP priorities through implementing particular projects. Indeed, at this relatively early stage, all but one of the flagship projects have been established, and a full-time RTP coordinator has been appointed by the WDA to support project funding bids and other aspects of implementation. In terms of ERDF funding and projects, the RTP process does appear to have contributed towards a range of new regional development activities which, it is expected, will be better tailored to the needs of firms.

The outcomes of the RTP process, however, are not all as tangible as those discussed above. For some participants the main impact of the RTP process may well consist largely of intangibles such as cognitive development, providing new ways of considering the role of innovation as it relates to their particular organisational context; new interactions, bringing together previously disparate organisations to exchange experiences and knowledge in novel ways. Nauwelaers (1996, p. 4) sums up this perspective neatly, suggesting that the RTP is a collective learning exercise in which 'private and public actors learn to work together, acquire a cumulative, shared knowledge of the issues at stake for the regional development through innovation...'. To understand whether the RTP has succeeded in this respect is really an empirical question which will require further research in the future. From our experience, however, we would tentatively suggest that where such learning has taken place in Wales, it has probably been among those most closely involved in the RTP process, such as the management and steering groups. For those with a less central position, the RTP appears to have impacted on them mainly by providing a framework in which to view existing support efforts and, perhaps equally important, the opportunity to justify activities in the field of innovation. A key challenge which has only recently begun to be given some consideration is the extent to which the knowledge and information developed during the RTP process can be communicated more widely throughout the regional economy.

In short, the early outcomes of the RTP process in Wales appear to vary from relatively 'soft' factors, such as new ways of thinking and interacting in the regional development sphere, to the more 'concrete' projects and changes in the Objective 2 plan. It is important, however, that we do not lose sight of the fact that the RTP in Wales was, and is, part of a wider regional development process. It is already apparent, for example, that the RTP has already begun to have a demonstrable effect on other areas of regional development.[13] Moreover, the experiences of the RTP suggests that the RTP principles and features could be usefully applied to other regional development activities in Wales. Again, time will tell whether the RTP approach has the potential to be 'elastic' in this respect.

CONCLUSIONS

In this chapter we have attempted to provide an objective view of the RTP exercise in Wales and its early impacts. While it is too early to give a conclusive judgement on the RTP it seems clear that the strategy process has proved to be an important exercise for regional actors, particularly those in the policy and business support sectors, helping to provide the opportunity for new insights into the innovation process, developing new interactions, and providing a framework for justifying new and existing activities in this area. It has also opened up the opportunity for more effective support for innovation activities under the region's Objective 2 plan.

In deriving wider lessons from the RTP exercise it is important that we maintain a certain amount of caution. Each RTP programme is necessarily unique and, in part, reflects the particular social, economic and political context in which it was developed. In this respect, it is vital that the useful suggestions and best-practice model contained in the European Commission guidelines (CEC 1994) are not viewed as the *only* way to build an RTP process. Such models may well fit particular environments, but it is important that regions take a reflective approach, assessing the best course of action given their specific regional context.

With these points in mind, the Welsh example appears to highlight the importance of setting realistic and practical objectives which command regional support. All too often regional strategy efforts in Wales have failed to give consideration to the serious activity of building any sort of regional consensus. The RTP exercise, however, has shown that consensus-building should be placed at the forefront of the strategy-making process, particularly where organisations are not compelled to implement the suggestions contained in the plan. For this reason, it is difficult to see how a broad-ranging strategy like the RTP action plan could ever be fully implemented. Research, alone, is not enough to build such support. This would misunderstand the true nature of the RTP as a social process, and one which requires regional stakeholders to collectively define the way forward.

The challenges facing Wales and other less-favoured regions in Europe in terms of alleviating unemployment and achieving economic growth are clearly significant. While the RTP and RIS exercises cannot be expected to hold all the answers to these problems, they do highlight the possibilities for a new, more participative approach to regional development based on a more sophisticated understanding of the needs of firms. This would, if achieved at the wider European level, represent an important step away from the top-down, supply-led approaches to regional development which have prevailed in recent decades.

NOTES

1. This interpretation of events is supported by both written and verbal evidence given to the Welsh Affairs Select Committee (1995).

2. This programme was launched in 1988 in response to the severe social, economic and environmental problems resulting from the decline of the coal and steel industries in the South Wales valleys.

3. The South Wales and Snowdonia Technopoles. These were both funded by the EC SPRINT programme during the early 1990s and focused on promoting stronger networking between firms and institutions.

4. This was a product of the fact that the Commission were, themselves, at the bottom of their learning curve in these early stages.

5. This was also perceived to be important for the regional support necessary for any changes to the region's Objective 2 plan.

6. Especially outcomes which could potentially criticise official government policy as well as embarrass the Welsh Office.

7. Strong efforts, however, were made to ensure that the wider RTP process was not exclusive to South Wales. Accordingly, consultation events, launch meetings and conferences were all held throughout the region.

8. 250 SME Audits undertaken in industrial South Wales (the Objective 2 area), supported by a further 100 SME and larger firm audits in other parts of the region.

9. This was evident from the experiences of the Wales 2010 exercise, which had failed to give significant attention to the difficulties of strategy implementation, treating it largely as an afterthought rather than an integral part of the strategy.

10. Approximately 40 per cent of these were firms.

11. The concept of 'flagship' projects was one of the suggestions made by the international experts panel.

12. As noted earlier, the role of the Welsh Office is largely one of delivering national government policy in the region. In other RTP/RIS regions which have close regional government involvement in the process it has proved more easy to translate the resulting priorities into policy.

13. The most prominent example of this is the EC-supported Wales Information Strategy (WIS) launched in July 1997. This has clearly drawn on some of the key lessons of the RTP exercise, particularly in the form of its organisational structure and process activities.

6 The Innovative-Region Strategy: Lessons from the Central Macedonia Regional Technology Plan

A new direction of European innovation strategies can be described and discussed as an 'Innovative Region Strategy'. This chapter provides a concrete example for this new orientation of European innovation policies. The presentation of this experience is divided into two parts. The first part is devoted to a detailed description of the structure and the major components of the Regional Technology Plan (RTP) of the region of Central Macedonia. The second part focuses upon both an assessment of this experience and an attempt to summarise whatever lessons can be drawn from its implementation.

The theoretical foundations of the 'Innovative Region Strategy' can be traced back to 1977, when Bagnasco (1977) published his study on Third Italy. Since then, the main concepts regarding innovation, industry and territory have evolved along the different approaches such as 'district theory', 'milieux innovateurs', 'new industrial spaces', 'technopolitan development' and 'regional systems of innovation'.

The concepts of 'industrial district', 'new industrial spaces' and 'technopoles', which had major influence during the 1980s, were in fact integral parts of the 'flexible specialisation' approach. Their conceptual core lies in the recognition of the capacity of the small, specialised company to develop external linkages and networks to the highest degree, and to acquire all the necessary technology and skill inputs from the agglomeration, itself composed of other specialised SMEs. In this way, horizontal and vertical disintegration of production activities are extended, while internal economies are substituted by external economies, and economies of scale by economies of scope. The spatial form of this complex is the cluster, because within the cluster external transactions costs are minimised. Thus, the district and the agglomeration composed of districts become the dominant spatial forms of flexible specialisation (Murray 1987; Piore and Sabel 1985; Scott 1988).

In the beginning of the 1990s a new theoretical contribution was added to the discussion on regional innovation, based upon the pioneering work of Lundvall (1992) on national systems of innovation, which widened the debate on districts, flexible specialisation, new industrial spaces, and technopoles. A number of tentative efforts have been made to utilise these insights on learning and innovation in urban and regional development theory. A sophisticated attempt, according to Morgan (1997), is to be found in the recent work of Storper (1997), who seeks to explain the rise of the local at a time when the forces of globalisation appear to be reducing the world to a 'placeless' mass. A key part of the explanation is the association between innovation, technological learning, and the agglomeration. In the same direction, Cooke and Morgan (1991) have coined the term 'intelligent region' in order to capture the complex web of relations, roles and functions of the different regional actors that promote innovation and regional development.

The Innovative Region Strategy is an evolutionary step in this ongoing debate. It focuses upon the regional innovation system in its totality, rather than on the more restricted notion of the cluster. In fact, it expands the content of the latter by introducing interventions that promote its adaptability, learning, networking, and both transfer and endogenous production of technology. On a practical level, it is based upon the experiences of innovation strategies promoted by the European Commission, namely, Regional Technology Plans (RTPs), Regional Innovation and Technology Transfer Strategies and Infrastructures (RITTS), and Regional Innovation Strategies (RIS).

The Innovative Region Strategy may be considered as an evolutionary step of technopolitan strategies, which were implemented on a broad scale in the 1980s with the development of large technology parks and 'technopolis' projects (Komninos 1992 and 1993). The new strategy attempts initially to bring to the surface the main factors behind the region's technology deficit: the archaic character of its small and medium-sized businesses, the inadequacies of its mechanisms for the diffusion of technology and the latent demand for technology and innovation services. It adopts a more integrated way of dealing with innovation, a systemic model of interaction between technology supply and demand, and a concept of innovation as a function of research, inventiveness and commercial exploitation. The basic difference between this strategy and the strategy of technology poles is in the promotion of a more decentralised regional innovation system, which exploits the existing industrial and research capability of the region, and seeks to integrate local technology supply and demand.

The Regional Technology Plan of Central Macedonia was a pilot project along these lines. It was a joint initiative of the European Commission, the Ministry of Macedonia and Thrace and the Aristotle University of Thessaloniki, which aimed to promote capacities for innovation in Central Macedonia. This goal was to be achieved through the elaboration of a regional innovation strategy and the forging of consensus among all the major regional partners involved with applied research, cooperation between research and industry, technology transfer, provision of technical skills and entrepreneurial capabilities under a strategic action plan defining the priorities for the renewal of products, production processes and the competitiveness of regional firms in global markets.

THE REGIONAL TECHNOLOGY PLAN (RTP) OF CENTRAL MACEDONIA

With a population of 1.7 million, Central Macedonia is a large and dynamic region in northern Greece that maintains a prominent role in the Greek regional system, especially as a pole of international significance in the wider Balkan area and a European Union gate region in its south-east borders. With a GDP of 2.3 trillion drachmas, the region represented 16.1 per cent of the national GDP in 1993, while its composition was 16.9 per cent primary-sector, 27.5 per cent secondary and 55.5 per cent tertiary. The employment structure of a total active population of 0.7 million was, in 1991, 20.9 per cent primary-sector, 27.6 per cent secondary and 46.5 tertiary, while unemployment was 7.6 per cent – below the 8.1 per cent national average. In the beginning of the 1990s Central Macedonia had a GDP per capita (in Purchase Power Units) of 46.8 (compared with the overall figure of 100 for the EU twelve), ranking fifth among the thirteen Greek regions but occupying one of the lowest positions among the European regions.

The region of Central Macedonia constitutes one of the thirteen programme regions of Greece and has three independent tiers of administration. The regional tier is part of the decentralised central state structure, while both the prefectural and the municipal tiers are represented by directly elected local authorities. Analytically, these tiers are:

- The regional tier: this is an administrative unit, headed by the general secretary of the region, who is appointed by central government, with nominal responsibility over the coordination and supervision of all state agencies decentralised at the peripheral level. Its most important function is its direct involvement in the formulation, monitoring and implementation of the Multifund Operational Programme (MOP) for regional development as an integral part of the European Community Support Framework.

- The prefectural tier: Central Macedonia is divided into seven distinct prefectures. They correspond to the second tier of local government and constitute a directly elected local state with various departments, offices and directorates possessing concrete administrative capacities. However, because it was established only recently (in 1994), and because the central state has been reluctant to devolve important administrative functions to the prefectural level, there exist many uncertainties and ambiguities over the exact range of its responsibilities.

- The municipal tier: the 626 municipalities in the region correspond to the first tier of self-government. They possess very limited resources and very few administrative capacities in relation to the management of specifically defined local issues such as the collection of garbage, the running of pre-school and primary education establishments, etc. There is an ongoing programme encouraging the drastic reduction of the number of municipalities in the region.

An important feature of the regional productive system is the dominant role of SMEs, which are characterised by generally low levels of organisation and considerable management deficiencies. The average size of regional manufacturing is 6.5 employees per firm. This is very low, even in comparison with the national figures. Small and medium-sized units account for 98 per cent of all manufacturing firms and absorb 72 per cent of total industrial employment. Industry covers most of its technology requirements by purchase from abroad, while most inward investment is focused on traditional industrial sectors (foods and beverages) or sectors with a wide consumer market (electrical machines and appliances). An equally important investment occurs in the tertiary sector (insurance companies, banks, transport companies), as well as in commerce, with a series of superstores which have located on the outskirts of Thessaloniki in order to tap the local consumer market and the markets of neighbouring prefectures as well.

The major tool of development planning and the channelling of public intervention is the Community Support Framework (CSF) 1994–99. This represents an amount of 30 billion ECU and consists of a regional component covering 25 per cent of the total (within which the Central Macedonia Multifund Operational Programme covers an amount of 977.4 million ECU) and a national component of 75 per cent of the total through which other Sectoral Operational Programmes finance a significant number of projects in Central Macedonia.

The regional innovation strategy for Central Macedonia was developed in five stages. The setting-up of the plan includes the methodological, institutional and organisational constitution of the Central Macedonia RTP. The analysis of the regional productive and innovation systems focuses on the productive system of Central Macedonia and the technology demand, supply and transfer in the region. The innovation support strategy deals with the formulation of a strategy supporting the innovation capacity in the region; it exploits the conclusions of the analytical approaches in order to identify and formulate problems and deficiencies, and to define interventions on the level of the regional innovation system. The action plan for an innovative region codifies the conclusions drawn from the previous steps and attempts to create an innovation-friendly environment supporting all businesses in the region. Finally, implementation examines the ways in which the regional innovation strategy can be interwoven with operational programmes of the second Community Support Framework and of the relevant community initiatives, which constitute principal financial sources for the implementation of the RTP priority projects.

Setting Up the Regional Technology Plan

The preparation of the Regional Technology Plan of Central Macedonia was a complex collective effort. It lasted for two years (1995–97), during which 39 specialised reports were produced, and more than 200 scientists, public officials and businessmen were involved in the process (see Komninos 1997). Recently, the plan has entered its implementation stage with the application of seven priority projects.

The objectives of the plan were:

- To investigate the processes of technological development in Central Macedonia and to define the strengths and weaknesses of the regional innovation system.

- To ensure an agreement between the principal bodies and agencies of government, the regional firms, the workers' organisations and the universities, on the priorities of technological development in the region.

- To select projects and actions that sustain the technology and innovation capacity of the regional firms and to investigate their feasibility.

- To implement these projects in cooperation with the Structural Funds and to attract funds towards actions sustaining the technology and innovation capability of the region.

- To establish a monitoring system to evaluate the effects of the plan and to diffuse information on innovation and development of Central Macedonia.

These objectives are closely related to EU regional policy. While EU policy adherence is not a prerequisite of the RTP concept, it arose here out of the actual development situation in Greece and Central Macedonia. The process of economic and monetary union and the intense effort of the country to meet the targets of the Maastricht Treaty connect most of the public and private investments to the Structural Funds and the Community Support Framework. The latter has become the dominant tool for the selection and implementation of projects and initiatives to renew the country's infrastructure and production capacity. In this sense, the principal problem in the development trajectory is to make a correct use of these resources, to sustain projects with major multiplier effects and to coordinate the public and private initiatives for modernisation and growth. The overall objective of the plan is to enable regional industry to work at best-practice level in the technologies relevant to it, to enhance the emergence and growth of new industrial branches, and to promote international technology cooperation and competitiveness to international markets.

A logical consequence of the objectives set was to focus the actions of the plan on the regional innovation system. The regional innovation system is part of the productive system of the region and the established mix of activities, linkages and institutional regulations. It is the system that drives technology and innovation to companies and intermediary organisations in the region. Focusing the plan on the regional innovation system was a principal methodological choice. The rest of the method was based on common planning approaches, such as the articulation of analysis and strategy, the specification of strategy into projects, the investigation of the implementation framework and the organisation of monitoring and evaluation.

The Central Macedonia Regional Technology Plan was managed by two bodies: the steering committee and the management unit. The steering committee was composed of sixteen representatives coming from the public sector (five members), the private sector (six members) and the scientific institutions (five members) and was responsible for the political orientation of the plan, ensuring an agreement on the character of technological development in the region.

The management unit provided scientific expertise and support for the policy guidelines of the plan and introduced proposals to the steering committee. It was composed of four persons from the Department of Urban and Regional Planning, Aristotle University of Thessaloniki, and the Department of European Programmes, Ministry of Macedonia-Thrace. The work of the management unit was supported by a large number of internal and external working groups, which provided scientific expertise and analysis on issues related to regional development, technology demand and supply, technology transfer and planning for innovation infrastructures.

The key issue in the overall decision-making process was the effort to create a broad base of regional support for the plan. Reaching consensus was a permanent concern of the management unit, and implied the preparation of all decisions, from the creation of working groups to the definition of priorities and the selection of projects, in consultation with the participants in the steering committee. Furthermore, to increase the motivation of the various parties involved in the planning process, we tried to assure their participation in the implementation and evaluation of the plan. The general support expressed for the RTP justifies these orientations and indicates a growing interest in its promotion and implementation.

FIGURE 6.1: MANAGEMENT AND ADMINISTRATION
STRUCTURE OF THE RTP

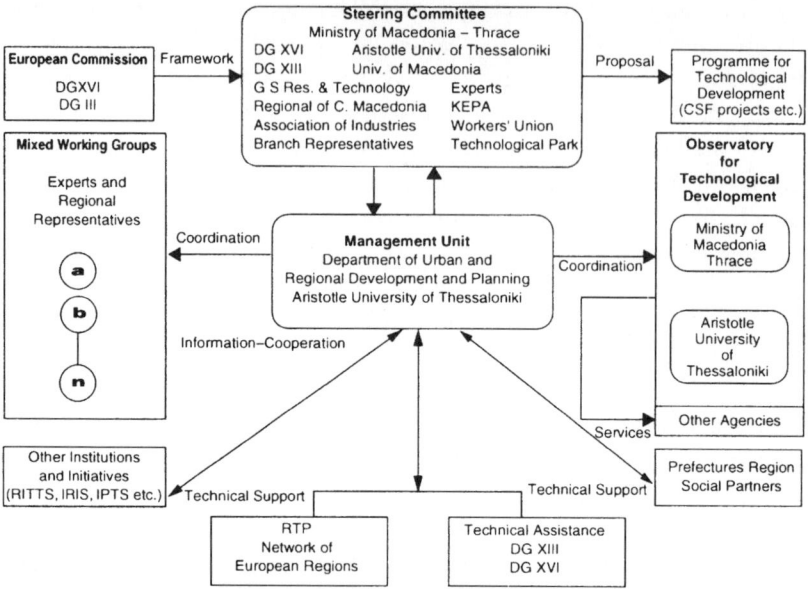

The Regional Productive and Innovation Systems

In Central Macedonia technology and innovation spring from the regional
innovation system. This can be considered as the 'brain' of the production
system, since it has the responsibility for the modernisation and adaptation of
regional activities to changing external conditions, technologies and competition. Understanding the innovation system in Central Macedonia was a
central issue of the Regional Technology Plan. In contrast to a long-standing
tradition of technology planning emphasising the supply side, on the assumption that industry would adapt to improved technology supply, this plan was
highly determined by demand, which defined both the strategic priorities and
the selection of projects within a framework of established priorities.

The regional innovation system in Central Macedonia (figure 6.2) has been
analysed from four different points of view, concerning the spread and application of generic technologies, the regional technology demand, the regional
technology supply, and the transfer of technology.

A multilevel survey (based on technology audits and experts reports) looked
at the main characteristics of regional technology demand and outlined the
technology needs of firms. For the companies participating in the survey, the
main source of technology was by the purchase of equipment. The development level of internal R&D departments was generally low, and only exists at

all in large and well-organised companies. Very few companies have special R&D departments, while in some companies R&D is carried out by either the production department or the quality control department. R&D levels are generally considered inadequate because the level of R&D is in many industrial branches fairly low, and information flow and dissemination of research results both from Greece and abroad are insufficient.

FIGURE 6.2: COMPONENTS OF A REGIONAL INNOVATION SYSTEM

Regional productive system

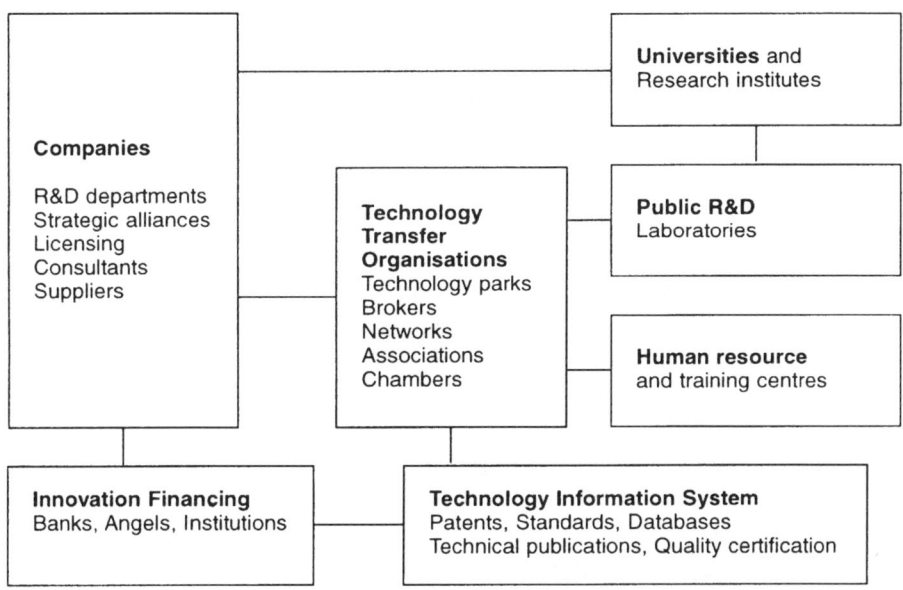

Regional productive system

For most companies, the idea of collaboration with other companies in the same branch has gained little ground, owing largely to lack of interest, suspicion, lack of finance and the absence of a spirit of collaboration within the business world. On the other hand, many companies subcontract and/or collaborate with producers of complementary products. Most companies surveyed lay great weight on producing quality products to meet market demands. Suggested ways of improving quality include automation and certification of production processes. A certain number of companies have already been awarded certification (mainly under ISO 9002), or are in the process of doing so. In fact, certification is one of the major company trends for the future. Most companies either already apply or are prepared to apply total quality management procedures, which reflect industry's realisation of the importance of the human factor in the production of quality products.

Technology objectives and requirements of the firms surveyed focus mainly on:

- product improvement, through the purchase of new equipment, the implementation of new technologies, the installation of automation systems, and better raw materials (new materials or better quality control);

- the development of new products via new technologies in accordance with market requirements;

- improved quality control procedures by the addition of supplementary equipment and trained personnel;

- improved product distribution.

At the same time, a major obstacle hindering innovation was stated as the high cost of money and the limited innovation funding available to companies.

There is also a clear need for qualified middle management, especially in the prefectures other than Thessaloniki. In certain sectors (textiles, non-metallic minerals) there is a tremendous need for middle-level and qualified staff (e.g. foremen, qualified technicians, etc.), who are usually trained on the job rather than in special schools.

Supplementary information on the regional technology needs was made available from an extended survey through questionnaire. This survey was based on a list of 1,900 businesses covering 92 per cent of the total number of businesses having more than ten employees in the Central Macedonia region. The data include information on the location of the firm, number of employees, turnover and industrial sector, as well as figures from their annual accounts and other quantitative indicators (current assets, net worth, gross income, investments, etc.). This survey permitted the description of the use and need for more specific technology and innovation areas. These included:

- industrial information technologies;

- automation;

- quality control;

- anti-pollution technologies;

- agro-technologies;

- funding for modernisation;

- funding for research, technology and innovation;

- participation in the Fourth European R&D Framework Programme;

- participation in business technology cooperation networks;

- improvement of human resource technology skills;

- cooperation with technology transfer organisms;

- technology cooperation with the universities;

- new infrastructure for telematics, professional premises and installations.

On the opposite side, the investigation into technology supply was designed to identify applied research activity in Central Macedonia and the potential for technology applications to companies stemming from non-company research centres.

Research activity in Central Macedonia is fragmented into a large number of small research units: 277 research units for applied R&D were identified and listed, of which 138 are university laboratories. The technology areas that concentrate most of the above units are related to agro-technologies, biology and biotechnology, and the technologies for materials.

Despite the significant number of research units providing technology services to companies, the degree of collaboration between research and enterprise does not appear to be very great. Only 30.6 per cent of the units polled felt that they provided substantial support services, replacing company R&D departments with their own R&D services. The main source of their inability to develop strong bonds with companies was considered to be the companies themselves. About half the research units attributed this low level of collaboration to a lack of interest on the part of the companies concerned. A significant number attribute the difficulty of collaborating to the lack of infrastructure and to the lack of personnel, equipment and space. Another restrictive factor was the institutional framework within which the public entities functioned, especially with regard to billing for services rendered.

A third important field for the innovation system in Central Macedonia concerns technology transfer mechanisms. Technology transfer was analysed from the point of view of the related public support, the university–industry interface, and the inter-firm technology cooperation in Central Macedonia. For the latter, a small survey was carried out covering the technology collaboration between companies (subcontracting, networks, licensing), as well the foreign direct investment in the region and the technology cooperation between local and foreign firms. The principal conclusions drawn from the technology supply analysis was the limited correlation between the scope of technology suppliers and the needs of regional companies:

- The provision of technology services was concentrated mainly on the Aristotle University of Thessaloniki and was fragmented into a large number of research laboratories.

- The overall organisation of technology services was not clear, and many entrepreneurs thought that information about and access to such services was difficult.

- Interest expressed by enterprises in the research activities carried out by the laboratories and their possible applications was limited.

- The number of laboratories that transferred technology to enterprises was minimal.

- There were no competence poles, especially in technologies with a broad range of applications.

These findings suggest that technology transfer constitutes the number one problem in Central Macedonia; on the one hand, companies cover their technology requirements by turning to external sources and, on the other hand, the external sources active in the region do not take into consideration the needs and the problems of local businesses. Regional firms lack both in-house technology capacity and external input from their immediate environment.

Innovation Support Strategy

The analysis of Central Macedonia's regional innovation system showed that the main problem in the region may be defined as the 'latent integration' of industry and technology that characterises both technology supply and technology demand.

By 'latent technology supply' we mean the informal operation of the system for the technology supply and transfer, in which the inflows of technology and innovation in the industrial sector are not recognised as distinct units. This is associated with three events:

- The main route by which businesses acquire new technology is through the purchase of mechanical equipment. In-house R&D departments are rare, although in some cases R&D is carried out by production and quality control departments.

- Inter-firm collaboration, which is a major source of technology know-how, is primarily in the form of subcontracting. The subcontractor works according to the plans, production methods and product specifications provided by the principal; this dependence seriously restricts motivation and the incentives for innovation.

- Technology dissemination and collaboration between industry and research are both limited. Research activity is concentrated primarily in university laboratories, and is fragmented among numerous small units without any specific clear industrial goal or connection. This is a structure that does not allow for the development of complementarity, interdisciplinary activity or the constitution of large-scale poles of competence.

All three routes for technology supply in industry are covered by broader activities and relationships: the purchase of technology by the purchase of equipment and machinery, the exchange of technology through subcontracting relationships between firms, and the technology dissemination via the loose relationships between industry and the universities. Academic activity, subcontracting relations, and machinery purchase are buffers to actions aiming to introduce innovations and restructuring into the technology transfer and supply system.

By *latent technology demand* we mean the lack of active technology demand and the low awareness in industry about the capabilities of new technologies to deal with production, competition and marketing problems. Lack of awareness and low information inputs prevent firms from understanding their real needs and developing adequate solutions to fulfil these needs. This concerns the spheres of both marketing and production.

On the other hand, the region's firms have a tendency to seek competitiveness through defensive strategies of deskilling, low use of human resources and excessive investment in equipment and automation. Innovation needs are concealed both in the production process, where automation problems prevail, and in product development, where the problems are those of quality rather than of new product design and development.

At the centre of these weaknesses lies the region's *industrial management* and its difficulties in following advanced business strategies. For the average European industrial firm, innovation is not an abstract concept, but is bound up with the firm's ability to apply new methods and technologies to production (automated machinery, flexible workshops, horizontal shop-floor structures), to the product (new products, small batches, short production runs, quality circles, total quality control), to inter-firm relationships (just-in-time delivery systems, production networking, externalisation of services, steady producer–supplier relationships) and to the work force (flexibility, upgrading of skills, multifunctional work culture). The gap between firms in Central Macedonia and their counterparts in Europe's more advanced regions reflects in miniature the true technology gap, which covers the fields of commercial strategy, technology inflow and individual ingenuity in adapting to an ever-changing international environment.

The strategy of the RTP will therefore focus on Central Macedonia's industrial firms, and especially on their latent research and technology integration. These constitute the plan's basic orientations for action. From this point of view the priorities finally established for the RTP are grouped into six different areas, each with a distinct thematic objective and goal. Of these, five pertain to Central Macedonia's businesses and the factors affecting their ability to innovate, while the sixth covers monitoring, evaluation and adjustment of the actions of the RTP.

FIGURE 6.3: PRIORITIES SET BY THE CENTRAL
MACEDONIAN RTP

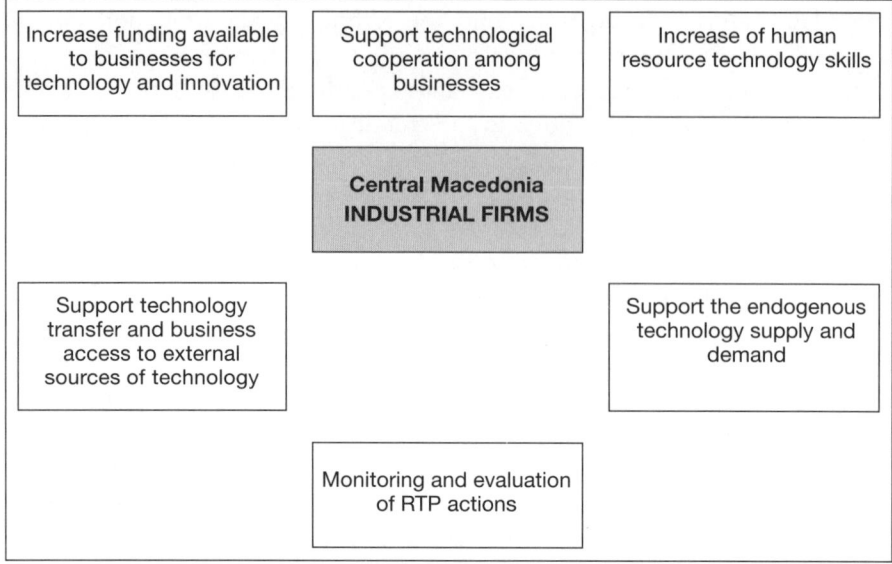

- Increased funding for research, technological development and innovation: this both promotes the modernisation of existing businesses and encourages the creation of new hi-tech firms. In numerous dynamic areas in Europe and the United States, forms of risk capital have greatly contributed to the development of high-tech industries. However, the actions recommended by the RTP have nothing to do with the creation of new institutions, like the venture capital measures included in the Operational Programme for Industry, but are instead addressed to the direct utilisation of existing funding mechanisms. More specifically, actions were designed to utilise funds available under the Second Community Support Framework and the Fourth R&D Framework Programme of the European Union.

- Support for technological cooperation among businesses: this constitutes a central priority for the expansion of innovative production methods and products. It is claimed that 'businesses learn better from other businesses', and on this basis inter-firm relationships, supplier–producer relations and networks are all crucial factors in innovation. In this area, RTP actions focus on the one hand on the development of technological collaboration networks within specific industrial branches, and on the other on attracting technology-intensive foreign investments that would then act as initial poles for new industrial sectors. The actions included in this area are designed to complement the actions for business networks included in the programme of the Ministry of Industry, 'The Future of Greek Industry'.

- Increase of human resource technology skills: this is designed to promote new business strategies that depend on the active participation and technology capability of the firm's executives and employees. The RTP emphasises in-house personnel training, and stresses the link between training and finding (or keeping) a job. Particular weight is given to training for entrepreneurs and senior executives on matters relating to innovation management, export promotion and risk management associated with investment in south-eastern European countries.

- Support for technology transfer and businesses' access to external sources of technology: this deals with the external technology and innovation environment of firms. The complexity and rapidity of technological change have shown that external sources and technology transfer are important factors in the technological structure of any business, be it large or small. Especially in Central Macedonia, the limited development of in-house R&D departments makes turning to external sources of technology even more important. RTP actions in this area focus on two principal orientations: on the one hand, they aim at the development of horizontal technology transfer mechanisms, in which all those involved in research, technology and business would cooperate in order to cover broad technological sectors; on the other hand, they seek to develop sectorial mechanisms for technology transfer, thus ensuring coverage of the technology requirements of the region's principal industrial branches.

- Supplementing these orientations is the *support of endogenous technology supply and demand,* which is concerned with the development of local applications within specific technology sectors (information technology, quality, environmental technologies, agro-technologies). A major problem to deal with is the latent technology demand. The RTP actions are designed to broaden the local market for a number of important technologies. However, these actions cannot be undertaken by the businesses themselves, since they require significant effort with no guarantee that they will pay off in the long run. Their effects are diffuse, making them collective actions from which all the businesses in the area will benefit, either as users or as providers of these technologies.

The five areas of priorities just mentioned focus on Central Macedonia's businesses. They promote innovations in the basic area of business strategies –

in production methods, in products, in inter-firm relationships and in personnel and executive training. At the same time, they facilitate access to various levels of technology: horizontal technologies, sectorial technologies, and specific technologies as well. The last priority area is different: it is associated with the application and effectiveness of the regional technology strategy promoted by the RTP. This includes monitoring the actions, developing criteria and evaluation coefficients and fine-tuning the plan while it is being implemented. In this case, the sole action is the expansion of the RTP Observatory, as a mechanism for the monitoring, evaluation and adjustment of all actions pertaining to the upgrading of the innovation system in Central Macedonia.

The Action Plan

The priorities of a plan provide a strategic framework of orientation. However, the decisive factor is the manner in which those priorities are specified and translated into particular action and projects. In this sense, the transition from priorities to projects is a process of evaluation by which specific projects are rejected or accepted. A system of evaluation is thus required, according to which a project may or may not be included within a priority.

A summary of the action plan is presented in figure 6.4, with indication of the priority projects that reflect the maturity and significance of the respective areas. The formulation of the action plan demanded three components: priorities, projects to specify the priorities, and evaluation to select the projects that best express the priorities. In the case of the Regional Technological Plan of Central Macedonia, the priorities resulted from the analysis of strengths and weakness of the regional innovation system, the projects emerged 'from below' (in the form of proposals submitted by political and economic agencies in the region), and evaluation of the projects was based on the investigation of the technological demand involved in them.

The procedures for assembling the projects that specified the priorities were relatively simple. The political and economic agencies of the area had been informed of the Regional Technological Plan and they were asked to propose appropriate projects. Each project was supposed to determine a set of services to support the technological and innovative capacity of the region (e.g. the funding of innovation, technology transfer, the dissemination of research, etc.) and an implementing agency as well.

Using this method, a large number of proposals were assembled. They were then systematically discussed at successive meetings of the steering committee and evaluated on the criterion of their feasibility and the interest that businesses in Central Macedonia might display in the services which they could offer. In total, 22 projects were selected.

FIGURE 6.4: ACTION PLAN SUMMARY

Priority 1

Lead project

- Funding businesses for technological modernisation.
- Funding businesses for research and technological development.
- Funding businesses from European R&D programmes.

Priority 2

Lead project

- Foreign direct investment and international technology cooperation.
- Networking in the food industry.
- Networking in the textile industry.

Priority 3

Lead project

- Employee technology training.
- Training in innovatiom management.
- Training in risk management and in the south-east European investment environment.
- Training in quality and exports.

Priority 4:

Lead projects

- Technology transfer department at the Thessaloniki Technology Park.
- Textile Institute of Northern Greece.
- Centre for Research Dissemination at the Aristotle University of Thessaloniki.
- Food Institute of Northern Greece.
- Local centres and network for technology services.
- Centre for Industrial and Developmental Studies of Northern Greece.

Priority 5

Lead project

- Association for Industrial Information Technologies.
- Association for Anti-Pollution Technologies.
- Association for Automation Systems.
- Association for Quality Control.
- Association for Agro-technologies.

Priority 6

Lead project

- Expansion of the RTP Observatory.

Implementation

Following the above strategy, the action plan was defined by six priorities and twenty-two projects. Each priority includes specific projects falling into two groups: lead projects, marking the character of the priority, and projects that fulfil the conditions for immediate implementation. Most projects are fairly elastic with respect to size: in other words, they can be implemented on different scales, from experimental through small to large. The extent of their application may be finalised once the initial stages of implementation have been completed and the evaluation by the recipients has been assessed.

The particularity of the Central Macedonia RTP as it is reflected in the action plan is that it is expected to be implemented via separate operational programmes within the Second Community Support Framework (CSF) and some relevant community initiatives (SME, Interreg, Adapt, etc). This decentralised implementation structure requires on the one hand the adjustment of the RTP Action Plan to the procedures of the Structural Funds, and on the other, the organisation of a central hub to record, monitor and assess the progress and the results of the various actions on the regional innovation system and the technological capacity of the regional firms.

An effort was made to identify and list all the actions of the operational programmes within the Second CSF and the Community Initiatives that may support the implementation of the RTP. This analysis led to a selection of the subprogrammes, measures and actions from various operational programmes, such as:

- the Central Macedonia Regional Operational Programme;

- the Operational Programme on Industry;

- the Operational Programme on Research and Technology;

- the Operational Programme of the Community Initiative for SMEs;

- the Operational Programme of the Community Initiative RETEX;

- the Operational Programme of the Community Initiative Interreg;

- the Operational Programme of the Community Initiative Adapt;

- the Operational Programme on Energy;

- the Operational Programme on the Environment;

- the Operational Programme on Education and Initial Vocational Training.

These programmes may sustain the projects described in the action plan and show that there is substantial potential for linkage with the RTP. It should also be noted that many of the projects and actions included in the above operational programmes have not yet progressed to the implementation stage, and in this sense the list remains 'open' for the introduction of new projects and actions.

For the monitoring of the plan, a Regional Innovation Observatory was developed as a local hub for the collection, evaluation and dissemination of information relating to the RTP and its results. This information system, accessible via the Internet, is composed of experimental infrastructure functioning at the Aristotle University of Thessaloniki and the Ministry of Macedonia-Thrace. This infrastructure supports the dissemination of information relating to the RTP, the innovation system in Central Macedonia, and the full presentation of the objectives, method, work packages, strategy and projects prepared within the framework of the plan. On an average, fifty-five hits per day have been recorded from 78 'visitors' from various countries of Europe, the USA and Australia. The thematic structure of the observatory includes three main sections, dealing with:

- the regional technology plan (objectives, administration, deliverables, working programme, work packages, action plan, interim and final reports);

- the economic and technological development in Central Macedonia (geographical units, population, employment, industrial structure, GDP, technology demand and supply, etc.);

- the innovation support infrastructure in the European Union (innovation infrastructures in Greece, innovative urban and regional development projects, support for innovation and technology from the R&D framework programme, etc.).

In a more developed form during the implementation, this information system will become part of the evaluation, by collecting and processing information from numerous observation points at the recipients of the RTP actions. Such information will permit a full development of on-line services, on the prefectures of Central Macedonia, the demand and supply of technologies, the industrial location areas, the innovation environment, the trends of industrial branches, and other more specific issues.

The implementation of the action plan is expected to be a long-term process. In effect, it will be an open-ended procedure leading to the formation of a more coherent Regional Innovation System.

THE INNOVATIVE REGION STRATEGY: LESSONS FROM THE RTP EXERCISE

Regions are complex socio-economic systems which are inserted in many different ways into the wider national and international regimes of overlapping and/or conflicting orders. It is common for regional development theorists to think of particular regions in terms of general models and concepts, while consultants and policy-makers tend also to provide general solutions to be applied in particular regions.

It might be true that all approaches have to face a common set of questions. Why do some regions succeed while others fail despite the similarity of targets, size of effort and political commitment? Why does the same set of measures seem to be effective in one region but totally ineffective in another? What is the appropriate mixture of actions in each case? However, as the 'Innovative Region Strategy' approach implies, regions are not passive containers or testing grounds for various kinds of theories and policies. Instead, regions react and participate in the evolution of their structures.

In the context of the above comments we should now turn to the particular lessons that can be learned from the Regional Technology Plan of Central Macedonia. These lessons are presented as a series of propositions or themes that summarise the experiences gained during the two years of continuous efforts to coordinate and cooperate with a large and diverse group of individual and institutional actors in order to forge a consensus concerning the priorities for the promotion of regional innovation capacities. These themes can be seen also as a list of warnings for anyone concerned with the development of regional innovation systems in either theoretical or practical policy-making terms.

The Clarity of the Initial Concept

It is important to develop an initial concept or idea around which to build a set of interlinked key targets. This initial idea should make almost self-evident its appropriateness and practical effectiveness to all or most of the prospective participants in order to launch the endeavour. For this to happen the initial idea should be an already mature issue that has aroused both the interest and the expectations in the region. In the case of Central Macedonia the key terms were 'technological innovation' and 'the community support framework'. Since the beginning of the 1990s most regional actors were perfectly aware that the regional prospects depend on the ability of the regional economy to respond effectively to the opportunities offered by the opening of the wider Balkan and East and Central European Markets. On the other hand the region had the experience of the First Community Support Framework (1989–93) and the perspective of the Second Community Support Framework (1994–99) that allocated important sums of public resources for the upgrading of the available social, technical and economic infrastructure. Thus when the management unit presented the draft proposal in response to the RTP initiative of the European Commission to the Ministry of Macedonia and Thrace for the construction of an action plan to orientate the existing operational programmes of the Community Support Framework, there was an immediate positive response.

Recognition of the Actual Interests of the Partners

The same was equally true for all the major partners in the RTP experiment that were approached by the management unit. As it happened there was a gradual build-up of the interest to participate and support the RTP efforts. The first to become involved were the representatives of regional business, the Industrial Workers Union, government agencies (the Ministry of Macedonia and Thrace, the general secretary of the region, the general secretary of research and technology) and major technological service providers such as the Aristotle and Macedonia Universities and the technology park. The interest of the European Commission was already given, as three Directorates (III, XIII and XVI) were to be represented in the steering committee of the project. The actual interest of each of the above players has a different origin and rationale. Business representatives were concerned particularly with the reorientation of the CSF funds for the provision of producer services and capital contribution to new ventures. The trade union representatives were explicitly concerned with the impact of the new policies upon the number and the content of jobs as well as with the potential to finance training and retraining. The government agencies were more sensitive to the political costs and benefits from their involvement and the possibility of employing the RTP for the reallocation and faster absorption of CSF funds. Technological service providers were keen to promote the selling of their research and development expertise and the upgrading of their research infrastructure through both public and private funding. Finally, the European Commission had an interest in monitoring the implementation of their policies and to guarantee the balanced presence of the respective DGs in the monitoring and evaluation of good and bad practices.

Competition and Cooperation Between Partners

It is easily understandable that such a mixture of interests does not lead automatically to a harmonious outcome. Indeed, there is need of an initial period for the bargaining between interests, the clarification of misunderstandings and the conclusion of agreements between the competing and/or cooperating partners. As it happened, the instances of competition were more numerous in the beginning, while at the later stages there was greater need to have time in order to elaborate the framework of cooperation. Furthermore, competition, at least in the beginning, was greater between the partners with similar interests such as, for example, competition between government agencies for political control and supervision, or between the technological service-providers for having priority access to R&D funding. It was very important to have the initial competition settled before any serious debate concerning the priorities of the action plan for the promotion of an Innovative Region Strategy. Once a balance had been achieved it was equally important to take the necessary measures in order to maintain the active participation of the partners. In the case of Central Macedonia RTP this was achieved through a constant flow of information and bilateral communication with the management unit playing the initiating or the catalyst role.

Clarifying the Meaning of Consensus

Despite the occasional ups and downs the forging of a consensus over priorities was a very demanding job, because in many cases the actual ground for concluding an agreement was not known in advance. As a result, consensus on particular issues was not always of the same quality nor had the same meaning for all the different partners. For example, the different partners were not all equally interested on the issue of whether to support more generic and horizontal measures for business support or to focus on specific sectoral and/or geographical clusters. Even depending on the specific concerns of the particular persons representing the various institutional partners, they were more or less willing to agree on one or the other option. This situation was foreseen by the management unit, which attempted to contain such casual decision-making by the careful preparation of specialised reports, to the elaboration of which all key partners were invited to contribute. Another qualification of consensus stems from the fact that many partners do not object to any priority in so far as their own particular concern remains on the agenda. Thus, the trade unions were very much concerned with the maintenance of employment and the provision of retraining, and to the extent that the RTP was particularly sensitive to the employment impact of innovation no other issues triggered significant objections on their part. Finally, a different qualification to consensus relates to the ways in which each partner sees its own position in relation to the distribution of costs and benefits from the implementation of the RTP priorities. In this respect, consensus was facilitated by the fact that in most cases no immediate costs are apparent, as most decisions were concerned with the formulation of guidelines for the distribution of public resources, while the expected future benefits were made conditional upon the implementation of the specific priority projects. Thus, in both cases neither direct nor opportunity costs were clearly visible to the partners because they had to compete only over the allocation of potential future benefits.

Assessment of the Actually Existing Capacities

The detailed monitoring of the actually existing capacities for innovation in the region of Central Macedonia was perhaps one of the major contributions of the RTP. The detailed systematisation of demand and supply of technological services has revealed both a wide under-utilised potential and the existence of serious structural obstacles for its utilisation. Among these obstacles are the lack of a cooperative tradition in the business sector, the inadequate inter-firm networking and vertical and horizontal integration of the productive system, the weak linkages and the general mistrust between business, academics and public administration, the lack of self-confidence on endogenous capacities for the production of innovations, the clientelistic ethos in political decision-making, the inadequate expertise in the implementation of soft infrastructural projects, the wide availability of copied or cheap second-hand technologies, and the inadequate integration between the different regional centres. The management unit recognised the importance of such knowledge and took steps first to monitor and then to disseminate information about the features and the potential of the regional innovation system with the establishment of a Regional Technology Observatory, with plans to develop antennae at the Ministry of Macedonia and Thrace, the General Secretary and the seven prefectures of the region.

Management and Implementation

There is no doubt that the RTP experiment owes its successful completion to the collective effort of all the partners in the steering committee as well as to the personal commitment and professional competence of the great number of people involved at various stages in the preparation and dissemination of information about the evolution of the plan. The management unit had a decisive role in maintaining clarity and cohesion of the initial concept as well as in coordinating the involvement of partners and the deliverables of the many specialised working groups at each stage. A major asset for the project was the fact that political authority on the one hand and scientific expertise and economic control on the other have remained separate from the beginning to the end of the exercise. There were many instances where this separation has saved the project from many unnecessary complications. Of equal significance was the fact that the particular interest of the management unit, based at the University Department of Urban and Regional Planning and Development, in the RTP project was the success of the project itself. Furthermore, the composition of the steering committee guaranteed that practically all those interested in the promotion of regional innovation potential were represented by at least one member. The above practices of the management unit are the background for the continuation of the efforts to implement the priorities of the Action Plan. It is not possible to provide a more comprehensive assessment, as the implementation has just entered its initial phase.

In concluding we should stress that the actual achievement of the RTP in drawing up an Action Plan of development priorities on the basis of a general consensus among all the major partners involved in the promotion of the innovative potential of the region was a very satisfactory outcome. However, this positive assessment should be qualified, because this consensus was due partially to the fact that each partner had a particular interest in the implementation of the plan without always a clear synergy between the different priorities. This additive character of the plan should be seen as the cost of political consensus compensated for by the in-depth analysis of the strengths and weaknesses of the regional innovation system and the promotion of projects fostering the innovative capacity and competitiveness of the regional enterprises. To the extent that the implementation of the RTP priorities will proceed smoothly, there is no doubt that the plan will promote the effective use of new technology and the upgrading of the technological capacity of both the region's businesses and the research centres. On the other hand, the attempt to construct an Innovative Region Strategy for Central Macedonia has left many unfulfilled expectations, mainly because the plan has made explicit the existing deep structural gaps and deficiencies in the regional innovation system, some of which are due to the lack of motivation and knowledge and not to the inadequacy of available capital, material resources or infrastructure. Thus, the major challenge for a successful Innovative Region Strategy is not to imitate what other more advanced regions have achieved, nor to apply in a formal way theoretical models and policy-making recipes, but to prepare the preconditions for a dynamic adaptation of the regional economy to a constantly changing international environment. That is, to make the region an innovative milieu of global significance.

NOTES

1. The authors wish to recognise the decisive contribution of Stamatis Tsiakiris, head of the European Programs Department of the Ministry of Macedonia and Thrace, with whom they shared the responsibility for the implementation of the RTP as members of its management unit. Nicos Komninos was the scientific coordinator of the RTP project while the Minister of Macedonia and Thrace (Constantions Triaridis at the launching phase and Philippos Petsalnikos at the completion phase) had the political responsibility as head of the steering committee. Special thanks are due to Mr G Durand and Mr M Landabaso of DG XVI for their commitment to the success of the RTP initiative. Finally, the development of our own views and practices on regional innovation have been greatly enhanced by our cooperation with Kevin Morgan and Meirion Thomas, both of the University of Wales, who acted as consultants to the RTP of Central Macedonia.

7 Regional Innovation Strategies: The Key Challenge for Castilla y León as One of Europe's Less-Favoured Regions

With its 94,224 square kilometres, Castilla y León is the largest region in Spain and indeed in the entire European Union. It accounts for 18.65 per cent of the surface area of Spain, and a full 4 per cent of the EU, some of whose member countries (notably Belgium, Denmark, Ireland, Luxemburg, Holland and Portugal) are smaller in size than this region.

The population of Castilla y León was only 2.5 million in 1991, representing 6.5 per cent of the Spanish population and 0.7 per cent of that of the EU. As such it can be considered, not only in relation to Spain but to Europe as a whole, as one of the regions with the lowest population density. It is also one of the EU's Objective 1 regions. Geographically, it lies strategically on a line connecting trade flows between the northern and southern ends of the Iberian peninsula, and between Portugal and the rest of Europe.

In institutional terms, Castilla y León is one of the seventeen autonomous communities that make up the Spanish state. It possesses a regional government which is controlled by a parliament elected democratically by universal suffrage. The government is made up of a series of regional ministries which include, among others, industry, tourism and trade, agriculture and stock-breeding, public works and telecommunications, budget and education and culture. Each ministry has wide powers to set down norms and guidelines and to intervene economically, which in some cases it does in conjunction with the central administration.

Specifically, the Ministry of Industry created the Economic Development Agency of Castilla y León in 1995, with the same objectives as other similar European institutions. As such, its aim was to help regional companies, via a flexible, operative and functional agency, to become more innovative and competitive.

At an organisational level, workers are grouped together in unions while the employers have their own organisation. There are also, in addition, the traditional chambers of commerce which offer services to companies, particularly those of a small and medium size. Nevertheless, none of these organisations is, in practice, particularly relevant to the everyday reality of the companies, nor are they in close contact with operational management needs. Moreover, there is a lack of organisational tradition in the private sphere which accounts for the existence of few company organisations within the sectors.

Since 1979, the secular decline of Castilla y León's economic fortunes in relation to Spain as a whole has given way to a progressive process of economic recuperation in which the future appears brighter. The industrial sector, taken as a whole, has emerged strengthened from the processes of restructuring and adjustment that took place throughout the 1970s and, in a less marked form, have been in operation since the beginning of the 1990s. Nevertheless, there is still a lot of important work to be done in terms of modernisation and adaptation to the new competitive situation in Europe.

Over the past several years, the Spanish Autonomous Community of Castilla y León has started working to meet the major challenges posed by the need to modernise and restructure its business and industry and to promote technological innovation in companies.

Against this general background, Castilla y León is beginning to enjoy positive growth, as seen by the rising regional GDP, which between the years 1988 and 1995 was above the OECD average. This reflects the capacity of the region and, particularly, of its industrial sector to adapt to the important changes taking place on the international economic front in recent years.

However, the panorama is not so encouraging when an analysis is made of the evolution of the regional GDP in the context of Spain as a whole. Here, the growth rate of Castilla y León tends to be below the national average, thereby revealing the existence of various problems of a structural nature in the region and a marked cyclical tendency in the regional economy.

Against this background, the industrial sector of Castilla y León is seen as a prime motor of economic development. The major subsectors contributing to this trend are energy, transport vehicles, and food and beverages, as reflected in the importance of their contribution to the economic growth of the regional GDP.

The role of the major regional groups stand out within these subsectors, as is the case of the energy subsector, the major national companies, especially within the food and agriculture sector, and the strong presence of foreign investment derived from multinationals within the transportation sector.

Indeed, the origins of multinationals in the region are linked strongly to the presence of companies such as FASA-Renault, Iveco-Fiat and Nissan Motor Ibérica, which have exercised a significant influence on the progressive development of a growing and dynamic auxiliary industry, and as such have acquired great importance in the industrial makeup of the region.

At the same time, along with the contribution of industry, the services sector is also becoming a major generator of wealth in Castilla y León, although up to now this sector is less developed than in European countries outside Spain. While the main activities carried out in the services sector are basically of a traditional nature, in recent years there have been the first signs of growth in business-related services and in trade and tourism.

Together with the development of the industrial and services sectors, the region also maintains a high level of agricultural activity. This sector has an enormous social and economic significance, which is reflected in both its high contribution to the regional gross added value, higher than the national average, and in its relative importance, which is considerably greater than that of countries with important agricultural sectors such as France, Italy and Denmark.

Nevertheless, Castilla y León's primary sector finds itself in fierce competition with other countries of the European Union, such as France, that possess agricultural and stockbreeding sectors that are more modern and advanced and which enjoy more favourable physical and climatic conditions.

For this reason, Castilla y León has been working in recent years to gain comparative advantage for the region from the size of its primary sector. To this end, the sector is at present immersed in a restructuring process and plans call for the incorporation of high-quality raw materials and the development of high-added value activities in the food and beverage industry, or other transformation activities.

Castilla y León in the National System of Innovation

The efforts made by Castilla y León during the last several years reveal the growing interest on the part of both the public and private sectors in keeping their eyes on the future to undertake the technological development necessary within a global framework of the internationalisation and globalisation of economic and technological activities.

These efforts have enabled the region to register a substantial improvement in its relative R&D expenditure, with growth rates that have been very favourable in recent years, on occasion even reaching figures above the national average (Hernandez and Del Olmo 1994). Indeed, the growth rate of R&D spending in the last ten years has been much higher (26 per cent) than the national overall rate (19.6 per cent). As a result, in R&D activities the region is making better progress than other Spanish regions afflicted with structural problems that keep them from improving regional competitiveness through the generation of new scientific and technological knowledge, possession of which would enable them to increase assimilation and adapt their structures to the changing technological trends operating at the national and international levels. But despite the significant progress made by Castilla y León in recent years, companies' expenditure on R&D activities and personnel remains well below the EU average. In fact, despite the positive evolution of R&D spending in Castilla y León, and in contrast to the regional GDP's relative importance as taken against the national total, this amount constitutes only 5 per cent of the national R&D budget, ranking it seventh among the seventeen other autonomous Spanish communities in terms of its expenditure (CDTI 1996).

Also, despite the spirit of innovation on the enterprise side, only 4.2 per cent of the Spanish R&D spent by companies has been made in Castilla y León. The differences become apparent if we compare the figures for Castilla y León with EU averages. Specifically, Castilla y León accounts for a mere 0.18 per cent of R&D expenditure and 0.14 per cent of R&D personnel in the EU (CDTI 1996).

However, despite this relative disadvantage, and taking into account the interest shown by regional agents and the public authorities, a trend towards the better can be detected in the composition of this expenditure. For one thing, the weight of the public sector in technological R&D activities is lower than in other Spanish regions, owing to companies playing a greater role in R&D spending, which is about 41.3 per cent of the total of regional expenses; this is an improvement over the performance of the rest of the Spanish Objective 1 regions, where companies account for a very small percentage of regional R&D, while public administrations help to make up for the deficit with their strong presence.

The high level of spending incurred by the business sector represents a potential source of competitive advantage for the industry of the autonomous community (CDTI 1995). Nevertheless, the greatest capacity and the highest spending are linked to the strongest regional economic sectors and to the large corporate groups set up by foreign investors in the region. This suggests that external capital, in the form of the subsidiaries of multinational companies, is actively contributing to the modernisation and technological development of the region, both directly and in terms of the multinationals' sphere of influence in the region where auxiliary companies act as their suppliers, as is the case particularly in the car industry. This leads to a situation where, on one hand, the level of R&D carried out is dependent on centres that have external decision-making powers, while, on the other, the level of R&D carried out locally within the regional network of small industrial companies is reduced, but is also one that increasingly generates the dissemination of advanced techniques among the economic forces operating in Castilla y León.

Along with the activity developed by the region's companies, there is also great potential in the universities of Castilla y León for undertaking R&D activities. This is reflected in the figures for university spending on R&D, which reached 15,000 million pesetas in 1993 (CDTI 1995). Even so, the university research carried out is of a basic nature. This is due to the limited contact that the universities of Castilla y León, along with the universities in Spain as a whole, have maintained with the business sector.

The Spanish government's 1986 Science Law represented an important milestone in the involvement of the universities in general, and of those in Castilla y León in particular, both as regards the R&D efforts carried out by the regional companies and also in promoting research and technological improvements and in applying and disseminating the results within the business community.

Despite the advances made on the legislative front, and the growing awareness of the need to strengthen relations between universities and companies, the limitations that still exist, whether of a legislative–administrative or a cultural type, hamper the effort to integrate the two worlds of business and science. The absence of an R&D strategy on the part of the universities, and the lack of a tradition of interaction and trust between the two worlds, constitute two of the barriers that have to be overcome. The universities of Castilla y León have recently adopted a positive attitude that has helped to open up new forms of collaboration between the two worlds. One example has been the emergence of a series of 'interfaces', such as Research Results Transfer Offices (OTRIs) and University-Business Foundations (FUEs) and, above all, the appearance of technological centres whose aim is to meet company needs, and which, despite being at an early phase, constitute an important step in strengthening the relations and forms of collaboration between the scientific and business worlds.

For all of these reasons, the outlook for Castilla y León is now quite favourable, particularly compared with the other regions affected by problems of structural backwardness in Spain. But the main problem continues to be the fact that many companies are still unaware of or make no use of the R&D available, and a tradition of cooperation on the part of the companies has still to take hold (Hernandez and Del Olmo 1994).

Institutional Context

In 1992, the regional government, conscious of the importance of technological development and innovation, launched for the first time a set of mechanisms provided for under the law creating the Castilla y León Network of Associated Technology Centres (RETECAL). These mechanisms are designed to establish a framework of action to facilitate the development and incorporation of technological research and development activities in the regional economy.

Since then, the regional administration has made a considerable effort in the field of technology policy. However, it should be pointed out that, owing to the low level it started from, Castilla y León's support of R&D has centred, up to now, on promoting the support infrastructure and has always given this priority over measures stimulating and articulating the needs of the companies in Castilla y León.

Today, the region has sufficient instruments to foster the development of innovative and technological activity, including the presence of five universities, a broad network of twenty-nine technology centres, a Castilla y León Economic Development Agency, a technology park at Boecillo and a science park in León.

However, given the relative newness of this infrastructure, it is still necessary to undertake considerable support efforts to help coordinate and rationalise its use, ensuring benefit to industry and promoting the creation of new companies to exploit the technical capacities and results of research. The idea, therefore, is to achieve a better connection between available technology and the needs of industry, and to bring companies closer to the centres generating new technologies and know-how in order to facilitate the diffusion and transfer of technology to all productive sectors and to all firms, particularly SMEs, so that innovation and technical change can take place and result in an improvement of the region's competitiveness.

The efforts being made, particularly by the RTP exercise, are increasing steadily through the promotion of a culture and environment of innovation, and through specific actions undertaken to facilitate the participation of all social and economic agents, creating a consensus that will make it possible to anticipate events and acquire a strategic vision with regard to the long-term trends. Within this general framework, the set of instruments implemented to date both at public and private levels, while very valuable, are nonetheless partial in their development. For this reason, it is necessary to achieve a greater degree of integration as a mechanism for developing local technological capacity through the stimulation of R&D activities and a technology infrastructure network focused on the real and latent needs of companies. Accordingly, the Regional Technology Plan of Castilla y León has become the key mechanism for integrating and coordinating all the promotion actions directly affecting the science–technology–industry system of the region.

It is against this background that the RTP of Castilla y León has been drawn up by the regional government acting in agreement with local business and industry. Under the plan, the region hopes to set up a technology framework that will serve as the reference for the design and planning of actions to be taken to favour the harmonious development of a process of modernisation and diversification of the region's productive structure.

THE REGIONAL CONTEXT FOR INNOVATION

As part of the technology infrastructure of the region, the RETECAL network is a prime example of the efforts to increase the technical and organisational capacity of the productive system and to effectively coordinate available technological resources. The RETECAL network, whose formation was co-financed by the European Union through funds made available by the STRIDE programme, has been working to disseminate technology to the productive sector for the express purpose of improving the competitiveness of the region's business and industry. Though a recent creation, the RETECAL network is linked closely to the universities of Castilla y León. This makes it possible for the network to serve as an intermediary within the scientific, technological and production communities, and to facilitate technology transfer.

However, the simultaneous existence of a large number of technology centres has highlighted the need for coordination to avoid duplication of efforts and to reinforce complementarity. The ultimate aim is to establish priorities and facilitate the emergence of a regional specialisation that will provide a competitive advantage over the rest of Spain and other regions in Europe. These efforts extend as well to business and industry, where activity clusters may be created to stimulate the comprehensive development of certain sectors. The RTP is generating the framework for the development of these innovative proposals and for rationalising the technology offer, to bring it more in line with actual requirements and available resources.

Moreover, Castilla y León also has a valuable scientific environment working for it. The region has five long-established universities with a stronger commitment to research than other Spanish universities. The universities of Castilla y León are actively engaged not only in the education of human resources but also in conducting scientific research and technological development projects. The evolution of the universities throughout the 1990s has been very favourable in terms of the growth of university expenditure on R&D. Clearly then, the universities form part of the science–technology–industry system and contribute to the modernisation of the region's productive structure, in addition to contributing a high proportion of qualified human resources capable of successfully seeing through innovative processes and guaranteeing enhanced competitiveness over the long term.

However, despite the efforts in cooperation between the universities and private sector, a large part of this university expenditure on research is concentrated on basic research activities. This is precisely one of the areas that the RTP has targeted for action to achieve a greater participation of universities in private R&D efforts, integrating existing regional capacities by publicising and promoting among the industrial sector opportunities that are available under the headings of education, training, research and technology in the universities of Castilla y León.

Especially worthy of note in this regard is the emergence of interface structures similar to those in other regions of Europe, such as Research Results Transfer Offices (OTRIs) and University-Business Foundations (FUEs), which help channel the universities' efforts to facilitate technology transfer to companies, training in the new technologies, the undertaking of R&D projects and the exchange of researchers between the scientific and business communities.

However, despite the progress made in this regard, university–business relations are still in their early stages. For this reason, the presence of a powerful instrument such as the RTP may help to change the logic of these relations and facilitate a better understanding that will improve industrial competitiveness over the long term.

As part of the effort to lay the groundwork for an environment favourable to innovation activities and to place research at the service of companies, the public authorities of Castilla y León supported the creation in the regional capital (Valladolid) of the Boecillo Technology Park, a facility seen as a quality enclave providing industrial land and first-class services to high-tech innovative companies. The presence of the Boecillo Technology Park has not only helped to create a positive, modern image of the region both at home and abroad, but has also served as an instrument for technological development. The park has been responsible for diffusing know-how and information, thus helping to intensify cooperation between companies, universities and technology centres. Furthermore, the Boecillo Technology Park has managed to achieve significant projection elsewhere, extending cooperation and technology transfer from the regional to the national and international scene. In addition, through its participation in cooperation and technological development programmes, it has been instrumental in establishing transnational cooperation networks. To these instruments must be added the financial support necessary for promoting the development of new activities and innovative technology projects. In this regard, the Economic Development Agency of Castilla y León manages a number of mutual guarantee and venture capital companies to provide backing for innovative projects and guarantees to SMEs requiring start-up capital under easy conditions.

Thus the Economic Development Agency deserves special mention as a key instrument for promoting modernisation and innovation among business and industry in Castilla y León, a region characterised by the predominance of small and medium-sized companies. Much of the effort has focused on involving these smaller firms, through different awareness processes and drives, in the design and drafting of the RTP, which is the instrument to introduce order, establish priorities and coordinate and rationalise the entire science and technology infrastructure of the region.

Within this general framework, the RTP of Castilla y León represents an effort to increase companies' awareness of what resources are available in the region and how they can make best use of them, at the same time as rationalising and coordinating the forms of technology on offer so as to respond, in the most efficient way possible, to the real needs of the companies.

In short, the RTP has been seen as an action to be taken over the short, medium and long term, whose aim is to establish the basis for the creation of an articulated and coherent environment for promoting technological innovation. This is in order to create the optimum conditions both for promoting those technological innovations that will enable companies in Castilla y León to modernise their activities and for diversifying the forms of production.

GENESIS AND OBJECTIVES OF THE RTP

The increasing awareness of the need for change in order to close the gap between Castilla y León and the rest of the European Union has resulted in a commitment on the part of the regional government to implement a policy of innovation and technological development aimed at the modernisation and economic revitalisation of this autonomous community. This in turn has meant the acceptance of the need to capitalise on the huge technological and scientific potential of the universities to the benefit of the productive sector, as a means of contributing to the modernisation of business and industry and, ultimately, to the development of the entire region.

It was in this context that the Autonomous Community of Castilla y León, aware of the need to improve its regional technology policy, agreed in the autumn of 1994 to accept financial and technical assistance in order to undertake a strategic study for the technological development and improvement of the region's innovative capacity.

The Commission's choice of Castilla y León as the Spanish region for developing the pilot RTP experiment was the result of a proposal by the Spanish Ministry of Industry through the Institute for Small and Medium-sized Industry (IMPI), combined with a set of factors such as the good use of STRIDE funds in the region, which had played a crucial role in the promotion of the RETECAL network. Other factors were the steady incorporation of the region into R&D programmes, the good management of actions already undertaken and the existence of an important reserve of know-how in the region's universities.

The proposal was handled by the Regional Department of Economy and Finance, which then assumed direct responsibility and leadership during the drafting of the plan. This was how Castilla y León initially took part in the Pilot Project launched by the Commission of the European Communities through Directorate-General XVI (Regional Policy) and Directorate-General XIII (Innovation), for the preparation and design of its RTP.

However, it should be borne in mind that, initially, the regional government only agreed to carry out a plan that had been proposed by the European Commission and the central government. That the initiative originated from the top down contributed to the fact that, in its first stages, the technology plan was not assumed to be relevant to Castilla y León and was not, therefore, given political priority within the regional government. This fact, together with the lack of prior experience with technology policy and the absence of clearly defined institutional responsibilities, made it difficult to launch the plan effectively.

When it came to defining which bodies were responsible for elaborating the plan, the participation of different agents was considered via representative organisations already in existence, such as the Economic and Social Council, the Commission for Monitoring the Pact for Industrial Development, and the Rectoral Council of the Associated Technological Centres. This resulted in an over-representation of institutions and a minimal participation on the part of companies, universities and other socio-economic organisations.

Nevertheless, even from the first, when the recommendations of the European Commission on the form of elaborating the plan were put into operation, timid attempts were made to open up the organisation, at first via a series of informative meetings attended by the rectors of all the universities in Castilla y León, and then later via a conference when the objectives of the plan were presented and a first diagnosis made of the regional economy. To this conference were invited all the different regional agents who could play a role in promoting innovation in the region.

However, the regional government continued to consider the plan as an imposition of the Commission and that this had to be carried out in order to keep those responsible for Structural Funds happy. The regional culture lacked any tradition of strategic planning, and immaterial policy aspects such as animation and political consensus were not considered important. For this reason, one of the main problems of implementing the plan in these initial stages was the absence of a political and socio-economical leadership committed to fulfilling its objectives. This was due to some extent to the lack of previous experience in this particular field, and also to a failure on the part of the Commission to put more effort into convincing the regional authorities that the project was theirs and not something owned by Brussels.

This situation, together with the ensuing regional elections and the subsequent transition of political power, which led to the dismantling of the old Economic and Industrial Ministry, created significant delays. People became sceptical about how the plan could be carried out in practice and began to lose faith in the possibilities of doing so in agreement with the premises laid down by the Commission, notwithstanding the opportunities presented by such a programme for improving the competitivity both of the companies and of the region as a whole.

Nevertheless, once the regional government was installed, and the new Ministry for Industry, Trade and Tourism created, decisions began to be taken in a more resolute fashion. One of the most important was the setting up of the Economic Development Agency of Castilla y León, whose creation and subsequent streamlining transformed it into a crucial instrument of governmental decisions.

With the decision of the governing Council of Castilla y León to clearly designate the responsibility for elaborating the technology plan to the recently created Ministry for Industry, Tourism and Trade, and with the minister himself assuming the role of supervising its implementation, treating it as the cornerstone of his political activity, a start was finally made on capitalising on the efforts made previously, and in a short period tangible results were achieved, in terms of both analytical research and the involvement of socio-economic agents.

Thus in practice the real starting date for the RTP exercise in Castilla y León was winter 1995, when the Economic Development Agency of Castilla y León became the operational instrument for drafting the plan.

After that, and in agreement with the directions given by the Commission, the steering committee was redefined in such a way as to include regional and national representatives operating in the socio-economical field. In addition, a process consultant was contracted to offer advice throughout the development process and to establish the guidelines for opening up the steering committee so as to include the regional companies, in particular those exercising a leading role in the region. This set up the framework for promoting consensus and cooperation between the key regional socio-economic agents, the main expression of which has been the Technological Forum, which enjoys the participation of more than 300 people, including all the universities, technological centres and more than 250 companies. The organs of central government involved in supporting research and innovation are also represented in the forum as a way of coordinating regional and national policies.

Once the political, institutional and social pre-conditions had been completed, the plan could be put into operation in a decisive form. Although the start of the technology plan was subject to considerable delay, when it eventually gained proper backing it became an authentic political priority.

Since its responsibilities have been clearly defined, the agency has played a strategic role not only in drafting the plan but also in serving as the intermediary between the different institutions and companies of Castilla y León. This in turn has given the plan greater prominence among the different productive sectors and agents in the science–technology–market system of the region. As devised, the plan not only contributes to and facilitates the process of promoting technological development, but also favours the participation of the region in leading international circuits, giving it access to the exchange of experiences and information with technological development and innovation support organisations facing similar challenges.

From the beginning, the Castilla y León Technology Plan has aimed at developing a consistent framework for providing long-term support for technological development and innovation, which is seen as crucial to attaining the modernisation and diversification of the region's business and industry, and to improving existing technological development and innovation support instruments, ensuring that each of the initiatives launched so far is consistent, comprehensive and a beneficiary of synergies.

These are the key strategic objectives adopted by a region with a clear predominance of small and medium-sized companies in the productive structure, requiring more and more processes that can help business and industry to adapt, participate in technology transfers and assimilate technological know-how, in order to facilitate the exploitation of the results of research and the discovery of new business opportunities.

In any case, the experts responsible for the plan were aware that these are very ambitious objectives and must be addressed over the long term, a period needed to break through the inertia of a business community dominated by patterns of behaviour that have only accentuated the region's technological dependency, and which, in many cases, have represented a big handicap in the attempt to initiate processes of cooperation and collaboration. Thus, from the very first, the RTP has aimed at rationalising and ranking the scientific and technological resources existing in the region, with particular emphasis on establishing an order of priorities that will enable planners to devote these resources to the most productive uses possible. The idea is to concentrate efforts on objectives defined with realistic criteria and capable of being maintained for sufficient time to produce significant results.

THE RTP PROCESS

The eagerness and commitment to provide the region with an instrument capable of introducing order and agreement, and of articulating actions designed to promote economic development and technological innovation in the autonomous community, can be seen clearly in the very process of elaborating the RTP. The process of defining the RTP, which is based on an open policy of communication, has given rise to an organisational structure responsible for galvanising public opinion and generating a collective awareness that will facilitate the social consensus necessary for developing a strategy of this kind.

At the same time, all efforts are being made to ensure that the technology plan closely addresses real needs, and that it is realistic, practical and operative. To achieve these objectives, as the agency responsible for designing the RTP, the Economic Development Agency of Castilla y León has equipped itself with a solid technical support structure, whose key figures are the steering committee and the Regional Technology Forum. The steering committee was defined as a body representative of the principal regional protagonists and capable of integrating and harmonising the diverse economical, political, commercial, scientific and technological strands that are necessarily present in a plan of this type. It is the maximum supervisory and decision-making organ and has always attempted to reflect the spirit of the region in terms of its strategy for innovation and technological development.

As a non-operational decision-making body, the steering committee is made up of representatives from the Economic Development Agency, the European Commission, the different departments of the Castilla y León regional government, business and industry, the technology centres, the universities, the central government and experts in technological innovation issues. Among those companies represented on the steering committee are not only small companies, but also big companies that in their capacity as regional leaders have exercised a highly positive influence on it in terms of generating and attaining consensus. Concretely, this committee, which was constituted in March 1996, brings together more than thirty-six individual members and is presided over by the Minister for Industry, Tourism and Trade.

The broad composition of the committee helps to ensure that this instrument will detect and identify the technology and R&D demands of companies in the region. Other responsibilities of the committee are: to seek the best possible balance between the demand for innovation from companies and the technology available at the regional, national and international levels; to concentrate resources according to a set of established strategic priorities; to seek more effective formulas for cooperation between universities and companies; and to build a consensus that will in turn strengthen the patterns of cooperation being laid down by the different agents.

Another important point to note is that the decisions taken by the steering committee must be debated and ratified by the Regional Technology Forum, which was constituted at the beginning of 1996 as a consultative body representing a broad range of the principal social and economic protagonists active in the region. The Regional Technology Forum is a body with a composition similar to that of the steering committee, but is made up of a larger number of representatives, more than 250 of whom are protagonists in the science–technology–industry system, thus entitling it to claim a broader representation of the regional innovation system.

The Economic Development Agency has set up a management unit that is directly responsible not only for the technical supervision of the project, but also for monitoring it and promoting it among the business community, universities, chambers of commerce and technology centres. Indeed, once the plan was launched, a dissemination period was initiated with the visit of representatives of the management unit to the nine provinces in the region in order for them to get to know not only the provincial authorities but also, most importantly, the companies in each of the provinces. Their objective was to get feedback on the work and activity being planned and thus catch the mood of the companies and test their response to the proposals, not only within the most important urban areas, where until then the economic promotion activities had been concentrated, but throughout the length and breadth of the region. Thus, in an explicit manner the plan was enriched by means of the territorial dissemination of innovation processes, whose aim has been to bring cohesion to a large region with great geographical inequalities.

The management unit must also see to it that the plan is publicised throughout the community, and is in short responsible for all external promotion activities aimed at promoting the plan.

During the development of the plan, the management unit has had at its disposal an important technical support, including two process consultants brought in to advise on methodology and on marshalling the different agents, as well as consultancy firms commissioned to make specific technology studies. The unit was then responsible for drawing up the first strategy proposals.

In this field of action, the process of drafting the regional technology plan was divided into two consecutive phases. During the first phase, in May 1996, work focused on analysing the regional technology offer and assessing the regional support infrastructure for innovation in Castilla y León. This was made possible through the elaboration of a preliminary diagnosis of the economic and technological situation of the region, including a profile of its industry and technology. This preliminary diagnosis, together with the analysis of major global economic patterns to forecast probable market, industrial organisation and technology trends, is what has made it possible to make the plan realistic, and suited not only to the needs of the region but also to the main currents of international change.

Once the major strengths and weaknesses were identified in relation to the environment, the first phase of drafting the plan was devoted to a series of technology audits to evaluate the capacities and requirements of the companies in the autonomous community. To this end, a selection was made of sectors strategic to the regional economy because of their growth potential and current ranking in terms of contribution to gross added value and to regional employment. These sectors were then organised into ten sector panels – made up of representatives of a significant number of companies, technological centres and other relevant organisations – which were made responsible for the checking and ratifying of the results of the demand study. The sectors from which the sector panels were made up were those considered the most significant in the region: chemical and pharmaceuticals, the environment and recyclable energy, food and agriculture, capital goods, tourism, timber and furniture, cars and components, culture and communications, energy, minerals and water. It is worth pointing out that these sectors were not only industrial ones, but that service sector activities, such as tourism and culture, also figured prominently.

To top off this first phase, a study was made to examine the connection between the technology on offer and the technology in demand in the region, assessing the degree of 'fit' between the two sides.

During this entire first phase, the socio-economic agents of the region were engaged in a major debate over the state of innovation and technology in Castilla y León. Over a thousand different organisations participated in the debate, including 800 companies, most of which were small and medium-sized firms.

Thus, this first phase of the plan made it possible to marshal all efforts and organisations in the pursuit of a common goal – the development of technological innovation with a view to enhancing the economic competitiveness of the region. In addition, all the activities conducted during the first phase were approved by both the steering committee and the technology forum, meaning that the plan is the result of wide discussion and agreement. Once the first phase of the plan had been concluded, its results were passed by the steering committee and ratified by the forum, and the second phase of the RTP was launched in January 1997.

This second phase has been devoted to: defining the specific objectives to be reached over the short, medium and long terms; devising the strategy, programmes and resources that make up the plan; calculating the financial commitment necessary to carry it out; and defining the monitoring and evaluation procedures.

Since discussion and agreement are constant points of reference in drafting the plan, during this second phase the different representatives of the region's innovation system were given draft lines of action to obtain the sort of feedback that will ultimately enrich the design of the plan. To this end, the sector panels were convened for a second time and asked to study the proposal.

The sector panels and provincial diagnoses formed part of the political strategy of a region as large as Castilla y León, where the aim is to ensure that all the provinces are fully aware of the repercussions of the plan so that they can help to develop synergies and achieve a high degree of internal coherence.

Once the information contributed by the sector panels was gathered concerning the proposed programmes and lines of action, and once the priority technologies had been identified, work began on developing an RTP management model and a definitive strategy proposal which was submitted to the steering committee and the Regional Technology Forum in July 1997.

Several results are expected from the plan. For one thing, it defines a clear framework for innovation support measures and instruments within the regional productive network. The plan is also expected to help in generating synergies, promoting interregional cooperation networks both inside and outside the region, preparing and implementing concrete technological innovation projects in companies, and strengthening regional technology centres.

Given that implementation of the RTP is expected to take place at a steady pace and with an eye to the future, the adoption of a methodology for monitoring it adequately has been considered necessary. This will take the form of a series of periodical revisions facilitated by the monitoring work carried out via programmes and *ad-hoc* methods. In this way, the norms for evaluating those operations carried out to date can be established, and any corrections considered necessary introduced in future operations.

With this in mind, a series of indicators have been identified in the context of the operation of the plan, such as proximity of the market, quality of R&D, target companies, investment in new technologies, companies that participate in the programmes, additional contributions from public funds, total spending on R&D/gross added value in Castilla y León, and the distribution of the funding of total expenditure on R&D. The aim has been both to obtain reliable information on a day-to-day basis on the specific operations contemplated in the plan, and to provide a mechanism for evaluating its global impact.

RESULTS AND LESSONS FROM THE RTP

In assessing the results of the RTP it is necessary to bear in mind that it is an open, live plan adapted to meet the actual needs of business and industry in Castilla y León. Moreover, the plan will be permanently updated to ensure its ability to respond to increasingly changing circumstances, where important technological innovation processes are currently under way.

The RTP exercise has helped to make the region's companies aware of the means at their disposal and the real possibilities of undertaking technological development activities within a comprehensive framework suited not only to the regional environment but also beyond, reaching national and international dimensions.

The excellent progress of the work undertaken so far has made it possible to begin the reordering of the science–technology–market system of the region, proposing specific mechanisms for rationalising the offer and achieving a higher degree of internal consistency among all the agents involved in the chain of innovation. This is expected to lead to greater coordination of existing infrastructures and of all the agents involved in processes of innovation.

One of the initial results of the Regional Technology Plan has been the success attained in involving companies in the plan's design by means of technological auditing and meetings by sectors. This has allowed validation of the analyses carried out and the establishment of priorities within a region whose inhabitants do not traditionally lend themselves to participation. This has not only provided first-hand information to define strategy, but has also created an atmosphere of credibility and trust within society and within the business world with regard to the importance of the innovation process.

One such important result of the plan has been the growing number of collaborative undertakings, with large international companies based in the region seeking the support of the regional authorities as a mechanism that will increase their competitiveness and thereby add to the region's development. It should be noted that this participation has taken place not only between companies but also between institutions, thanks to the teamwork of all departments of the regional government of Castilla y León and other social and economic bodies. The plan has likewise allowed the regional Economic Development Agency to keep the know-how and extensive internal relations created by the plan within the region.

Having involved so many agents, the plan has created sensitivity and clearer ideas as to the need for cooperation between these agents, and for coordination of the various policies for the promotion of technology and innovation within the region. The plan brings together various means of back-up for technological development and innovation and the efforts made by the region's various autonomous ministries. An example of this is the fact that other activities that are currently being promoted by the Castilla y León government (the Business Competitiveness Plan, now being defined at the Ministry of Industry, Commerce and Tourism, and the Science Law, being elaborated by the Ministry of Education and Science), and that are aimed at improving regional competitiveness, were designed to extend the work begun by the plan.

The involvement of business and industry, which have traditionally remained detached from political action and sceptical about their effectiveness, has also been achieved throughout the community by publicising the need for a Regional Technology Plan in the various provinces of Castila y León. This has helped to secure political acceptance of the plan, and to ensure that the specific issues affecting each different sector and/or geographical location of the area will be taken into account.

Perhaps the greatest achievement of the plan is its ability to provide an ordered framework for future technological development. This would guarantee its own continuity as a dynamic force in time, bringing together as it does measures designed to take effect in the short, medium and long terms.

This plan is the regional government's first planning experience in an attempt to provide overall coherence for all current and future technological activity within the region. Although it is but a first step and there is still much to do, the plan offers the region its own self-defined strategy as a reference to coordinate the supply of technology and prevent dispersion and overlapping of effort, and to help mobilise demand.

The final result to date has been a comprehensive strategic and integrated 'bottom-up' framework, which reinforces actions in technological innovation already present within the region with other measures. Action planned within this framework is to take place gradually, and only certain priority courses of action are to be taken immediately in accordance with their importance and the ability to take such measures. Action taken with the future in mind falls into five programmes: infrastructure, innovation, training, awareness and structuring of demand. Together they considerably increase the resources used by the region to create technology, and will mobilise 73,780 million pesetas (460m. ECUs) in both public and private funds in the first four years (1997–2000).

The plan's main aims are as follows:

- to realign and strengthen the technology infrastructure;

- to articulate the needs and requirements of the enterprises with a view to strategically strengthening the sectors;

- to develop collaboration at all levels of the innovation system;

- to optimise and increase the availability of human potential;

- to facilitate Castilla y León accessing the technological benefits available at a national and international level;

- to promote an integral approach to innovation;

- the continuous monitoring and evaluation of the results obtained as the plan is put into operation.

Out of all these programmes and measures, the infrastructures programme deserves special mention, given its importance in Castilla y León's science and technology system. This system takes account of public support through the regional definition of a model of a technology and innovation infrastructure in order to act in a global way on the regional network of Associated Technology Centres as a whole. In this way it is able to determine its role and its future development strategy by deciding which centres should be given more support and which should fuse with others, or even disappear. Thus, the number in existence can be rationalised and they can be assigned realistic objectives in specialised areas, while measures can also be adapted according to the needs of the companies and the level of competition in an international context. For this to happen, it is considered fundamental to define a stable framework for the funding of the centres.

The other basic element of the plan is the priority given to stimulating the companies to seek out technological advances by means of distinct instruments. The spirit of the plan is to gradually increase the number of companies benefiting from the measures supporting innovation, in such a way that the number of innovative companies increases year by year. The plan takes into account that its innovation policies are aimed at all companies and not an elite. Thus, in the course of elaborating the Regional Technological Plan, the need has been revealed for a specific regional policy on technology to take account of companies of a medium size which, having more than 250 employees, still cannot be considered large in terms of enterprises operating in European markets.

Finally, it is possible to establish some operational conclusions:

- The plan was not able to achieve real force until it was taken up by the regional authorities as something pertaining to them. When this happened, with clear leadership from the Minister of Industry, and the designation of an operational body, the Economic Development Agency of Castilla y León, the RTP process got underway in earnest.

- The plan is important in the sense that it has mobilised a great number of socio-economic agents and created a framework for discussion and for building up contacts that has made it possible for a consensus to be reached over the main problems and best solutions. Moreover, there has been a notable increase in the collective awareness of the importance of research and innovation.

- The lack of major conflicts throughout is probably due to two factors:

  - The government's positive response to the opinions and suggestions made by those agents which have been involved in the process; it was said that the plan was going to be a matter concerning all the region and not just the government, and that is how it has been in practice.

  - The policy for supporting innovation in the region is still in its early stages, which makes it is easier to achieve consensus on its basic aims and measures.

- The speed and extent of the social participation generated indicate that the plan has been defined at a moment when awareness in the region provided favourable conditions for it to be carried out. This is due to the challenges represented by the Single European Market and expansion to the east, and the possibility that these factors could put in question the present bases of the regional economy.

- The fact that the technology plan was the first public task to be carried out by the Economic Development Agency of Castilla y León has been a positive feature both in terms of the agency's visibility and legitimacy. It also explains the priority given to it by the agency, in terms of personal dedication and financial commitment, which has been much higher than the grant made by the Commission and higher than the amount initially stipulated.

8 From Planned Economy to Global Markets: The RITTS Project in South Brandenburg

The European Commission has recently launched a variety of regional innovation programmes and schemes. The Regional Technology Transfer Strategies and Infrastructures (RITTS), an initiative of the Innovation Programme (DG XIII), has many similarities with the Regional Technology Plans described in this book. It follows the same structure: an assessment of the strengths and weaknesses of the region, a definition of priority actions and the development of a demand-led, consensus-based, regional strategy for innovation. This chapter discusses the case of a German region where such a RITTS project was conducted. In 1994 the Technologie und Innovations-Agentur Brandenburg (the Technology and Innovation Agency Brandenburg or TINA) successfully applied for a RITTS project for South Brandenburg. The project started at the end of 1994 and finished in the summer of 1996.

Brandenburg, formerly a GDR state, is one of the new Länder in Germany. South Brandenburg is a subregion of that federal state. The RITTS project was intended to be a pilot project for this subregion and would fit into the CITI '99 Initiative, a six-year initiative to launch an innovation strategy in the sub-region jointly undertaken by a number of key organisations. The following chapter will describe the background of the region, the start of the RITTS project and the findings of the assessment of the economic situation, company needs and the innovation support infrastructure; the process of strategy-building in the RITTS project is also described later. The international dimension of learning from other RITTS projects was of limited importance in this case, since exchange of experience took place mainly within Germany. The results of the project, and a summary of some of the lessons learned, are described in the final section.

THE SOUTH BRANDENBURG REGION

Brandenburg is the German federal state (Bundesland) that surrounds Berlin. As all German Länder, it has authority and resources to formulate and implement economic policy on the regional level. Brandenburg's governing bodies are located in the capital, Potsdam. The department responsible for innovation policy is the Ministry for Economic Affairs, Trades and Technology, which co-funded the RITTS project. The regional innovation support policy is a mix of implementation of national programmes and specific regional support activities, some funded by European (Structural) Funds.

The RITTS project covered only the south part of this Bundesland, called South Brandenburg. This subregion borders Poland in the east and the Länder Sachsen and Sachsen-Anhalt in the south and south-west. The neighbouring Sachsen, with its cities Leipzig and Dresden, has a strong industrial tradition and with centres of technological expertise, and these are focal points for innovative firms in South Brandenburg. South Brandenburg has approximately 1 million inhabitants and covers 22 per cent of the surface of Brandenburg. It is designated as an Objective 1 area and has special status in German innovation policy, which allows firms to receive a higher level of support from the national R&D programmes. Although acknowledged as a subregion, South Brandenburg has no governing authority. On a lower geographical level, the municipalities (Kreise) have some administrative power and adopt an economic development policy, which is focused mainly on the planning and management of industrial estates.

The present socio-economic problems of the region originate from its history as part of the GDR economy and its recent transition from a planned economy into a market-oriented economy. This transition had its impact on both the economic fabric and the region's institutional environment.

Travelling through South Brandenburg, one can see why this region is an area with very specific problems. A moon-like landscape full of barren open fields, occasionally covered with deep holes, hardly any vegetation, are the visible signs that reflect the region's past booming industry: energy production based on the mining of lignite (*Braunkohle*). The region had a number of power plants, fuelled by local lignite. The lignite-mining industry, a form of mining where the immediate surface is dug out by huge excavators, also caused severe environmental damage. The lignite fields were excavated in areas a couple of kilometres in width and much longer in length. Villages in the path of the excavators were simply 'relocated'. Underground water was pumped out in a large area surrounding the mining fields, changing the vegetation in the wider environment. The large-scale energy plants were very unproductive, and consumed a trainload of lignite every ten minutes. Both activities, the energy supply and the mining, were severely downsized after unification, leaving thousands unemployed. At present some lignite-mining fields are still in operation, but most have been closed together with the closure of energy plants and factories for lignite briquettes, a common household energy source in the GDR. Service and engineering sectors linked to the energy and mining activities suffered from these closures as well. Another regional stronghold, the clothing industry, based on products fabricated from artificial fibres, experienced a similar sudden downsizing after unification because of lack of demand.

Brandenburg is seen as one of the regions where so many problems – environmental, industrial and social – come together that, compared with the other GDR regions, it is one of the most challenged (Wegner 1993). Its economic structure is in transition, consisting of mainly small and medium-sized companies, which are having to catch up in terms of productivity, management skills and business links. In addition it has an institutional landscape that has almost started from scratch, after old institutional networks were dissolved. Targeted public–private actions such as the RITTS project aimed to find solutions to these challenges.

THE ORIGINS AND OBJECTIVES OF THE RITTS PROJECT

For policy-makers the attraction of a RITTS project is that it is more than a study: it provides an opportunity to instigate a strategic debate in the region, to implement new initiatives, and to involve various public and private stakeholders. The second stage of the RITTS project is precisely aimed at starting up the implementation process of various 'priority actions'. At the beginning of a RITTS project, it is not clear what types of priority actions will emerge from the first stages of the exercise. It depends on the analysis of strengths and weaknesses of the innovation system, the needs of the companies expressed in the first stage assessment, and the objectives of actors that shape the innovation policy in the region.

As we have seen, the initiator of the RITTS project was TINA, the intermediary technology support agency in the region. TINA Brandenburg is a public intermediary organisation, supported by the Federal Ministry of Economic Affairs and the Minister for Economic Affairs and Technology of the federal state of Brandenburg. The agency covers the complete federal state, with offices in each of its subregions. The RITTS project was implemented and managed by one of the TINA offices, with its seat in Cottbus, the administrative centre in the south part of the federal state.

A consensus-based group of regional actors had established an association in its subregion Cottbus, to encourage innovation in the region. The initiative Cottbus Innovation and Technology Initiative (CITI '99) has as its primary goal 'to stimulate and encourage enterprises to realise innovations in southern Brandenburg, through business expansion, establishment of subsidiaries and new start ups' (TINA 1993). The strategy was mainly aimed at creating new businesses in 'future markets'. The background paper described the strategy as a technology-push approach, to prepare the firms for more innovation-oriented challenges. Economic objectives were to attract external investors and to encourage the local firms to engage in international 'future markets'.

The RITTS project was intended to function as a pilot to give additional impetus to this initiative. The precise objectives of the RITTS project were not defined at the start of the project, but developed in the process between consultants, TINA and the steering committee. From the start the expert team and the project promoter agreed that the RITTS project should lead to clear concrete and feasible proposals for action, rather than to become (another) strategic policy document.

The RITTS project followed the structure as proposed by the European Commission at the time. Phase 1 consisted of an assessment of the SME needs, the supply side and the strategies of the main actors. Phase 2 aimed to translate the results of Phase 1 into Priority Actions. Finally, an evaluation and monitoring system would be put in place to follow the implementation. Unlike in the present second-generation RITTS projects, there was no Phase 0 to finalise the work programme, define the objectives and commit a broad set of actors to be involved in the project's steering committee. In hindsight this created problems for the further phases of the project, because divisions of tasks and methodologies were decided 'along the way', while allocations of time and money were set at the start.

The objective of the RITTS project was to make those organisations that support companies in achieving greater competitiveness and better performance more effective, in particular in their efforts to produce new, commercially viable and possibly innovative products and services. These targets would be achieved through:

- the increase of interaction/collaboration between the organisations in the innovation support structure;

- more demand-led, business-oriented operations of the organisations, following the findings of the needs analysis;

- improvement of operations and competencies of the organisations in the infrastructure and better definition of core business and targets;

- removal of bottlenecks, improvement of information flows, division of tasks and cooperation in the innovation support infrastructure to create a coherent regional network

The structure of the project and the actors involved in the different activities are shown in figure 8.1. It follows the given structure of a RITTS project, with several moments of interaction with the regional stakeholders in between the phases of the project. The only major change to the original plan was to build in more time for the implementation phase – final definition of priority actions and preparations for their launch – and thus to extend the entire time schedule. This decision was made at the start of this phase when it became clear that the process of committing actors and elaborating plans needed more than the planned three months.

FIGURE 8.1: THE STUCTURE OF THE SOUTH
BRANDENBURG RITTS

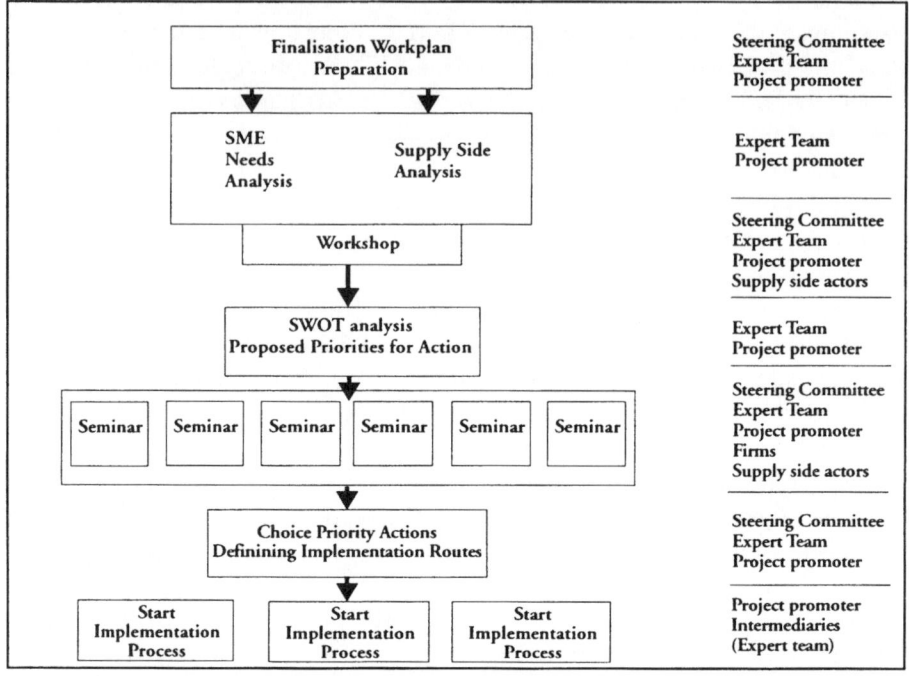

THE REGIONAL CONTEXT FOR INNOVATION

South Brandenburg is not only a peripheral region on the border of the
European Community; it also has to deal with a heritage from its GDR past
and the transition process into the West European market. To understand the
specific issues of this economy we need to describe some of the typical problems of these new Länder.

The restructuring of the eastern German economy after unification has had
an enormous impact on the industrial fabric, employment, research and development and the institutional framework in general.

The GDR economy was organised around large, highly specialised and primarily vertically integrated *Kombinate* based on product-value chains.
Economies of scale would allow for greater efficiency in production. Gernot
Grabher describes how this system had two disastrous consequences for the
regions. First, it favoured the deepening of already existing and new regional
monostructures. Second, as a result of the internalisation of economic interactions, the notion of the region as a supply base for firms no longer had any
meaning.

> In other words, the rationalisation of production within the Kombinate and
> across regional boundaries ... ended up destroying a flexibility once provided
> by localised production clusters. Beyond the utilisation of the local labour force,

the individual plants of the Kombinate had no economic relation with the region in which they were located. (Grabher 1995)

Indeed, in the case of South Brandenburg the monoculture in economic activities was clearly visible: it was designated as the energy supplier of almost the entire GDR. With its huge lignite mining fields and energy plants, it provided electricity for a large part of the GDR. The gross production of electric power in 1990 was 53 per cent of all electricity generated in the new Länder.

The economic transition has had a dramatic impact on employment in the region. One of the major sources of employment in South Brandenburg, the mining and energy industry, had seen a drastic decline, despite the fact that in 1994 the former coal mining company Laubag was by far the largest employer in the region with approximately 29,100 employees. In 1991 the mining industry produced 27 per cent of the industrial turnover, but in 1993 this share had dropped to 18 per cent. Many supporting and related industries, from mining engineering through rail transport and the manufacture of mining equipment to fabrication of lignite briquettes, suffered from the closures of many of the lignite mines. Another major source of employment, agriculture, collapsed as well. Up to 1993, 140,000 people lost their jobs in agriculture (78 per cent of workforce in that sector) in the federal state of Brandenburg alone.

The total unemployment rate in South Brandenburg increased from 6.4 per cent in January 1991 to 14.2 per cent in 1992 and to 17.6 per cent in January 1994. This does not include the hidden unemployment of many people in public-supported schemes (*Arbeitsbeschaffungsmassnahmen*) launched in East Germany to soften the severe consequences of the privatisation and closure of many firms. Some experts state that if this is taken into account the unemployment rate should be doubled.

Within the RITTS project one of the consultants developed a competitive advantage analysis of South Brandenburg as a business location, using comparative database analysis. This revealed that the industrial density of many parts of the region is very low compared with other German regions. At the same time, there was a relatively high proportion of firms with less than 50 employees and very low export rates. Other studies showed a relatively low level of productivity in East German firms compared with West Germany.

The RITTS exercise also uncovered some competitive advantages of the region:

- the possibility of the region acting as a bridging area between West European markets and Eastern European industries. Many firms have business links with Eastern European companies, as partners, clients or suppliers;

- the proximity to Berlin offering firms a large consumer market;

- geographic factors such as the availability of space, and some minerals.

One striking feature that emerged during the RITTS project was a lack of networks and linkages, both between firms and between firms and the innovation support infrastructure. Inter-firm relations appeared to exist on a very limited scale. Most firms had only a very short history, either in terms of management or in terms of their existence. This was due to the changes in ownership after unification, where the local firms were:

- bought by West German or foreign companies and in most cases restructured;

- newly located subsidiaries of West German and foreign companies;

- existing firms taken over through a management buyout by local East German entrepreneurs; or

- new start-ups, of which many were *'Existenzgründer'*, companies that were set up because the entrepreneur had lost his or her position in one of the former GDR companies.

Thus, the economic fabric had little chance to develop a tradition of inter-firm networking. The RITTS SMEs analysis confirmed this picture. In the face-to-face interviews companies had a tendency to look at their difficulties to survive as an individual problem. What was striking was the answer to the survey question about what companies judged to be the main source of ideas for innovation. In many European studies customers and suppliers are mentioned as a key source, but in South Brandenburg an overwhelming majority of almost 60 per cent of the firms said that internal development was a major source for obtaining (technological) knowledge. External sources of knowledge scored less than 30 per cent.

This does not mean that networking never existed in the economy of the GDR, despite the establishment of the strictly organised *Kombinate*. Grabher describes how the gap between the (in theory) very thoroughly rationalised *Kombinate* and the reality of chronic shortage of intermediate goods and spare parts provided the basis for intense informal networking within and between *Kombinate*:

> [I]nformal exchange networks within and between the Kombinate played a key role in not only compensating for the chronic shortages of raw material, spare parts and equipment, but also dealing with the continual ad hoc interventions of various power groups, such as local party members and trade unionists... Although the larger part of such exchange took place in the grey area of personal networks reinforced by mutual obligations, some Kombinate turned it into an auxiliary organizational device: they circulated special 'pendulum lists' (*Pendellisten*) among different production sites of the Kombinate, indicating the resources and capacities that were idle and of potential use as a buffer inventory to cope with unforseeable shortages. (Grabher 1995)

An extensive informal system of linkages between people and parts of the economy emerged, creating its own local supply system. This informal exchange system shows many similarities with the 'Favour Bank' in the New York criminal justice system, so eloquently described in Tom Wolfe's novel *The Bonfire of the Vanities*, where mutual favours were mentally mapped to be called upon when needed.

It appears that the abrupt dismantling of the *Kombinate* by the Treuhand after unification,[2] separating the individual plants, downscaling and closing of departments such as R&D, had a detrimental effect on economic and social networks in the East German states. Grabher states that:

> [I]t is becoming more and more clear that this strategy has resulted in not only a dramatic loss of training and R&D capacities… but also in the dissolution of basic social institutions which could have formed a nucleus for developing the institutional fabric of a modern (local) civil society. A technology transfer and innovation support system as we know it in most European countries was built up almost from scratch in the early 1990s. The preference for the Western economic model … reduced the transformation of Eastern Germany to a mere cloning of the Western German institutional framework. (Grabher 1995).

This also applies to the innovation support infrastructure in South Brandenburg.

Research and development in the GDR were conducted within the *Kombinate*. After unification the industrial R&D expenditures dropped to 15 per cent of the previous GDR level. The R&D skills were embodied in the engineers employed by the large *Kombinate*. With the acquisition of many of these eastern companies by larger companies in Western Europe, the engineering and R&D capacities were in many cases shut down and concentrated in the company head offices outside the region. Brandenburg had 14,000 people engaged in industrial R&D in the GDR era, while in 1992 only 2,500 to 3,000 were active and the number was still going down. The downsizing was particularly strong in those companies (in the process of being) privatised or sold under the supervision of the Treuhand (Schulze, undated).

Given the restructuring both on the company side and on the institutional side, the team of experts decided that the core RITTS model linking the supply side with the needs of SMEs was not addressing the core problems in the region sufficiently. First, the firms were struggling with many internal problems, and for most of them access to R&D facilities was not (yet) an issue. Second, since the university and research system in general had been severely restructured, with new people – often West Germans – leading new departments, the technology transfer infrastructure was in its infancy.

The SME Needs Analysis

Most RTP and RITTS projects can start on the basis of previous data and analyses of the regional economy and its firms. One of the problems in the

South Brandenburg case was a lack of information and data on these subjects. The reasons for this were as follows:

- The transition of the economy was in full progress. The population of firms (ownership, new start-ups, collapses) was changing rapidly. Many firms were in the process of being sold or privatised by the Treuhand. Reliable and up-to-date information on the economy was not readily available, nor was there any history in the data material, given the recent privatisations, acquisitions and so on. Even for key actors in the region it was difficult to keep an overview of the industrial fabric.

- The database of firms managed by the Industrie und Handelskammer (IHK – Chamber of Commerce) was considered to be confidential and could not be accessed for analysis in the RITTS project. Eventually a random selection of addresses could be used for the postal survey.

- South Brandenburg is not an administrative region. Most statistics on the economy were collected on the federal state level and not aggregated for subregion level.

This meant that a large part of the RITTS team's effort was focused on retrieving information on the regional firms. The research method chosen was a combination of data analysis, face-to-face company interviews and a postal survey. During the project there were face-to-face interviews in 45 firms.

In an early stage of the project, in discussions with the project team and TINA, consensus was reached that the RITTS strategy should be built on the existing strengths in the region and not only target on generic technology issues for all industrial and service sectors. The CITI '99 initiative had already identified some focal points for encouragement such as medical technology and environmental technologies. Given the limited financial resources in the subregion, targeting specific areas was felt to be necessary. The idea of developing parts of the regional priority actions around clusters of firms with growth potential was accepted with interest by the team and the steering committee. In the course of the needs analysis, the apparent isolation of many firms – in terms of possibilities of sharing experience, exchanging ideas or using local firms as a supplier base – confirmed the idea that encouraging networking among the firms could help to diffuse (technological) know-how and market information. At the same time, the face-to-face interviews revealed a high degree of disquiet about the idea of exposing the firm to outsiders, including innovation support consultants. Part of this disquiet can be explained by the role of private consultants during the Treuhand privatisation exercises in the early 1990s. The consultants had had full access to all the companies' information systems, which were then strategically used and sold to interested investors. Another explanation could be a deep-rooted distrust of state-owned organisations.

One of the first tasks was to identify the (potential) clusters. Previous experience of the international consultant with cluster studies was brought into practice in the South Brandenburg region. (Boekholt 1994). The company interviews were also used as an information source to identify clusters of economic activity. From economic data and the face-to-face interviews with intermediaries and firms, a first 'cluster pattern' emerged. This pattern was presented in a workshop where representatives from economic development agencies and the technological infrastructure were invited to discuss whether the picture was accurate. The industrial branches with a higher than average presence or future potential in the region are shown in figure 8.2. In the implementation phase the expert team developed the first steps for specific actions that could be taken in those areas, particularly in network awareness-raising.

FIGURE 8.2: CLUSTERS IN SOUTH BRANDENBURG

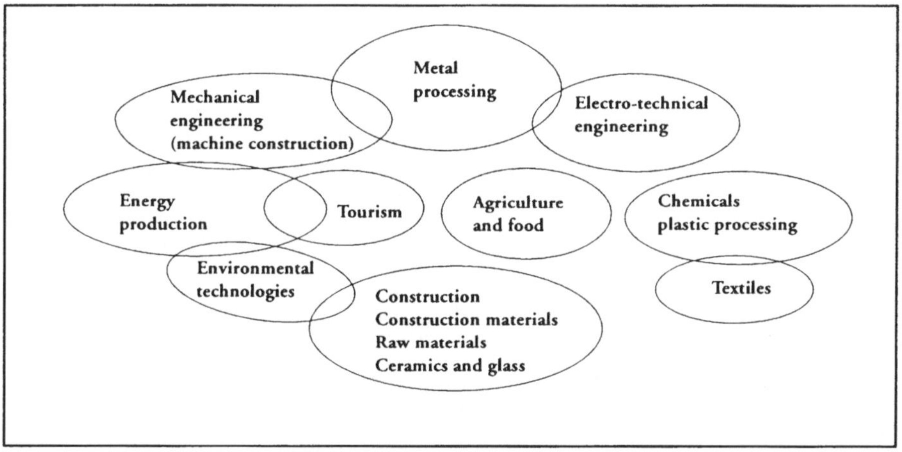

The clusters that overlap are thought to have opportunities for synergy effects, especially in the traditional areas of mechanical engineering, electronic engineering and metal-processing. The overlap between energy and tourism, at first sight a strange combination, relates to the possibilities for water tourism in the artificial lakes left behind after lignite-mining. The regional authorities have high hopes of encouraging leading-edge local firms in the area of environmental technologies with large-scale projects in land reclamation and the recycling of contaminated soil. The problem in developing this into a real opportunity is the funding of the redevelopment of this land and the lack of other tourist resources that can attract visitors from outside the area. Strengths in the chemical industry are centred around two major plants in the region, now owned by BASF and Hoechst. Especially around the first firm, the large-scale downsizing and outsourcing has encouraged many spinoffs, supported partly by BASF. The number of employees dropped from 5,500 in 1990 to 2,150 in 1995. R&D facilities previously in these plants have been

downsized and in the case of Hoechst closed. The RITTS assessment concluded that building a network of firms on the industrial sites around BASF
could offer opportunities for inter-firm technology transfer. BASF provided
initial support to the new start-ups that resulted from the outsourcing of many
of the previous internal business functions. BASF's higher standards also
helped them to increase their product and service quality.

The textile industry was specialised in artificial fabrics, for which demand
fell drastically after reunification. New initiatives were taken up by local firms
using natural materials such as flax and hemp to manufacture clothes. In fact,
a successful 'cluster initiative' was set up by the remaining textile companies,
in collaboration with Polish textile companies just over the border. With the
organisational efforts of a local technology centre, the textile companies share
information systems, design facilities and present themselves with a common
fashion line in the West European fashion markets.

The only wide and deep supply chain in the region can be found in the
construction cluster: it ranges from the mining of raw materials through the
production of a wide range of building materials (also in the metal-processing
sector) to the presence of many construction firms. After an initial boom in
the years following unification, this sector is now suffering a severe recession.

The seminars organised on the topic of clusters and collaboration as a solution to economic problems raised a lively debate among a number of
entrepreneurs on the issue of competition versus collaboration. There was
consensus that fierce regional competition, where companies tried to sell their
products below cost price in order to survive, in the end damaged all companies. The entrepreneurs showed interest in the concept of networking, but
were hesitant to start initiatives themselves. This confirmed the idea in the
RITTS team that an independent organisation has a better chance of acting as
broker and to build up more trust between the companies.

In addition to the face-to-face interviews with firms and some key actors in
the regional economy, the RITTS team decided to conduct a postal survey
among a wider range of industrial firms (500 firms). We found this necessary,
first, because of the lack of key data on firms in the manufacturing industries
and industry-related services on the level of South Brandenburg, and, sec-
ondly, because the survey aimed to obtain information from a larger
population than could be covered with face-to-face interviews.

The results of the survey confirmed in broad lines the conclusions from the
other parts of this RITTS analysis. A general conclusion from the survey is
that the South Brandenburg firms revealed an awareness that innovation, in
particular the modernisation and improvement of their production processes,
was crucial for their existence in the medium and long term. Three-quarters
of the firms intended to modernise their production process in the coming
year. Even more remarkable is that almost 60 per cent stated that they would
work on the development of a new product. On the other hand, almost half
the firms had no staff engaged with research or development and another third

had one or two people involved in this. We found in the face-to-face interviews that this was often the task of the manager or owner, alongside all their other managerial responsibilities.

In terms of bottlenecks for an innovative development, over 60 per cent of the entrepreneurs experience market entry, finding their way to new customers and assessing their relative position towards their competitors as (very) important or very important problems. Three-quarters of them also judged cost-effective production as a major bottleneck. In the face-to-face interviews entrepreneurs often spoke about their (perceived) difficulties of getting into supplier networks. They observed that West German and foreign firms investing in the region brought their suppliers with them, even for the most simple products or services that could have been provided locally. Entry to the competitive and quality-oriented West German market was seen to be even more difficult. The entrepreneurs were convinced that the West German markets were tight-knit networks of customers and suppliers, where East German companies had great difficulties breaking in.

The survey suggested that, in easing the firms' problems, technology transfer played a modest role: access to research knowledge and know-how for development were regarded as an important bottleneck by about a third of the firms. Asked to rate the possibility for R&D to solve their innovation problems, only 10 per cent had a strong feeling that it could help here. Given the urgency of adaptations to production, most firms are in search of applied research as well as knowledge and information on existing technologies.

The financial situation of the firms, in particular their lack of capital, was judged a major bottleneck by more than 60 per cent of the firms. This type of survey result is not unusual for SMEs. Again the face-to-face interviews gave the story that traditional banks were very reluctant to provide finance, particularly for risk-bearing innovative firms. The East German entrepreneurs with start-up or management buyout firms experienced the greatest difficulties in accessing finance. In the early 1990s the banks invested heavily in the local retail sector (motor companies, do-it-yourself chains, carpet halls and shopping malls), which after an initial boom was starting to hit the first recession in the mid-1990s. This made the banks even more cautious in investing in local businesses, especially if they were engaged in risk-bearing innovative activities.

In answering questions about which type of support was most urgently needed, help with making improvements in the production process, and/or its organisation, and the implementation of technologies scored high with most of the firms. It is striking that support in finding new markets or improve marketing was not high on the agenda, in spite of the fact that market entry was put forward as the largest bottleneck.

One of the conclusions from our interviews was very clearly confirmed by the survey: the South Brandenburg firms had a strong tendency to invent or reinvent things themselves. Asked what the firms' main sources for their innovative technologies and know-how were, a large majority said they developed these for themselves. Very few regarded suppliers or customers as an important source of innovative ideas. One explanation could be that the South Brandenburg firms had not yet managed to establish stable inter-firm networks – within and outside the region – as was explained earlier.

A remarkable result of the survey was the relatively high number of firms (44 per cent) who were involved with a technology supplier (i.e. a higher-education institute or research organisation), inside or outside South Brandenburg. The Technical University of Cottbus (BTU Cottbus) is the best-known higher-education institute in South Brandenburg, and a fifth of the interviewees worked with them. We do not know from the survey what type of collaborations are considered. Most likely, both informal contacts and formal research contracts are included. In the face-to-face interviews we found several cases in which firms had organised working groups with university professors to study certain topics. The entrepreneurs indicated that the large advantage of these regional contacts was that they did not necessarily involve contracts from the very start. These links seemed to be organised on personal contacts, rather than on official and systematic technology transfer activities. Although the technology transfer agencies of the university and Hochschule were familiar to many firms, only a small number of firms used their services. One explanation is that these technology transfer services are very young and still have to establish their activities. Another explanation can be found in the answer that so few companies said the R&D could solve their problems, which is not surprising for young and small firms.

The firms were familiar with some intermediaries such as TINA, the IHK and the Handwerkskammer (Chamber of Trades). Although the number of firms that had received consultancy services from the intermediaries was quite small, in general they were satisfied about the collaboration. What is striking is that although finance was a major bottleneck for innovation, only two out of seventy-nine firms had heard of the Brandenburger Seed Capital Fund, a publicly funded body set up to help innovative firms in the region.

To summarise, the combination of face-to-face interviews and survey results showed that the main bottlenecks for the South Brandenburg firms were:

- developing a market strategy and finding market entries;

- access to finance;

- access to technological know-how in particular applied technologies;

- isolation from competitors, suppliers and markets;

- lack of personnel with commercial expertise;

- insufficient managerial capacity;

- lagging production processes in terms of productivity and quality control.

The Supply Analysis: Institutional Shake-up

As mentioned already, the institutional framework for innovation support and R&D experienced a thorough restructuring as well. Old structures disappeared and new institutions were put in place according to the West German model. In 1992, two Frauenhofer Institutes, with a specialisation in materials research, were located in the region, just on the border of Berlin and Brandenburg. The RITTS analysis showed that there were hardly any institutional or business links with the South Brandenburg region.

In the higher-education institutes and universities, faculty structures and staff have been severely reorganised. South Brandenburg has one technical university and two specialised technical *Fachhochschule*. These three have a strong tradition in engineering, construction research and electronics. After the unification, East German professors and lecturers in the university and *Fachhochschule*, did not keep their positions as a matter of course. On the contrary, they had to apply for their old jobs if these were still in place after the reorganisations of faculties and departments. In the Technical University of Cottbus for example, of those lecturers appointed in 1995, 60 per cent came from West Germany, and the remaining 40 per cent from East Germany. Many posts were still vacant. Formal networks between the technology supplying institutes and the regional economy hardly had time to develop.

The University of Cottbus and the two technically oriented *Fachhochschule* set up technology transfer centres to link their expertise with industry. They were all in the process of defining strategies and learning how to 'market' their skills. The RITTS study showed that it was very difficult to interest local firms in their activities. Part of the problem is related to academic regulations; in the German university system, sideline activities of professors are not encouraged and are difficult to arrange administratively.

The public innovation support agencies were modelled according to experiences in West Germany. Technology centres were established locally as incubators to support technology-oriented start-up firms, with consultancy and favourable business locations. Although their managers were committed to playing a role in the RITTS implementation process, their hands were tied by lack of finance.

The project promoter TINA has as its main task identifying and assisting firms to participate in the federal and national support schemes. In 1994 TINA transferred 6 million Deutchmarks to the regional economy. The schemes offered are a mix of national and regional programmes and have a wide range, from R&D support and management support to investment credits.

TINA's advisory expertise is focused mainly on helping firms to tackle technological issues and to developing ideas as to how public support schemes fit these technological and R&D-related issues. The background of its counsellors was in a range of technological fields. The survey and face-to-face interviews revealed that most of the problems in the companies were related to management issues, finance, market entry and organisation of production. Few firms could make the step to performing internal R&D, because they lacked resources, capabilities and so on. The assessment of the supply of innovation support found that the level of business use of public innovation programmes and technology transfer was very low and was one of the lowest in the new German Länder. There appeared to be a mismatch between the type of support offered (mostly upstream and R&D related) and the type of support needed according to the SME analysis. The company survey showed that almost two-thirds of the companies did not believe that R&D could help them solve their problems. Therefore many of the national and regional support programmes did not fit their immediate needs. The RITTS project helped to increase awareness that additional skills were necessary – with TINA's advisory expertise – to assist the companies, particularly in the area of commercial and technology management. One of the RITTS actions implemented by TINA is precisely on this subject: company audits and management training.

The proposals for actions were focused on gaps in the support structure: access to available technology, management support linked to check-ups and quality improvement, finance for innovation, the encouragement of networking and cluster-building and the encouragement of entrepreneurship with university graduates.

THE RITTS PROCESS OF REGIONAL STRATEGY-BUILDING

Unlike in many RTP and RITTS projects, where the project promoter is a regional authority with a certain degree of decision-making power over policies and financial resources, TINA was a local intermediary with hardly any direct powers to change the innovation policy or innovation support structures in the South Brandenburg region. In this case, the objectives were far too ambitious, since none of the organisations actively involved has any power to 'enforce' changes in the innovation support network. Despite that limited power, the RITTS project did manage to bring together many actors in the region, thus sharing a feeling of responsibility over the project and its implementation. However, the organisations that did not cooperate smoothly before the RITTS project were still on the same terms at the end of the project.

The steering committee in the RITTS project overlapped with the advisory board of TINA. It consisted of representatives from the Federal Ministry for Economy, SMEs and Technology, the Ministry of Science, the Technical University of Cottbus, the regional technical college, two regional technology centres, the chamber of industry and trade, the chamber of trades, and a local government in a subregion of South Brandenburg. There was no direct company representative. The steering committee met whenever there was a stage report finished or in combination with seminars organised in the framework of RITTS. For instance, the results of Phase 1 were discussed in a seminar with members of the steering committee and also with a wider audience of regional actors.

The team of experts that undertook the tasks in the project consisted of three German consultancies and one international consultant. They were responsible for the analyses and the translation into priority actions. The project promoter had an important task of supporting the expert team in setting up meetings and interviews, providing data and organising seminars. One of the lessons learned from this project was that the time and effort that the project promoter had to invest in the project were seriously underestimated. The project manager needs to allocate sufficient capacity to keep the project running and support the expert team. In the first generation of RITTS projects, the budget was allocated completely to the external experts. Time spent on the RITTS project was an additional investment to be made by the project promoter. This was often a heavy burden on the project manager, who was supposed to do this alongside their normal tasks. In the course of the project TINA, with the financial support of a European exchange programme, employed a French trainee who could take over part of the organisational work for the project.

The European Commission has learned from the experiences of this first generation of RITTS projects and now allows the project promoter to allocate part of the RITTS funding to the management time spent by its own staff.

Defining the Priority Actions and Implementation

A crucial point in a RITTS project is the translation from the analyses in Phase 1 into priority actions. The initial choice of priority actions was very much a consultancy-led exercise. The priority actions were chosen on the basis of the findings of the studies on the firm's needs and the strengths and weaknesses of the innovation support structure. For each type of action, the most appropriate organisations and people were identified to take on responsibility for the elaboration of the implementation process.

On the basis of the analyses in Phase 1 a list of bottlenecks emerged both on the side of the firms and on the supply side. The expert team found that those public-support mechanisms focused very much on creating R&D capabilities and on linking research knowledge with regional firms. The needs analysis had pointed out that many companies had more 'down-to-earth' problems acting as primary bottlenecks. These prevented the many attempts to link the R&D system with the local companies from being very successful. The expert team came up with the following list of proposed actions and areas of encouragement:

- 'Brandenburg Invents!' An innovation offensive, i.e. a media-oriented awareness campaign for invention.

- Licence brokerage and support for import of applied technologies.

- Building 'clusters' of regional cooperation in the following areas:

  - general awareness-building and the design of concepts;

  - future-oriented building in the construction sector;

  - development of system suppliers in the metal–electronics sector;

  - environmental technologies;

  - biological materials.

- Start-ups in the *Hochschule* and university (HEIs).

- An 'Innovation Finance Forum'.

- Strategy development in companies: management training courses.

- Company audits.

- Collaboration with Sächsichen Lausitz, the neighbouring region.

In collaboration with the expert team, TINA organised a strategic seminar on each topic, inviting relevant stakeholders from industry and the supply side. A series of seminars was organised over two days, where each of these topics was presented and discussed. Local actors and firms were invited to come to specific meetings and express their thoughts on the proposed actions. Unfortunately, for logistical reasons, the invitations were not sent to companies on a theme-by-theme base, explaining the background of each of the proposed seminars. This must have affected the number of entrepreneurs in the region who felt addressed by a particular theme of a proposed action. Although some company representatives did participate in the seminars, their level of participation in general was not high. The main innovation support institutions and policy agencies were well represented. Although interest from industry was only moderate, some potential project champions for further actions were in the audience. The steering committee meetings appeared very useful for engaging people in the process and to identify project leaders, committed to elaborate a given action. For each action, a preliminary cost calculation was made, including a first indication of possible sources of funding.

In a steering committee meeting the results of the first elaborations of action plans were discussed and tasks divided. A striking result was that most organisations present were eager to take on board one or more actions. TINA was not the only organisation to initiate actions. Representatives from technology centres and the local *Hochschule*, in particular the business studies department, were willing to start with some of the proposed cluster initiatives. The Technical University of Cotbus was prepared to start a pilot project for the support of start-ups by university graduates. The head office of TINA in Potsdam took responsibility for the initiative for Brandenburg. TINA in South Brandenburg implemented the Innovation Finance Forum plans, bringing together firms, banks and public investors – after an initial meeting, TINA assists the firms to develop a coherent business plan or plan to finance an innovation project. TINA also commissioned a consultant to develop the management training and individual audit schemes after the end of the RITTS project. Thus the steering committee was a good vehicle to achieve agreement on priorities and spread the responsibility for taking action. The disadvantage of this spread of responsibility was that after the project's end, there was no single organisation that could keep the momentum going on all of the actions taken up. The RITTS resulted in a number of individual projects taken up by individual organisations, but hardly as a coordinated regional strategy.

THE INTERNATIONAL DIMENSION

The RITTS project was foremost an internal strategy exercise; linking the exercise with external and international experience was of secondary importance. The RITTS initiative did not have a network similar to that run by the RTP secretariat. Two workshops were organised by the European Commission, one at the very start of projects and one halfway through them. The South Brandenburg project promoters gave a presentation of the preliminary results (it was one of the first RITTS projects to start effectively and to finish on schedule) and learned of the experiences in other projects.

There are a number of explanations for the limited international networking during the project:

- The region was still in the middle of a far-reaching restructuring of economy and institutions. The new industrial fabric and knowledge about innovation issues had still to settle down, though they were just about to do so. The focus of the main actors was on finding out about the situation in their own region.

- Given the limited orientation towards Western Europe in the past, language was a substantial barrier. German was the only language spoken by many of the regional actors, which limited the possibilities for exchange of experience with other EU regions.

The international dimension was brought into the project mainly through the international consultant. Some international comparisons added to the needs analysis. In the implementation phase, a seminar was organised where two Dutch experts were invited who were directly involved in the process of building a supplier network in a Dutch region. Those intermediaries who had committed themselves to involvement in the cluster initiatives were able to exchange experience with these experts. At the same seminar, the South Brandenburg example of a successful cluster initiative in the textile sector was presented by the intermediary involved in setting up this initiative.

THE MAIN RESULTS AND LESSONS LEARNT

In terms of *defining a regional strategy,* the main lesson is that it requires a certain degree of empowerment of the main actors involved in the RITTS project. South Brandenburg is a subregion lacking authority in policy formulation and policy design. It depends on initiatives taken at the Land or even the federal state level. Although the ministries were involved in the steering committee, their actual involvement in the project was limited. The impact from the RITTS output on developing new strategies for the use of structural funds or other existing funds was therefore minimal. The project promoter, in practice TINA Cottbus, a subregional office of an intermediary agency based in the capital Potsdam, also lacked the authority to change the mode of operation, definition of tasks and collaboration of the innovation support infrastructure in South Brandenburg. In the course of the project the ambitions in terms of outcomes were changed towards initiating some concrete actions, involving companies. An additional bottleneck was that TINA did not have any financial resources to implement the proposed actions. Nor did the ministries commit themselves to additional funding for actions. TINA had high expectations that the RITTS expert team would manage to locate and arrange these resources. Although some explorations were made by the team, it was felt that this was the task of those who took responsibility for the implementation of the actions.

What the project did succeed in was embedding the cooperation between certain local organisations represented in the steering committee. A good collaboration was reinforced between TINA, the university and *Hochschule,* technology centres, and local authorities. This was confirmed by the eagerness of these organisations to be actively involved in the implementation of certain priority actions. The cooperation was on a voluntary basis where key actors were convinced that more should be done to cooperate and explore opportunities for economic development. The near-to-business organisations such as the chambers of commerce and trade associations were less involved in taking up the RITTS as an opportunity in the region. A 'culture gap' between the technology and research-oriented organisations and the business development organisations was still very strong after the RITTS project. As said before, the RITTS resulted in a set of individual projects rather than in a coherent joint strategy. The limited room for manoeuvre for each of the actors and the situation where no central governance was involved left the very largely bottom-up strategy-building process in an indecisive position. Decisions on solving possible frictions in the support system or new approaches to innovation support were hardly within the authority of the actors involved. For the project promoter some actions could be developed with additional support from their central office, with the help of the RITTS results.

It proved difficult in the South Brandenburg case to involve firms actively in the strategy-building process. The organisations on the intermediary and supply side do not have a tradition of involving firms in the regional debates or of developing public–private partnerships. The fact that there were no firms in the steering committee reflected this lack of public–private cooperation. Some initiatives suggested by the RITTS team, such as making better use of the opportunities offered by one of the two multinational companies in the region, were not taken on board as part of the strategy. The firms from their side, when present in the seminars, were mostly interested in concrete schemes in which they could participate.

In terms of *providing demand-led services* to businesses, the RITTS project had the effect that technology support organisations, and particularly TINA, became more aware of the need for a more systemic approach to innovation problems: technology (or R&D) is only one aspect of dealing with the firm's problems. Adaptation of a new technology will fail if this is not embedded in the firm's management and organisation. The actions that TINA launched as a result of the RITTS project are partly on these 'softer' areas of management, finance and providing information technology linkages. The original regional CITI '99 initiative aimed to make local firms operate in future high-tech markets through better use of (regional) technological expertise. The RITTS project focused more on the present strengths and problems of the indigenous firms, which were in many cases not ready for the leap to future high-tech markets.

In terms of *project management* several lessons can be learned:

- The investment of time and effort by the project promoter is easily underestimated. In the South Brandenburg case the project promoter did much to assist the expert team to do its work well. In the first-generation RITTS, the project promoter was not allocated any funding for this task, which created some problems in internal capacity and funding of events. The European Commission has learned from this problem and encourages the second-generation RITTS managers to allocate time and money for their role in the project and for organising events.

- The original work programme allowed too little time (three months) for the implementation phase. Since this phase involves obtaining the commitment of several organisations, exploring financial resources, and fine-tuning proposed actions to local circumstances, six to nine months appeared more appropriate.

- The original work programme was defined in great detail, with very strict time schedules at the very start of the project. Although this had the advantage of providing clarity between the experts (four consultancies) about tasks, it also limited the flexibility of the project. For the project promoter it was a gradual learning process that deviation from the original plan was not necessarily a negative development.

- Since project management was conducted by one of the consultants, and the project promoter was not allocated a role other than that of client of the project, the RITTS exercise had the tendency to be consultancy-led. Although interactions between the expert team, the project promoter and the steering committee were regularly organised, the initiative for setting the priorities came from the consultants. They also took the lead in writing the reports, which led to a focus on the contents of their assessment work and provided relatively little documentation on the socio-political process of consensus-building. Since this appeared to be a common feature in RITTS projects, the European Commission has put in place several mechanisms that increase the RITTS 'ownership' of project promoters.

- The insistence of the project promoter on finishing the project according to schedule, in combination with the underestimation of tasks performed by all team members in previous phases, resulted in the neglect of the putting into place of a structural evaluation or monitoring system. The RITTS team members developed some performance criteria for each of the individual projects. A more robust regional innovation monitoring system would have been difficult to establish because of the fragmentation of data resources. For instance, the organisation with access to company data was not willing to share this information with other organisations, owing to data protection rules.

The experiences in the *implementation process* showed that:

- It is crucial to find 'project champions' who are committed to take responsibility for the implementation and keep the momentum after its initial start and the formal end of the RITTS project.

- One should begin at an early stage to assess the possibilities for the allocation of funding for proposed priority actions. RITTS itself does not provide additional funding, and it is not necessarily linked to Structural Funds as with RTPs. In the South Brandenburg case, several proposed actions with dedicated project champions are halted because no funding could be found to implement them. Some financial backing is necessary, especially for those actions that are a start of a long process of awareness-raising, such as cluster-building

- Companies and particular SMEs will be willing to participate only when the objectives of actions are sufficiently concrete, and in such a manner that they can identify the benefits for their day-to-day business. We found that involving SMEs too early risked losing their interest because of lack of concreteness in the proposed priority actions; it was difficult to attract the same companies in later stages of the RITTS project

The project promoter TINA considers the main result of the RITTS project to be the fact that a start has been made to implement concrete actions that include firms, and that several organisations have taken initiatives to function as project champions. Not all initiatives have been equally successful. The actions that have showed real progress are Brandenburg Invents! (which receives funding from the European ADAPT programme), the Innovation Finance Forum, and the management training and check-ups. The initiatives in the area of cluster-building have been taken up by the technology centres, but lack of additional resources prevents them from doing more than general awareness-building of the opportunities of networking.

An indirect effect is that there is an acceptance by a larger set of institutions that a common strategy is possible and that all those who have been involved in the RITTS project take up part of the responsibility.

NOTES

1. The author would like to acknowledge the contribution of the other members of the RITTS expert team, who have enabled the writing of this chapter: Heyo Mennenga (Rational), Hans Troje and Dieter Jentzsch (Troje Beratung) and Karl-Heinz Klinger (Technostart); also the organisational and financial support and expertise of the project promoter of this RITTS project, TINA. Cottbus and its staff were an indispensable factor for the success of the project. The author conducted the RITTS project as senior consultant for TNO – the Centre for Technology and Policy Studies. The RITTS project was conducted with the financial support of the European Commission, under the framework of the Innovation Programme.

2. The Treuhand was established by the German government after unification in 1990 to privatise or close former East German businesses.

9 Prospects for Building Technology Policy in Central and Eastern Europe[1]

The transformation of the post-socialist economies of Central and Eastern Europe (CEE) has till now been dominated by transition policies. These include privatisation, the restructuring of enterprises and the liberalisation of prices, trade, foreign exchange and banking. The aim is institutional transformation of these economies towards the open market model. Issues of growth and of industrial, technological or regional restructuring are not explicitly addressed (see EBRD 1995, 1996).

As it became clear that the link between progress in institutional reform towards the model of open market economy and economic recovery is much more complex than originally assumed (see Economist Intelligence Unit 1996), it emerged that a stage of searching for alternative policy models had begun. Policies that explicitly address growth are coming onto the policy agenda. An alternative policy perspective should build on successes in institutional transformation, but also should take into account the fact that growth will occur only through industrial and technological change.

Elsewhere we have analysed these issues through the perspective of strategic policies for growth (Radosevic 1997a) and strategic technology policy in particular (Radosevic 1994b, 1997b). Common to both concepts is that they draw their rationale not from a simple argument about market failure but from the perspective of evolutionary economics (Teubal 1997; Teubal *et al.* 1996).

In this chapter I analyse the prospects for the development of regional technology policy (RTP) in CEE as the policy that forms a part of the strategic policies for growth. My inquiry is partly empirical and partly conceptual. In the second section I analyse the historical heritage of RTP in the CEE. The third section analyses the main restructuring processes in R&D infrastructure. This factor is considered here to be an important potential advantage of the CEE, and I analyse the restructuring of this sector from a regional perspective. The fourth section explores the relevance of conventional RTP, as implemented through the EC STRIDE initiative, for the CEE and also explores what would be the appropriate features of RTP in CEE. Here the basic idea is that 'catching up' in terms of RTP requires 'forging ahead' within some of its elements. What is crucial to our assumption is that in a regional context learning is dependent on mutual interaction between the accumulated capabilities as well as the accumulation of social capital. This raises several policy issues, which are discussed. The main arguments are summarised in conclusions.

POST-SOCIALIST TRANSFORMATION AND REGIONAL TECHNOLOGY POLICY

A neglect of the region as a locus of innovation has not been entirely a social-ist phenomenon. While some factors that led to this could be exclusively ascribed to socialist features, others seem to have been more general. The dom-inance of mass production and a subsequent shift towards flexible mass production or flexible specialisation are techno-economic factors common to all economies and are factors that strongly shape the region as an innovative milieu (Storper 1995). Specific socialist factors that contributed to the neglect of the region are rooted in the basic features of the socialist economic system: its property rights and its mechanisms of centralised political and economic control. These have reduced the diversity of regional development and tech-nology opportunities. Before moving to the RTP aspects of this socialist heritage we will, first, outline briefly the general regional aspects of such a heritage.

Regional Aspects of Socialist Heritage

As a result of systematic neglect of the region as an innovative milieu, regions in the administrative sense in the CEE are usually weakly developed. Long-term lack of responsibility led to a situation whereby local and regional authorities were not equal to the tasks they face today. The need for regional structures and regional policies is not matched by the administrative structures or the institutionalisation of regional policy. While variations in this respect are present across CEE countries, we believe that they do not undermine this general conclusion. For example, in Hungary the communes were given more responsibilities, and in 1989 no less than 41.6 per cent of all investments in the non-material sphere were by municipalities (van Zoon 1992). However, even in the Hungarian case the business activities of local governments were not extensive, even according to 1991 data. The surveys completed at that time indicated that 25 per cent of local governments participated in various production or service enterprises and that half of those enterprises operated with very low capital (Peteri 1993). In Poland, because of stronger centralis-ation, administrative capabilities at the regional level were even lower. Furthermore, in Slovakia there are still no regional governments, and district authorities wield only administrative and executive powers, as do officials in cities and villages (OECD 1994). As there is no organised political and administrative machinery at regional level, and as a result of transition policies which effectively ignore the regional component, OECD studies on industrial policies in CEE countries have concluded that it is still too soon to speak of any regional policy in CEE (see OECD 1994, 1995). On the other hand, economic differences across regions are likely to increase, which further reinforces the need for regional policy.

The current situation is characterised by increasing tensions between regional and central levels, which in some countries have become major political issues. For example, in Russia, 'local budget outcomes stem from games of tug-of-war between regions and the centre, without the regions having much formal autonomy in the determination of their own tax bases and tax rates' (Hanson 1995, p. 51). This lack of clarity about the distribution of powers and responsibilities between regions and centres has led to a situation where individual regions have gone a fair way towards creating distinct economic environments.

Given the lack of labour mobility in CEE countries, the regional differentiation in unemployment rates is very likely both to intensify and to persist for many years. Also, areas with the highest unemployment rates have the highest rates of long-term unemployment, indicating strong structural features of CEE unemployment. This means that high levels of unemployment might not exert much of a dampening effect on wage inflation, which again reinforces the case for a regional policy, and especially help with retraining and assistance in finding new jobs. This calls for an active, regionally based industrial policy.

The sector system – a branch system of organisation of the economy, which prevailed over the territorial system – has led to a situation in which intra-sectoral input–output linkages are less developed than in comparable market economies. This system enabled mainly vertical links between geographically dislocated enterprises or else ensured a high degree of vertical concentration in localities within a specialised and narrow economic structure (Grabher 1997).

While in some branches production is spread relatively evenly across most or all regions, in many the output is strongly concentrated. In such cases the economic fate of local communities is likely to be closely associated with the fate of one or other branch of industry. It was the responsibility of the production and corporate sector to contribute to local services. The types of contribution included local payroll taxes, the compulsory transfer of funds, and the development of local infrastructure (housing, kindergartens, public utilities, etc.) (Peteri, 1993). In such regions and localities social life usually centred around one or a few large enterprises. Large, vertically organised enterprises were economically isolated from their locality in terms of input–output links. However, in social and welfare terms these factories were crucial to localities.

The number of regions with a diversified economic structure in CEE seems to be lower than in the EU. Few SMEs existed, but this is now changing because of the rapid growth of small firms. However, their linkages to large companies are not widespread, which has led some analysts to point to emerging signs of a dual economy whereby SMEs are technologically stagnant and not driving the economy (see Gabor 1996 for the case of Hungary and Sutherland 1997 for the case of Russia). In Hungary, this was partly enabled through a very permissive system of registration of new businesses. Instead of the registration system being subject to strict criteria, government has attempted only to establish concrete regulation in specific areas where there was the strongest demand for regulation (Gulacsi 1993).

The removal of regional disparities in the economy was high on the political agenda in socialist times and new enterprises were established in regions that were lagging. Within localities, efforts were made to promote the development of the industrial sector. The result was over-industrialisation and under-urbanisation of localities. This created an economic structure with limited agglomeration economies and led to a very difficult regional problem – small or medium-sized towns each dependent on a single factory. Belief in the endogenous potential of regions, so prevalent in the EU RTP policy initiatives, may be the most difficult aspect to translate into a viable policy response, especially if solutions are sought in new areas that lie outside the competence spectrum of the region (for such a case-study see Lorentzen 1996).

Starting from such a historical perspective, regional and local governments have tried to strengthen their position by what Peteri (1993) has called 'enterprising local government' or transferring the rules of the private sector into areas of public services. Since there were no significant local income sources, the only way local governments could survive was to act as market participants or as if they were 'corporate entities' with their own production units. In this respect, the establishment of production and service companies (owned partially by councils) became a general objective, along with an increase in institutional and council rents and revenues.[2] This is coupled with a new opportunity to increase local government revenues by sales of assets (flats and land) and through local taxes. However, as Peteri (1993) points out, 'the development of the local economy, as a basic task of local governments, requires the development of a more comprehensive local policy than the simple entrepreneurial mentality' (p. 40).

The economic role of regions in CEE will differ significantly with the type of region. There are several classifications of regions in CEE countries (see van Zoon 1992, Grabher 1997, Treyvish as quoted by Hanson 1995 Hausner et al. 1996). Either they are relevant only to specific countries or they appear somewhat inconsistent (van Zoon 1992). To make the diversity in the CEE situation simpler we would suggest a very rough but illustrative grouping of regions as follows:

- Capital towns and regional centres with a diversified economic structure and developed infrastructure. Examples of the latter group would be Gyor (Hungary), Plzen (Czech Republic) and Varna (Bulgaria).

- Regions with more diversified economic structure where a lower industry share enabled them to start post-socialist transformation with less structural problems. This was then followed by either intensive formation of new firms and foreign investments. Examples are the Poznan province in Poland and Csongrad (Szeged) in Hungary.

- Monostructural regions are those where a single sector heritage (defence; agricultural, heavy industry) makes restructuring based entirely on endogenous resources very difficult if not impossible. Such cases abound in Russia, for example in the Perm region, a centre of the defence industry (see Cronberg 1994). An example of the old industrial centre in Hungary is the BAZ region (see Lorentzen 1996). However, even in very small CEE countries, like Slovenia, with its old industrial centre of Maribor, such cases can be found.

If we approach regional restructuring by taking into account only the state of tangible regional endowments of labour, capital and natural resources we would hypothesise that difficulties in regional restructuring would follow in ascending order from one to three. However, more detailed regional situations within individual countries would show that this is probably not the case. An analysis of Russian regions by Hanson (1995) shows clearly the limitations of such an approach and the much more complex dynamics of regional restructuring. The example of Nizhnii Novgorod, a region greatly dependent on heavy and defence industries but a front-runner in reforms in Russia, beautifully illustrates this point, which we elaborate in the fourth section. Any regional comparative advantage or disadvantage is conditional upon the existence or non-existence of knowledge networks or social capital, which may or may not turn this conditional advantage into a real absolute advantage. Often crisis acts as a window of opportunity that catalyses collective action and produces regional leapfrogging through intensive public–private cooperation and the growth of learning networks (see Kuznetsov 1997b).

The difficulty of the regional transformation in CEE lies not only in deficiencies of capital, infrastructure and knowledge but also in the enormous scale of coordination failures. For example, in defence-based regions, traditional links of defence companies with defence ministries have collapsed, and new links both between the regional administration and enterprises and among enterprises, should emerge in the regional context. However, this transformation is influenced strongly by national factors, which, much as in the less-developed regions of the EU, play a major role in determining these outcomes. For example, stability in the growth of SMEs cannot be achieved by activities at the local level if they are to become suppliers to the big companies that are themselves in difficulty. Inter-country differences in terms of economic recovery among CEE nations are increasing, which sets limits to RTP in some of them.

Despite the great variety of country-specific regional situations we would hypothesise that there are some common features of regional transformation in CEE. These lie in the lack of horizontal information flows, which is a consequence of temporary social fragmentation and the break-up of previously vertical channels of communication and economic management. This lack of horizontal communication channels is being addressed through the building up of a layer of new agencies that should assist regional enterprises, though these are still very weak and hence unable to make any significant changes in a structurally very difficult situation. This process is also being helped by newly emerging enterprise forms like holding companies, financial–industrial groups, and new private conglomerates that are primarily horizontal structures that strengthen horizontal communication and form new input–output linkages (see Grabher and Stark 1997). Foreign investors, for example the Suzuki supplier system in Hungary, are also encouraging the relationship between the now fragmented large enterprises and SMEs.

Regional Innovation Systems and Socialist Heritage

In the socialist period the local nature of the innovation process was not taken into account. Users, user–producer links, in-house R&D and the innovation activities of enterprises were not sources of innovation (see Hanson and Pavitt 1987). The main source of innovation was the externalised RTD system, which was branch- and sector-oriented and whose core lay in industry-oriented research–technology organisations (RTOs) (R&D institutes, design centres, centralised R&D institutes) (Radosevic 1996a).

While national factors did, and still do, play an important role in the national technology accumulation process in the CEE, the same cannot be said for regions. Proximity was no asset under socialism, and hence productivity improvements that could accrue through localised collective technology activities were not given a place in the system. The tendency towards regional horizontal and vertical integration was limited. Links were vertical, and factories producing components for other parts of larger systems often did not know the other suppliers but only the factory to which they delivered parts (Cronberg 1994). Although the degree to which this was true varied significantly across different CEE countries, the problem was common to all socialist countries. Accordingly, in the 1970s and 1980s there was a general wave of attempts to remedy this problem by decentralisation through different horizontal amalgamations of enterprises (science–production associations in Russia, *Kombinate* in eastern Germany, VJH in Czechoslovakia, etc.; see von Hirschhausen 1996).

The individual plants of the *Kombinate* had no economic relations with the region in which they were located, but they had strong social links with the local community. Regions were deprived of agglomeration economies – economies arising from a diversified regional economic structure which was essential for the long-term adaptability of the region (Grabher 1997).

A rare empirical test of the irrelevance of proximity in socialism is developed by Hare and Oakey (1993), who show the centralised pattern of service provision in the machine tool industry in Hungary, with companies strongly concentrated around the Budapest area. Respondents from plants located near or in Budapest experienced greater problems with local service agents than with their peripheral counterparts. The plants with the best access to service agents were those that recorded the greatest service problems. This paradoxical outcome is logical in conditions where the availability of a service outlet with an inferior level of service provision causes more difficulties than the complete absence of such provision. When no local servicing facilities exist, this leads to greater self-reliance, which ensures better repair and maintenance of the machines.

In terms of national RTD capacities (employment, funding), CEE countries have inherited quite large R&D systems, especially when we take into account their GDP levels. This is clearly visible in relation to less-developed EU countries and holds to some extent even after a period of significant downsizing of their R&D systems (see Auriol and Radosevic 1996).

While these capacities were, and are still, significant nationally they are at the same time very concentrated. We are unable to provide a systematic picture of concentration. However, a few examples may illustrate this point: Budapest has 77 per cent of all the research personnel in Hungary (van Zoon 1992), in Russia only 1 per cent of government expenditure for R&D goes towards regions, while in Poland *voivods* (counties) do not have R&D budgets (van Zoon 1992).

Because R&D capacities were geared towards the needs of closed economies, the extent to which they are relevant and of a quality appropriate to the needs of the market economy is not clear. From analyses of RTD systems in CEE we conclude that the supply of RTD is not the main problem (see Auriol and Radosevic 1996a). Policy issues are not building capacities but are contributing to their restructuring. At the core of this restructuring is the growing relevance of RTD in increasing the quality of the local environment, which in the closed economy of the past was of no concern.

TAPPING THE POTENTIAL: THE RTC INFRASTRUCTURE

Various studies of systems of innovation have shown that R&D is only a part of innovation and that innovation dynamics are a highly complex process with numerous sources and complex feedbacks closely linked to institutional features of the system in which innovation occurs (see Edquist 1997). The technological history of socialism is full of illustrative cases that indicate the limitations of R&D-driven and technology-push-based innovation systems (see OECD 1969, Amman *et al.* 1977). Any attempt to rebuild the innovative capabilities of CEE regions should therefore start from these experiences and try to build on a policy that supports highly diversified sets of functions and activities. These functions and activities should go beyond R&D and take into account knowledge-creation and diffusion – not just innovation *per se* – which matter so much for regional performance. However, despite these arguments it would be equally misleading to ignore the problem of institutionalised R&D systems, which in CEE were involved to a great extent in design, product and process engineering and often in the problem-solving of enterprises. Besides broadening the perspective on all aspects of knowledge creation and diffusion, RTP in CEE should equally address the restructuring of the existing RTOs as one of the main tasks. Exploring the ways in which this can be approached requires an understanding of the main causes of the current problems that research and technology organisations (RTOs) are experiencing. This requires a brief reminder of the basic features of innovation in socialism.

The former socialist economy should be considered as having been one large, complex enterprise in which separate enterprises existed not as businesses but only as production units. The marketing function was removed to the Ministry for Planning, the export function to the large foreign trade organisations, the finance function to the Ministry of Finance, and the R&D function to R&D institutes, which most often were not integrated to enterprises. Enterprises were production units that neither discharged any R&D functions nor engaged in any engineering, design or technical problem-solving. Such tasks, and the production of specialised parts and components, were performed by industrial institutes within which all these different activities were conglomerated.

Although R&D systems in socialist economies were oriented very much towards the needs of industry, they were not organisations *in* industry but *for* industry (see Radosevic 1994a). R&D was externalised and treated as a separate activity, with enterprises seen as passive recipients of 'R&D achievements ready for implementation' previously developed by the R&D institutes.[3] The neglect of the role of enterprises as a source of technology and the emphasis on extramural R&D were at the root of the problems of the innovation deficit in the socialist system.

Given such a heritage, we would argue that the basic problem lies in reconstructing enterprises as the main generators of innovation rather than in reconstructing links between RTOs and enterprises. Under the old system these linkages were functional (from R&D and design towards production) and one-way (from RTOs to enterprises). Their reconstruction today may take place only in parallel with the reconstruction of actors (enterprises, RTOs, supporting organisations). This implies that RTP should be focused equally on assisting enterprises and RTOs. The problem is that regions in CEE are too weak to assist in the restructuring of organisations whose streams of income, customers and suppliers come from elsewhere, and who are seen by regions as those who should actually be assisting *them*. Although this puts serious limitations on the viability of RTP in CEE, we believe that there is room for manoeuvre (even though this is not always obvious), in that regions could do something for enterprises and RTOs, and that the latter could do something for the regions.

From Branch-Oriented to Regional RTD Infrastructure

In this section we analyse the situation of RTD infrastructure in CEE, from a survey of 560 organisations undertaken by Segal Quince Wicksted (1994) for the EC Sprint programme in several CEE countries.

The activities of RTOs cover a wide spectrum that includes R&D and non-R&D activity (see figures 9.1 and 9.2). Dominant in these R&D activities are basic research, applied research and product development, which account for 50 to 80 per cent of working time. Among non-R&D activities microproduction has a significant share (from 8 to 24 per cent) and in some countries was actually somewhat higher in 1994 than it was in 1988. Microproduction generally comprises small series of specialised components, which were essential in the former system where RTOs substituted for the lack of specialised suppliers. In market conditions they are often a source of cash.

FIGURE 9.1: MAIN ACTIVITIES OF THE CENTRAL AND EASTERN EUROPE RTOS (IN % OF TIME, 1988)

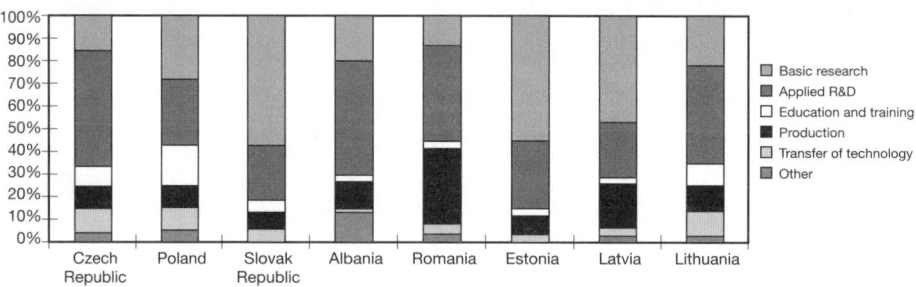

FIGURE 9.2: MAIN ACTIVITIES OF THE CENTRAL AND EASTERN EUROPE RTOS (IN % OF TIME, 1994)

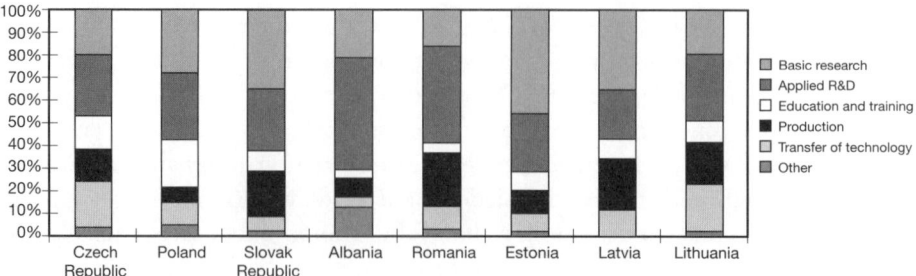

From an RTP perspective it is important to note that technology transfer does not play a significant part in RTOs' activities (from 5 to 22 per cent). This indicates the lack of links with their local environment, and shows that these organisations are still dominantly R&D organisations. However, except in Romania and Albania, a gradual shift towards non-R&D activities can be seen, which leads to further diversification of the activity profile of RTOs. The diversification is towards an increase in non-R&D activities at the expense of R&D activities. This is a demand-driven trend, which in many cases leads to the transformation of RTOs into industrial or services enterprises.

Increased diversification often results in rather incoherent organisations. However, as I have argued elsewhere, this is a temporary diversification, which will result eventually in significant organisational restructuring in terms of splitting, mergers and liquidations (Radosevic 1996b).

Diversification in terms of activities is accompanied by diversification from basically state and state enterprise funds towards funding from the now privatised enterprises, foreign and new private enterprises. These new sources of funding range from 41 per cent (Czech Republic) to 5 per cent (Romania). The share of privatised enterprises is dependent on the general process of privatisation in individual countries and the distinction between state-owned and privatised enterprises shares may not always be meaningful. Nevertheless, there is a clear shift from pure state funding, which reflects the efforts on the part of RTOs to meet new demand. These new sources of foreign funding are relatively significant in certain countries (Czech Republic, Hungary, Slovak Republic, Bulgaria, Slovenia, Latvia and Lithuania) and in the case of Estonia quite significant. This reflects a possible new role for RTOs as intermediaries between foreign and domestic enterprises fulfilling the role of distributor, customer or simply consultant. In some cases they operate as R&D subcontractors. Demand coming from new private enterprises is still marginal in most countries, reflecting either low technological sophistication in the newly formed enterprises or problems encountered by RTOs in meeting the criteria of the newly emerging demand. In summary, RTOs still survive, thanks mainly to state funds, which contribute on average from 40 to 60 per cent of their revenues.

The relatively small share of technology transfer activities in the overall activities of RTOs is further characterised by their diversity. This may be partly the result of the available aggregate data, which hide specific institutional specialisations, but reflects the search of RTOs for new, non-R&D sources of revenues. In any case the low share of transfer activities underlies the lack of competencies and experience in undertaking such activities in a market context. Although there are country differences in terms of frequency of types of activities, in all countries the most frequent activity is consultancy followed by technical assistance and testing and certification. The dominance of consultancy has resulted in a new consultancy service sector in CEE, but also in rather 'shallow' demand for technology transfer activities. This may reflect the need for problem-solving and the inability to pay for more complex support. The frequency of more demanding and complex types of transfer activities, like licensing technology, promotion and marketing, and improving the absorption of technology and quality initiatives, is still fairly low.

Estimates of future demand for transfer activities by RTOs indicate that the trend will be moving towards more complex transfer activities. RTOs in all countries state that testing, certification and quality initiatives are the most frequent activities, although consultancy and technical activities are likely to be the most frequent activities in the future.

From a regional perspective it is important that RTOs should be more geared towards satisfying regional needs. By far the most often cited barrier to this is the lack of finance. The main barriers in transfer activities could be classed as external and internal. Among external barriers, the most important are the low absorptive capabilities of enterprises (lack of skilled personnel in enterprises; deficit in learning capabilities of enterprises) and the lack of infrastructure for technology transfer (finance; lack of market information on enterprises). Among internal barriers, RTOs indicate their own lack of experience in transfer activities. It can be seen therefore that problems in enhancing RTOs' transfer function cannot be solved by mere linkage activities, because the major problems are internal to RTOs and enterprises.

Two major findings emerge from our survey that will have implications for RTP in the CEE. First, the main problem does not seem to be the lack of transfer institutions. The RTOs themselves, if restructured, could operate as transfer agents. Building a new layer of intermediate or bridging institutions would be hard to justify as a general solution. Second, the main barriers to transfer are not the lack of bridging institutions but the lack of transfer capabilities in RTOs themselves, coupled with the low absorptive capabilities of enterprises. Again, building a new layer of bridging institutions would not solve any of these problems. Enhancing the absorptive capabilities of industry and the transfer activities within RTOs themselves seems to be a more sensible solution (on this see Radosevic 1996b).

In summary, survey data have reinforced some of the arguments advanced in the previous section. RTOs are still operating in the main as R&D organisations funded by government. They are shifting towards new areas of demand that are primarily in non-R&D activities. This points to a strong need for assistance in restructuring RTOs towards new demand. Rather than building linkages, this can be achieved by enhancing the absorption capabilities of enterprises and the transfer activities of RTOs themselves. I would argue that the specific problem of CEE RTD is not the supply of RTD *per se* but the relevance and quality of RTD activities.

In the shift towards relevant and quality RTD activities it may not always be best to push RTOs entirely towards local industry. In many cases organisations that in the past served branches and specific national sectors may not have the competencies to serve only a wide range of local SMEs. Regional policy may not be the best answer to what are actually problems of national technology and industrial policy. This implies that there are limits to which RTOs can be used as mechanisms for enhancing regional innovation activities.

BUILDING CAPACITIES FOR ACTION: COORDINATION FAILURES AND SOCIAL CAPITAL FOR RTP IN CEE

A still relatively large sector of RTOs represents one of the elements of conditional comparative advantages of CEE. Whether this potential may be turned into real advantage at the regional level depends on many factors. Here I touch upon those factors which are of concern for building up RTP in CEE. My argument is that technology catch-up of CEE will require forging ahead in policy in general, and in the present case, in the area of RTP in particular. I argue that in order to represent forging ahead, RTP in CEE would have to be conceptually new and it would need to address the key constraint of conventional RTP policy – its inability to address an issue of the emergence of collective action, which is indispensable to regional change.

Following Storper *et al.*(1995), we may distinguish four areas of RTP of relevance to CEE. The first three can be considered as conventional RTP policy responses, while the fourth represents a new conceptual understanding of regional change that, in my view, has not yet been translated into a policy response:

- Strengthening input–output linkages through physical investments, and opening new markets and trade links, should be important areas of RTP for CEE. The disintegration of previously vertical production links managed by ministries has raised the transaction costs of building new input–output relations significantly. This applies equally to intra-regional and to new inter-regional links, particularly horizontal ones. An RTP response to this may be two-fold. The first response would be activities in establishing regional business centres and development agencies that would act as promotion agents for the region; this response is already spreading throughout the CEE. The alternative would be giving support to those enterprises and organisations that are themselves input–output linkage creators; instead of promoting linkages *per se,* the policy answer would be to support those agents whose activities are linkage-intensive (see EBRD, 1995). However, as pointed out by Storper *et al.* (1995), localisation of input–output linkages (traded interdependencies) may not be enough to regenerate the regional economy.

- Provision of skills and training is considered to be an important part of RTP. In CEE there is a deficiency in some skills as a result of their socialist heritage. Management training, accounting, marketing, organisation, etc. are those areas that have been already addressed through international programmes as well as through private provision of training services. While these activities are necessary in the process of transformation towards a market economy, they are often fairly general and do not answer to specific regional needs. As shown by Porter (1990), the sectors in which countries are catching up are those where there is an intensive process of building up industry-specific human capital. Finally, the main constraint in CEE lies not in their general education level but in sector- or firm-specific knowledge and know-how (see World Bank 1996). In addition, such knowledge deficits cannot be addressed through publicly funded programmes, because they cannot be justified by the market failure argument. Supply and demand for such skills and training is very much industry-specific and users must be actively involved in their development. This requires numerous coordination problems to be resolved, which may not be possible on the regional level.

- Assistance in institution-building and institution transfer is quite often the form of assistance given to the CEE regions. From an RTP perspective, an important form of this transfer is innovation centres, incubators and technology parks. Although we have not come across a comprehensive review of these initiatives, there is enough evidence to suggest that their effects and results in the CEE context are not very encouraging (see Webster 1996; Segal Quince Wicksted 1994). Frequently, the areas which originally were meant to strengthen knowledge exchange operate as renting areas. Most often, they are initiated through foreign assistance programmes and operate successfully only as long as foreign assistance is in place.[4] What is wrong with these forms of institutional transfer is that only very seldom do they represent the response of the locality to their own problems. They are no more than a transfer of institutions, which does not resolve the main constraint – the lack of collective action implicit in institutions like innovation centres.

- In the above three areas of the conventional RTP that is under implementation in CEE I have pointed out one common weakness – that of not addressing the crucial element of managing regional change, namely collective action. This constraint is not specific only to technical innovation, although, owing to pervasive uncertainties and information asymmetries among the social actors involved in the innovation and learning process, it may be in this case the most visible. As technical innovation is always a localised change, and involves the embodiment of technical opportunities in a local context, deterrents to it are not always linked directly to technology but to the capability or incapability of collective action.

Such capability is defined by some authors as social capital (see Kuznetsov 1997, Grabher and Stark 1997), and in the regional context (Storper *et al.* 1995) as 'untraded interdependencies'. Irrespective of the differences between these views they all share one common view, namely that alongside the accumulation of technological and other capabilities the accumulation of social capital is essential. Moreover, Kuznetsov (1997) hypothesises that social capital predicts long-term economic performance better than do economic factors (natural resources, fixed capital investments, etc.). Whether or not this is the case, there is an emerging agreement that the existence of social capital, or the capability to undertake collective action – the ability of people to work together in groups and organisations towards a common purpose – is a necessary ingredient of catching up. As just mentioned, at the regional level Storper defines this capital as untraded interdependencies, which he treats as assets whose scarcity is essential for understanding the dynamics of contemporary capitalism (Storper *et al.* 1995).[5]

A post-socialist economic transformation and the prospects of catching up, falling behind or forging ahead by CEE countries depend much not only on the available fixed assets and human capital but also on the capability to undertake collective action or social capital. While this proposition by itself is not something entirely new in the social sciences (see Olson 1965; Storper *et al.* 1995; Granovetter 1985; Grabher and Stark 1997) or even economics (see Dosi *et al.* 1990), what is new is the attempt to translate this conceptual understanding into policy activities. Storper *et al.* (1995) claims that untraded interdependencies may be created by policy actions, although he warns of the complexities involved. Morgan (1996), himself also a practitioner of regional policy, is more optimistic regarding the possibilities for policy induced activities in 'building capacities for collective action'. On the other hand, as Kuznetsov argues (1997a), spontaneous sociability, which is at the core of collective action, cannot be organised but only facilitated.

In the context of RTP there is a close complementarity between the formation of this social capability and the formation of RTP. Owing to the pervasive nature of RTP, which involves a wide range of actors whose boundaries cannot be confined to RTD supply alone, its implementation is inconceivable without developed social capital. On the other hand, rapid spontaneous formation of social capital may be the outcome of the formation of RTP.

If, as pointed out by Morgan (1997), 'the main objective of the RTP exercise is to develop a regional innovation process, in which regional stakeholders are enjoined to define a commonly agreed, bottom up strategy for their regions', then the question is: how can it be done? When it comes to 'translation' of such understanding into policy activities the dominant view is that of 'removing barriers' for generating change. It is assumed that the policy problem is one of removing obstacles to knowledge exchange and the creation of learning networks. However, as pointed out by Kuznetsov (1997b), this approach tended to overshadow the central issues of priorities (what to do first) and strategy (time sequencing in alleviation of constraints) to such a degree that implied policy implications – 'remove constraints' (when?, how?) – were sometimes perceived by relevant stakeholders as trivial or irrelevant. (p. 3)

Priorities and strategies are important in inducing the emergence of collective action, as this by itself involves high fixed costs and cannot be resolved by focusing on 'removing barriers' to generating change. The process of the emergence of public–private learning networks, 'on which private investors are able to bet their future' (Kuznetsov 1997a), is not something that can be developed incrementally. The creation of such networks is a highly non-linear phenomenon and depends on the emergence of a network entrepreneur. Its non-linearity comes from initially high fixed costs which, after a critical mass of understanding and consensus is reached, may generate a collective learning process with increasing returns.

'Removing barriers' as if they were spread around the region in fairly equal proportions does not address the main problem of RTP – which is how to support the network entrepreneurs and how to cover the fixed costs of the formation of learning networks. While this may never be resolved in the form of normative propositions to RTP-makers, a better understanding of the dynamics of formation of social capital or private–public learning networks may be helpful in this process.

From the Specific to the General: Supporting the Process of Collective Action at the Regional Level

In this section I argue that RTP that would serve as a catalyst for regional change should start from support to specific actors (enterprises, informal networks, public bodies, RTOs, etc.) in whose interest it is to act as network entrepreneurs. Policy should compensate for the high fixed costs that these entrepreneurs will incur in the process of broadening their networks. Through the process of expanding learning networks this specific support will be amplified into general support as more organisations get involved in learning networks. On the basis of Kuznetsov (1997a), I now outline how this process might operate in the case of RTP.

The initial stage in the process of development of RTP should be the identification of potential network entrepreneurs. These will be organisations, individuals or groupings of individuals who would benefit from the expansion in the region of learning networks in their specific areas of activity. They should be able to act as catalysts for change. The idea is to support the potential network organiser and not linkages *per se*. Thus, it would make more sense to support technology transfer and the networking capability of specific enterprises, universities and RTOs rather than set up new standalone organisations to perform these functions. Who are the potential network entrepreneurs? They could be large regional or national firms that could act as promoters of linkages. Regional public bodies could also learn to harness large firms to act as 'tutors' to local SMEs. Further, foreign firms could act as promoters of linkages. In some cases these could be RTOs. For example, in the case of the Russian Perm region, Cronberg (1994) points to the lack of funding for the research institutes and design bureaux, that potentially could have been functioning as networking agents for the new, more civilian-oriented innovation system in the region.

In this phase we would need a methodology that would analyse who potential network organisers might be. Although we should not expect too much of them, they are necessary tools for rationalising the dialogue between the funders and the beneficiaries of RTP support. Once network entrepreneurs are identified they should be given technical assistance and grants towards part of the fixed costs of setting up and broadening such networks. In the next stage, we should see the broadening of networks through different forms appropriate to each network entrepreneur, be they supplier networks, deliberation councils in case of public bodies, local RTD projects in the case of RTOs, investment consortia, etc. Finally, this process may result in the emergence of formal institutions, like suppliers' associations, that are basically institutionalisations of previously informal networks. If the network entrepreneur is a public body then we should see the creation of institutional structures that promote a dialogue among the main economic actors of the region.

The Problem with Policy Rationale for RTP

Such a process of RTP development becomes problematic against a background of conventional RTP. This type of RTP cannot be justified on the basis of the market failure argument. It would require very specific support to individual organisations, and sometimes even to informal networks of individuals, that would be difficult to justify with a market failure rationale. Here we come to the internal paradox of the market failure argument and to the fact that regional change, to become general, usually starts as specific change that is then amplified through learning networks. One of the basic principles of conventional RTP is that it has to be demand-driven (bottom-up), and based on consensus at the regional level. The best RTP is the one that is specific to the region. Also, capacity for collective action starts always as a specific activity that then diffuses into other sectors and becomes generalised. For example, the good behaviour of foreign investors in setting up local subcontracting networks is replicated by other investors. Similarly, diffusion of the best practice comes about through demonstration effects by domestic firms. This implies that RTP should be specific in its support. RTP should support specific industry-relevant capabilities, and there are limits to the extent to which RTP based on the market failure argument and provision of 'general-purpose public goods' can serve as a solution to this. RTP should assist in the articulation of supply and demand for the relevant technological capabilities, which are usually firm-specific (see Justman and Teubal 1996). General public goods are in most cases removed from users' core needs and are providing only 'commodified' services or standard packages.

Application of the 'general public goods' formula through RTP may be misplaced for a second reason pointed out by Storper *et al.* (1995). The application of RTP that provides 'general-purpose public goods' has little chance of success because 'the political and economic conventions of action' – the untraded interdependencies – may be wrong in the sense that they do not amplify learning networks and do not support activities of potential network organisers. This does not mean that such polices are entirely inappropriate but simply that they are ineffective.

For example, passing a law on decentralisation in CEE will not suffice to build anything resembling collective capacities. It may result in a system of political governance at regional level rich in subsidies, price controls and intervention in enterprise restructuring that will have to be dismantled (see, for the case of Novosibirsk region, Kirkow 1997). As argued by Storper *et al.* (1995), the decentralisation laws may simply reinforce the power of local notables and allow them to broker the locality's interests *vis à vis* the centre. This is exactly what is happening in Russia today, where regional notables operate as brokers between central government and regional organisations. In such cases, providing 'general public goods' in the form of innovation centres or regional technology plans, without any understanding of the structure of existing public–private learning networks, and without an appreciation of who the potential network entrepreneurs are, could result in the legitimisation of the existing structures, which may actually be a major barrier to change. Rather than promoting innovation in the region, these innovation centres may remain isolated from the regional economy and be merely surrogates for modernisation. Instead of reinforcing the existing public–private networks through interactive exercises between enterprises, RTOs and public bodies it might be more sensible to support potential network entrepreneurs in concrete projects through which they can create new, more dynamic public–private learning networks. This again reinforces the role of priorities and strategies in RTP, as opposed to 'an approach based on removing barriers to change'.

CONCLUSIONS

In this chapter I have tried to analyse the prospects for building RTP in post-socialist CEE. Inevitably the analysis has been seriously limited by lack of empirical evidence and case-studies, and in many respects has had to rely on very partial insights. However, I believe that even at this level of empirical analysis it has been possible to provide an informed basis for discussion on the prospects for building up RTP in CEE.

In socialism, the notion of the region had no economic meaning, because intra-regional linkages were superseded by inter-regional linkages (Grabher 1997). In post-socialism we are witnessing a growing number of local actors and regions that are trying to find their position in the national and global economy through actions that go beyond the plan and the market (Grabher and Stark 1997). However, the dominant policy context of post-socialism – transition policy – considers the region to be irrelevant in the transformation process. My argument is that RTP is not a panacea, but that it is an essential ingredient if economic renewal is to be developed in CEE.

Analysis of the role of R&D infrastructure in CEE has been conducted through survey data on RTOs. My conclusion is that RTOs represent a conditional comparative advantage of CEE. Their main problem does not seem to be capacities but relevance and quality. We noted several adjustment processes within RTOs, but it seems that the process of their reorientation towards regional needs (through technology transfer functions) is still very limited. On the other hand, it would be unrealistic to expect that organisations that are still all dominantly public-funded R&D institutes could serve only regional needs.

I have outlined the main areas of conventional RTP, input–output linkages, training, and institution-building. When it comes to their application to CEE, the concern must be that none of these areas *per se* addresses the main constraint to development of RTP – capability for collective action or social capital. On the basis of Kuznetsov (1997b) I then outlined the process of development of RTP that would directly address this problem. The core of my approach is the importance of support through RTP to potential network entrepreneurs in the regions. This raises important issues of priorities and strategies as opposed to RTP, which is focused on removing the barriers to generate change. I am aware that 'translation' of these conceptual insights into RTP practice may not be straightforward owing to serious problems of policy rationale. Elsewhere, I have tried to answer the problem of policy rationale and insufficiency of the market failure argument for post-socialist economies at the conceptual and empirical level through the concept of strategic technology policy (see Radosevic 1994b, 1997a, 1997b). I hope that future work along these lines may provide answers that are applicable in the context of RTP.

NOTES

1. This research is funded by the EC DG XII TSER programme project 'Restructuring and Reintegration of S&T Systems in Economies in Transition'.

2. Half of the local officials stated that 'the local government is unable to operate without property for its own production use' (59 per cent of mayors, 50 per cent of local government members, 48 per cent notaries; Peteri 1993 (p. 38).

3. This was the actual definition of innovations in Bulgarian statistics.

4. Illustrative of these misunderstandings are the examples of Tallinn (Estonia) Technology Park and EKTA, Tallinn (an association of small electronics companies attached to the ex-Academy Institute of Cybernetics). While the former operates as a collection of unrelated businesses the latter operates as a mutually reinforcing group of companies which share mutual complementarities and synergies. While the first was undertaken as an act of modernisation of the country, the second is an expression of the bottom-up-driven survival strategy and vision of its chairman.

5. The reason they are so scarce lies in the properties of untraded interdependencies. They 'permit actors to travel along superior technological trajectories (or to do so more rapidly than others), [thus] creating the absolute advantages which shelter them, at least temporarily, from Ricardian competition' (Storper *et al.* 1995, p. 17).

STUART ROSENFELD

10 Regional Technology and Innovation Strategies in the United States: Small Steps, High Expectations

Technology and innovation policies in the US come in so many different shapes and sizes that this often confounds and frustrates visitors trying to understand the US system. Technology and innovation policies range from free-standing technology or industry-targeted initiatives, such as North Carolina's Biotechnology Center, to regionally targeted, broad-based strategies spanning R&D, technology transfer and technology diffusion, such as Arkansas's Science and Technology Authority. Further, priorities change, and programmes rise and fall with changes in regional economies and/or state governments. This diversity and flexibility are consequences of the fact that responsibility for much of the funding and most of the implemention of technology and innovation policies rests with the fifty states. Although the federal government spends large sums of money on research and innovation, the states control the purse-strings and make the decisions concerning which programmes to apply for and, within generally broad guidelines, how and where to use the resources. Because states have different economies, government structures, technological capacities, resources, priorities and political orientations, they have adopted a variety of objectives, programmes, and organisations.

This is not to understate the importance of the federal government which, by virtue of its funding, influences states to develop technology and innovation programmes that would not have been considered in the absence of federal resources. The federal government is a vital catalyst for starting new programmes. It is also the major source of funds for basic and pre-competitive R&D. Further, it influences private-sector participation through its tax and regulatory policies.

Multi-state and sub-state regions have less discretion and authority but are also actors. Multi-state agencies, which are generally voluntary and non-binding, periodically establish plans and use their collective strength to leverage federal and state resource. Sub-state regions, which exhibit even more diversity in economies, resources and wealth than states, devise ways to compete for and use the state and federal funds to fit their own circumstances and meet their own special needs.

This chapter briefly traces the recent history of innovation policy and then describes strategies in two contiguous states in the south-eastern United States – North Carolina and Virginia – to illustrate innovation policies at the state and sub-state areas and show how they can be influenced by multi-state regional bodies. Each of these states is moving from a historic dependence on agriculture and low-wage, non-durable manufacturing goods to highly skilled high-tech industries and services. Each is advantaged by many strong research universities and each now has an urban concentration with an international rep-utation as a Mecca for high technology. Each state also retains some of the unfortunate legacies of its past, like relatively low levels of education and weak public schools (compared with US averages), and rural areas with low incomes and large disadvantaged minority populations that are slow to embrace technol-ogy. To understand the strategies of North Carolina and Virginia, it is first useful to appreciate the national context and influences under which they evolved.

An Evolving View of Technology and Innovation

Large-scale public sector research, technology, development and innovation strategies began with the first element of those strategies following a path-breaking report by Vannevar Bush in 1945 that legitimated scientific research as a public responsibility and social good (England 1982). One result was the formation of the National Science Foundation, the main source of support for basic research in the US. To the extent that technology and innovation were accepted as factors in regional development, they were linked to research and development. Regional development was associated with regions' research capabilities, which, in turn, were tied to their universities and research labs. Economic outcomes were expected to be eventually derived from the trans-formation of R&D into new commercial products. In this paradigm, public policy debates and strategic plans were about investments in and quality of R&D, and enrolment patterns in collegiate science and engineering pro-grammes. The participants and primary beneficiaries were generally those with vested interests in the outcomes: the universities, large corporations with R&D divisions, banks, government agencies and the communities with R&D facilities.

Individual states took a different view of technology and innovation policy and saw it as an opportunity to attract federal R&D dollars to their educa-tional and research institutions, which were assumed to be the wellsprings of technology-based growth, usually by attracting new companies. Industry was a customer for research contracts with universities and for communities' plant sites, not a source of innovation. The public benefit was akin to GE's old slogan 'progress is our most important product'. Although a few far-sighted planners foresaw the connection between technology and innovation and economic growth, for the most part states' interest was mainly in the contributions research institutions could make to local employment and to improve the overall attractiveness in marketing a region to industry.

FIGURE 10.1: STRUCTURE OF TECHNOLOGY AND INNOVATION POLICY IN THE UNITED STATES

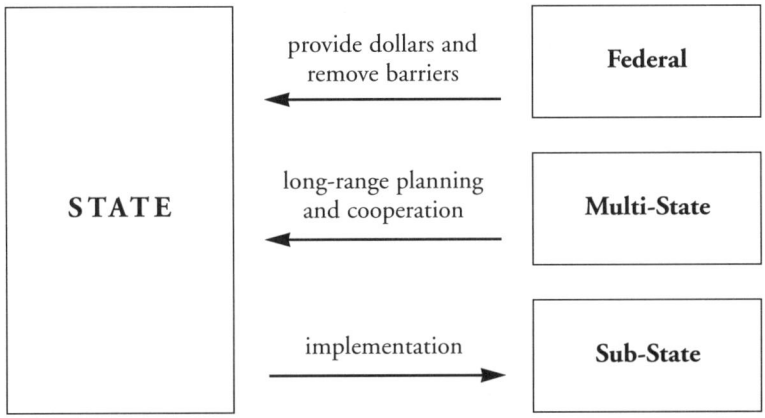

Rising Interest in High-Tech Industries

In the early 1980s, as emerging economies became more cost-competitive for traditional industry sites, states turned to technology and high-tech industries, where they still had an advantage, for economic growth. This led to a whole host of state technology-based strategies likely to produce jobs, generally assumed to be tied to what was loosely designated 'high-tech' industry. (Glasmeier *et al.* 1983) A survey by the US Congress's Office of Technology Assessment (OTA) in 1983 found 153 state programmes aimed at stimulating the growth of new and existing technology-dependent businesses, e.g. applied research and development funds, seed and venture capital, technology transfer agents, science parks and business incubators (Office of Technology Assessment 1984). One project that often attracted government dollars was the 'Center of Excellence', a title taken by research centres across the nation to promise (but not always produce) high quality and commercial results. In 1983 a National Governors' Association (NGA) survey produced 27 states that had appointed special bodies to report on state capabilities and recommend policies to promote technology and innovation during the previous three years (National Governors' Association 1983). States' strategies took on a more regional and economic development focus than did federal efforts, because state legislative bodies insisted that the benefits of the appropriations be captured locally. No state wanted to support a programme that created jobs or wealth outside its borders unless it was reciprocated.

That desire to have the 'best' resources in so many common technology areas led to considerable duplication of effort, and states competed intensely for what they considered to be emerging, high-growth, high-tech industries. In 1987, for example, the NGA found state funding for 38 research centres for microelectronics, which came to symbolise high technology, in 20 states (Rees and Lewington 1990). This emphasis on microelectronics was in large part a response to the competition in 1980 for the location of the Microelectronics Technology and Computer Consortium (MTCC), an alliance of large corporations' R&D operations that acted and was treated like a branch-plant in its site selection process – eventually settled in Austin, Texas. Many states that unsuccessfully wooed the MTCC with large portfolios of incentives and subsidies subsequently established their own microelectronics centres hoping both to compete with Texas and to capture a share of the anticipated spinoffs.

The benefits of this multitude of programmes accrued mainly to the already advantaged regions and companies, not the less-advantaged regions. First, targeted high-tech industries were classified by their products and tended to be in places where levels of education were high. Second, these programmes were supply-driven by the R&D labs and often ended up where the capital and intellectual capacities were most highly concentrated. Large corporations and areas with strong economies, bolstered by the necessary resources to exploit technological advances, gained the most from technology and innovation programmes. Rural areas and inner cities where skill levels were low and technological infrastructures weak did not. In fact these areas lost jobs, as their local employers, unable to either modernise or compete on the basis of costs, either closed or moved to lower-labour-cost regions.

Establishing Technology as State Policy

In 1983, the NGA – after reviewing states' programmes – concluded that 'no State has yet devised a fully integrated, comprehensive policy' for promoting high-technology development (NGA 1983). By the late 1980s nearly every state had created some organisation or office with responsibility for technology and innovation efforts, but still few were truly 'comprehensive'. Some states heavily endowed with science and technology, such as New York and Michigan, increased their efforts to turn them into economic advantage, and other rural and agricultural states, such as Montana and Maine, began to look to technology and innovation to transform themselves into modern industrial economies. The state governance structures of these organisations range from independent, non-profit, quasi-governmental agencies with independent boards and programmatic responsibilities to state commissions or councils with authority limited to planning and oversight and with no programmes to operate.

The Feds Crack Open Doors

The federal government supported states' efforts with the Stevenson-Wydler Act of 1980 requiring all federal laboratories to make greater efforts to transfer their technologies to commercial arenas; the Small Business Innovation Act of 1982 setting aside at least 1.25 per cent of all federal research dollars for SMEs; the National Cooperative Research Act of 1984 protecting companies in joint research agreements from anti-trust litigation; and the Federal Technology Transfer Act of 1986 authorising and supporting cooperative agreements between federal labs and businesses or states. The federal government also provided funds, mainly through the National Science Foundation (e.g. basic research, science and technology centres, university – industry partnerships), the Department of Defense (military R&D) and the National Aeronautics and Space Administration. To help the states with the weakest economies and least wealth – which nearly always also had fewest technological resources measured by rankings of per capita in R&D and scientists and engineers – the government established the Experimental Program to Stimulate Competitive Research (EPSCR). It provided qualifying states with R&D funds, which had to be matched, to build its capacity for research and technology development. The federal government also began to try to pinpoint the technologies critical to its national security or economy and target R&D funds to their development.

At this point in time, each state still viewed technology and innovation as an outgrowth of R&D and dependent largely on the strength of and tied to its research universities. In 1986, a report carried out with an agency of the National Governors' Association identified six innovation policy options for states: R&D tax credits, direct support for R&D, joint university – corporate R&D, science parks, small-business incubators, and technology extension programmes (Jones 1986). Only the last option was aimed at existing small and mid-sized enterprises (SMEs), but it too was generally described as university-based and primarily technology transfer. Further, many of the states supported these initiatives not for what they would produce but for what they would attract, i.e. federal R&D dollars and new technology dependent businesses. Industrial recruitment remained the strongest argument for state technology and innovation policy.

New Interest in Technology Diffusion

By the end of the 1980s, technology and innovation policies were beginning to shift away from the most advanced technologies to more practical, down-to-earth applications. America's competitive edge in manufacturing was seen as slipping, and critics placed some of the blame on the nation's low investments in process development and applications of advanced technologies (Dertouzos Lester Solow 1989). Simultaneously, the downsizing of industry placed more importance on the nation's 360,000 small and mid-sized suppliers and niche producers, which had been bypassed in all previous innovation strategies. This resulted in the current paradigm in which the technology and innovation strategies gain legitimacy and command more attention as public strategies. New technology-based initiatives include process research and development, adopting more technologically advanced production processes, but they also recognised the multi-dimensional needs of SMEs in order to adopt new technologies, which include management, organisation, marketing, financing and training. The primary national goal of the new – and more pragmatic – strategies for technology and innovation is improving the competitive advantage of industry.

The US Congress, in the Omnibus Trade and Competitiveness Act in 1988, authorised a new set of initiatives to facilitate the technological modernisation of SMEs. The Act provided the financial incentives and national leadership to energise states and regions enough to start or scale up technology support programmes for industry. At the outset, the federal legislation was designed as a traditional R&D-driven programme, a means to transfer technologies and know-how from university and federal research labs to SMEs more effectively. But before long the administering agency realised that cutting-edge technologies were not what most SMEs needed most, and that to serve them the programme had to be much more customer-driven and decentralised. As the Office of Technology Assessment noted, 'What small manufacturers need more than the newest technologies fresh out of the laboratory is off-the-shelf hardware and software and individual help in choosing and managing them' (Office of Technology Assessment 1990).

Collectively, the resulting set of programmes became known as the National Manufacturing Extension Partnership (MEP), and the title that attracted federal dollars was the 'manufacturing technology centre'. In the early stage of implementation, the architects of the strategies decided that states ought to be full partners, and that federal funds ought to require state endorsements as well as matching funds. Thus, the resulting MEP became an alliance between the federal government and the states to establish – and fund for a limited time until they achieved self-sufficiency – manufacturing technology centres and field-based technology extension services. A few of these existed before the federal initiative, but they were small and university-based and were having little impact on SMEs or regional economies. Compared with earlier, more traditional, research-oriented strategies that aim to advance the state of the technology, these technology-based strategies aim to advance the state of the firm, to allow firms to catch up with the technological advances already made. By 1992, 37 states had created programmes of technology-focused assistance to manufacturers (Phelps and Brockman 1992) This was significantly up from only 13 programmes in nine states found in a similar survey in 1988–89 (Office of Technology Assessment 1990).

The ways states initially chose to organise these services also held certain attributes in common but with important distinctions. One such attribute was a clearly defined organisational setting but with substantial differences in the degree of institutional autonomy. Some programmes were tightly controlled by universities or state agencies, such as New York, South Carolina and Wisconsin, while others were set up under autonomous non-profit organisations, such as Minnesota Technolog, Inc. and Kansas' Mid-America Manufacturing Technology Center. Some states assigned responsibility to the same agency that manages other technology and innovation programmes, such as Arkansas, Delaware, and Minnesota, while others, like Virginia and Massachusetts, separated responsibilities for technology diffusion from those for R&D and technology development. The current trend across the nation, however, is toward independent, non-profit entities unfettered by bureaucracy.

A second attribute is the source of industry expertise. Some states, like North Carolina and Georgia, rely on resident experts while others, like Minnesota, refer SMEs to consultants for technology solutions. Another attribute is the way an area of activity is defined and circumscribed; some states have developed special expertise around specific business clusters, such as Indiana with plastics or Michigan with the auto industry, while others address a geographic region.

Finally, all programmes charge some fees for services. But just how much is still a subject of controversy. States are expected – and often directed – by the national support programmes to recover all their costs. For example, the National Institute for Standards and Technology (NIST) expects programmes it starts to eventually become financially independent, not only from federal funds but from state funds. Yet many states view technology and innovation as a form of economic development and are quite willing to share costs of services that benefit their economies. This tension between self-sufficiency, which turns programmes into erstwhile consultancies, and public goods, has created conflicts in states farsighted enough to embrace technology and innovation as an ongoing economic development strategy.

Thinking About and Acting on Clusters

The latest shift in states' views of technology and innovation policy is to address businesses as production systems rather than as independent atomistic employers and develop cluster-targeted strategies. This newest of the technology and innovation paradigms is based on the tendency for businesses to cluster regionally, where they can utilise specialised technology services, learn from each other, attract other related firms and produce synergy. Therefore, technology and innovation strategies will be more effective if directed toward the needs of clusters that are dominant or prominent because of their present or potential contribution to the regional economy.

This observation, that technology-based businesses and resources tend to cluster, is not new. The 1984 OTA report on technology and innovation noted the tendency of high-tech businesses toward agglomeration, or 'proximity to complementary and competitive enterprises as well as distributors and customers' (Office of Technology Assessment 1984). Concentration, the OTA wrote, 'enhances productivity by creating external economies of scale, in both production and marketing, similar to the internal economies created by the size and vertical integration of much larger corporations' (ibid.). Yet at that time state and federal governments were reluctant to make choices that appeared to be industrial policies. Instead they focused on accelerating the development of 'critical technologies', which loosely related to specific industries but were theoretically available to help all US businesses.

In the 1990s, states began to accept industry-specific policies, in part because the most prestigious business schools were promoting the value of clusters and in part because states were defining 'clusters' broadly enough to include a large proportion of the state's jobs. The report by DRI-McGraw Hill (1995) called *America's Clusters*, for example, claims its 380 clusters include 57 per cent of all jobs in the US. A growing number of states – including North Carolina and Virginia – took steps to encourage and support business clusters. The ostensible goal of these strategies is to increase regional synergy by developing the conditions that enable geographically clustered businesses to interact more easily with one another. Cluster strategies in place in Arizona, Oregon, Illinois and New York, and emerging in a number of other states as small-scale experiments, cut across both technology and innovation and economic development organisations.

International Influences

Technology policy, and particularly technology diffusion and cluster approaches – especially when targeted to SMEs – have been heavily influenced by European and Japanese models. The US, which had little experience and less success in assisting SMEs in traditional industries, looked to Europe for their models. Every region of the US sent delegations of policy-makers to Europe between in 1987 and 1996. This author, for example, led delegations of state legislators, government officials, and business and technology programme executives from the Southern Technology Council and the states of Delaware, Kentucky, North Carolina and Oklahoma. Most visited such highly regarded technology diffusion programmes as the Danish Technology Institute, the Netherlands' TNO, and Germany's Steinbeis Foundation and Fraunhofer Institutes. Federal agencies such as the National Institute of Standards and Technology and the US Department of Commerce's Economic Development Agency commissioned studies of these and other European programmes. The operating principles of the most successful European technology diffusion programmes were ultimately adopted by many new state and federal programmes. For example, the concepts of inter-firm collaboration and industry clusters, now included in some fashion in most state technology policies, were based directly on European experiences, and the increasingly popular concept of the teaching factory was a European import.

REGIONAL (MULTI-STATE) STRATEGIES: USING THE POWER OF PERSUASION

The competition for federal dollars led groups of states to formal regional alliances in order to strengthen their comparative positions, and a few multi-state efforts to attract federal dollars and accelerate technology adoption and innovation developed. The first was the Midwest, where the governors formed a short-lived technology alliance that died because it lacked a sound basis for cooperation and tried too quickly to name the 'winners', the sites within the region that would become hubs of R&D and innovation. Perhaps the most prominent success was in the US South. Owing largely to its strong cultural identity and common economic problems, technological disadvantages and more unified political environment, it had in place an established regional organisation that enabled it to respond regionally to technology and innovation.

That organisation is the Southern Growth Policies Board (SGPB), a 14-state organisation created in 1971 by a group of progressive southern leaders from business and government to plan for orderly growth in the region. Its by-laws direct it to establish a Commission on the Future every six years and set priorities for the region. The 1986 Commission, led by the SGPB Chairman, Arkansas Governor Bill Clinton, was the first to explicitly address technology and innovation. Southern states were just beginning to recognise both the importance of technology to emerging industries and the weakness of their technological infrastructure and resources. Eighteen months earlier, a summit meeting of the directors of the region's fledgling or potential state science and technology organisations produced a plan to use the collective strength of the region to increase its science and technology capacities. It set out some of the guiding principles for the Commission.

The 1986 Commission produced a plan called *Halfway Home and a Long Way to Go*, which lent legitimacy and credibility to a newly formed arm of SGPB dedicated specifically to technology policy called the Southern Technology Council (STC). In 1988, the STC began a process to develop the nation's first multi-state plan for science and technology, in a region that on average considers itself disadvantaged in this arena but that also has pockets of emerging strength. The region includes, for example, the states of Florida and North Carolina, rich in research capacities and high-tech companies, but also the states of Mississippi, Louisiana, Kentucky and Arkansas, among the nation's weakest states in science and technology. The plan had to balance the needs of all 14 southern states, which meant finding a broad set of objectives and flexibility in implementation strategies.

The STC's plan, *Turning to Technology*, created a framework that projected a new structure for technology development. It added technology diffusion to the conventional technology transfer, and it addressed the needs of poor and rural areas and populations likely to be left behind in technology-based strategies (Southern Technology Council 1989). Some of the recommendations were new to the region, such as increasing 'cooperation among firms to achieve economies of scale and scope' to meet the goal of widespread deployment of technology and 'enlarge multi-institutional collaboration and international exchange' to meet the desired goal of improvement and expansion of research and technology development. The plan also included a strategy for implementation that assigned responsibilities to various levels of government, business, labour, trade associations and non-profit organisations, but since regional organisations have no legislative authority – only the power of persuasion – each state was responsible for setting its own priorities.

The STC was successful in presenting a united regional front to both federal government and industry. It sponsored the first regional studies, noting the need for modernisation among the region's many rural SMEs, which led to a host of state programmes around industrial modernisation. Most important, the STC provides a forum for heads of state technology and innovation programmes to get to know each other, exchange information, and even share resources and has led to a number of multi-state initiatives around technology and innovation. Yet this body is mainly a network for raising visibility, learning and forging alliances among operating bodies. Resources require action by individual member states.

WHERE THE ACTION IS: NORTH CAROLINA AND VIRGINIA

North Carolina and Virginia are two states now noted for their successes in using technology and innovation to promote regional development (Virginia is actually a 'commonwealth' rather than a state, but I use the term 'state', the more common US term, throughout this chapter to avoid confusion). This is particularly significant given their histories. Both were sleepy southern states through the 1950s, steeped in southern customs and culture. They were racially segregated and their economies were highly dependent on agriculture and on traditional manufacturing industries recruited to the South with the promise of subsidies, lower wages and freedom from unions. The last was important because average wages did not rise as quickly as did the economies. As late as the 1970s, some areas were turning away companies that paid above-average wages or were likely to be unionised (Luebke 1990). In later years, however, both were fortunate to have progressive governors that sought to modernise their economies, improve education and increase the standards of living.

Today, North Carolina is the nation's tenth largest state with about 7 million people and growing, and the nation's most industrialised state, with the highest proportion of its workforce in manufacturing. Virginia is a state of about 5 million with the nation's capital on its north-eastern border and it benefits from the overflow of federal agencies such as the Pentagon and National Science Foundation inside its borders, the highly educated technical workforce living in its suburban communities, and from the resulting business spinoffs. Both states however still have substantial pockets of poverty in their Appalachian regions to the west and the coastal regions in the east.

The Story of North Carolina: A Round-up of High-tech Plants

In North Carolina the hub of technology-based development is the Research Triangle Park (RTP), widely acknowledged as one of America's two most successful planned research parks (the other being at Stanford University in California). The RTP was conceived in 1955, when Governor Luther Hodges formed a committee of business leaders and university officials to investigate the strengths of the three top universities (Duke, North Carolina State University and the University of North Carolina) for economic development. At that time, the state ranked 49th among the 50 states in income per capita and a large part of its employment was in textiles, tobacco and furniture. Their report suggested that these universities had sufficient strength in science and technology to attract a cluster of high-tech companies (Luger and Goldstein 1991). In 1956, a group of citizens and corporations bought the 6,700 acres in the middle of the triangle formed by the three universities. With a half-million-dollar grant from the state and 157 acres, the foundation established the Research Triangle Institute as a non-profit contract research company with interlocking boards drawn from the universities. Thus, the park became more than just a real estate operation. But even with the early state support for the research institute and the formation of a state Board of Science and Technology in 1963 to make small research grants, RTP remained largely empty for eight years until 1966 when IBM and then the US Environmental Health Sciences located large facilities there. With those two tenants as anchors to inspire other companies, RTP eventually reached its current size of 34,000 employees.

The RTP stands as North Carolina's most visible technology and innovation policy for two decades. While the RTP prospered, much of the rest of the state's economy remained mired in the past and dependent on traditional industries and branch-plants using low-skilled labour. The next phase of technology and innovation began in 1980, when the young, newly-elected Governor Jim Hunt assembled a 'blue-ribbon panel' of state leaders to see whether the state could replicate California's success in microelectronics and attract a cluster of electronics companies. It recommended the formation of an independent non-profit R&D centre in RTP to attract industry. The governor said that 'the microelectronics industry is our chance – perhaps the only chance that will come in our lifetime – to make a dramatic breakthrough in elevating wages and per capita income of the people of the state' (Whittington 1985). General Electric quickly announced plans to build an electronics plant there, citing the new Microelectronics Center of North Carolina (MCNC) as a major factor in its decision.

But North Carolina did not stop with this major investment. Between 1980 and 1982 the state legislature established the North Carolina Biotechnology Center to support the growing high-tech industry, the Technological Development Authority to help new high-tech business start-ups through incubators and risk capital, the North Carolina School of Science and Mathematics to produce a cadre of young scientists and raise the state's image in public education, and, with federal support, a North Carolina Small Business Technology and Development Center. The state already had various research centres in its universities, a small industrial extension service operating out of its state university, and a nationally renowned system of fifty-eight vocationally-oriented community and technical colleges. With the plethora of high-tech programmes to back up its recruitment efforts, high-tech employment in the state nearly doubled, from 132,209 in 1977 to 262,863 in 1994.

North Carolina was still considered surprisingly weak in coordination and planning. The state now had more than thirty independently administered, publicly supported and sometimes competing public and private organisations addressing specific research and technology-based needs of the state's economy, and the customer-companies were confused, with little connection to the state's Department of Commerce. A survey of companies found that even among electronics companies, only one in seven was aware of MCNC, and fewer than half were aware of any public support service, including the state's industrial extension service, community colleges and small business centres (North Carolina State University 1996). There was little coordination among agencies and no state body responsible for coordinating, rationalising, and supporting technology and innovation policies.

Many technology programmes receive substantial investments from the state but were also expected to produce measurable results and eventually become self-supporting through memberships and fees generated by services. The various programmes competed fiercely with each other for state funds allocated by a legislature that had little understanding or appreciation of technology and innovation policy other than for attracting new industry to the state. Ongoing operating funds from the state were quite small and getting smaller, not larger, as the political climate grew more conservative. It was in this climate that the governor decided to act.

Forming a State Coordinating Body: The North Carolina Alliance for Competitive Technologies (NC ACTs)

Frustrated by the lack of coordination and cooperation among technology and innovation agencies and their failure to reach SMEs, Governor Jim Hunt, who established many of the state's leading programmes and who was re-elected after an eight-year absence, created a new agency. Its purpose was to better organise the existing set of technology and innovation programmes and make them more user-friendly for industry. The state was now considered rich in technology and innovation resources; its universities had established themselves in R&D, and centres, and the much-publicised Research Triangle Park, which anchored a large number of high-tech companies, had become an international success story.

In 1995, the governor, through an executive order, established the North Carolina Alliance for Competitive Technologies (NC ACTs) as a partnership to coordinate, plan and rationalise the state's technology programmes. He appointed a twenty-member Board of Directors, composed of leaders from industry, government and education, and hired Walt Plosila, a highly respected technology policy expert and former architect and director of Pennsylvania's Ben Franklin Technology Program, as its first director.

NC ACTs' three overriding objectives were to develop a comprehensive strategy and vision to guide the use of state public resources devoted to technology development and deployment, organise public and private entities involved in technology to ensure a rationale customer-driven delivery system that measures and rewards results, and match state investments with other public and private investments. A state-wide plan was its first order of business, and toward this end NC ACTs created an advisory board which it divided into working committees around manufacturing modernisation; human resources; R&D technology infrastructure; technology transfer and commercialisation; technological innovation and entrepreneurship; and structure, organisation and financing. Staff gathered most of the relevant information, including a detailed inventory and assessment of all technology and innovation programmes and a survey of businesses' needs and views.

The various committees studied the data and information, applied their own experiences, and wrote committee reports with recommendations. These findings were compiled into a plan for the state called *Making Manufacturing and Technology Work for North Carolina: Strategies for a Competitive Future* (1995). Many of the recommendations included the words 'partnerships', 'relationships', 'alliances' and 'linkages', emphasising the desire for collaboration. But cooperation proved difficult to achieve, in part because of past organisational autonomy and independence and in part because of past competition for funding, competition that was even more fierce in the face of diminishing state resources. But it was accomplished. The plan included a set of 10 'principles of implementation', such as 'be client-driven, accessible, and responsive to industry needs', 'invest in performance-based incentives, not grants', and 'there should be an industry sector or regional geographic focus to the effort'. Implementing the plan, however, required not just consensus and cooperation among the players, but legislative support.

Some agencies found ways to cooperate to strengthen their positions, while others continued to follow old patterns undermining the state's efforts to harmonise programmes. Today, 24 of the state's 35 technology organisations meet bi-monthly with NC ACTs and are using the plan to programme their resources. North Carolina State University's Technology Extension Service has formed an alliance with the state's community college system and located its agents at the colleges to work with continuing education staff.

Furthermore, and, perhaps most importantly, the state is coordinating its agencies and resources around cluster-based strategies, beginning with efforts to support the formulation of industry 'roadmaps'. Industries are selected by the state based on seven criteria – critical mass, economic growth impact and potential, retention and expansion of current employment base, dominance by SMEs, market changes, dependence on technology, and industry interest and support. Although most of these are based on quantitative analyses, the last is considered vital, and industry leaders must support the effort. Industry clusters submit proposals to NC ACTs, which the board of directors weighs against its criteria.

The first cluster to be funded was somewhat of a surprise because historically it had few connections to the state's universities, did little research, and was not considered either technology-based or a particularly good prospect for growth. That is, the hosiery industry. Despite the fact that North Carolina produced 60 per cent of the hosiery made in the entire United States, the cluster was given little attention by the state. Traditional industries like textiles, apparel and, to a lesser extent, even furniture were considered millstones that dragged down wages and were more likely to lose jobs than to grow. In 1995 the Catawba Valley Hosiery Association (recently renamed the Carolina Hosiery Association), with help from NC ACTs, led its members through a process that produced this industry's first strategic plan (Carolina Hosiery Association 1995). As a result, members reached consensus on a need to expand markets and agreed that their success depended on cooperation in both vertical production networks and marketing alliances. The cluster's ability to develop a clear plan, reach consensus, and present a collective vision has helped it win continued support from the state legislature and from the state's technology programmes. Today, the industry appears poised to compete in world markets. Other sectors that followed suit were manufactured housing, environmental technologies and plastics.

Despite the apparent success of NC ACTs in establishing a plan, in building support within the private sector through its industry initiatives and in creating a coordinating body, the traditional independence and autonomy of the state's many programmes and the absence of strong and influential champions in the legislature (or Governor), resulted in a major change in the programme. After a substantial budget reduction that made it difficult to function in the role originally intended, the original president of NC ACTs resigned. Subsequently the organisation was renamed the Center for Entrepreneurship and Technology and reconfigured under the Department of Commerce. The organisation, though in operation, is still not official although the Governor is expected to sign an executive order authorising the new agency soon. Although it has many of the same goals as its predecessor, the emphasis has shifted somewhat from technology transfer and diffusion to new business start-ups, particularly in more rural areas.

Part of the reason for the change in focus may have been that the major building blocks of the state's policy, e.g. the biotechnology centre and technology development authority, are on solid ground and there is less need for a central agency. Those that have been able to continue by attracting federal dollars, such as MCNC, the Small Business Technology and Development Center, and the manufacturing extension programme, remain viable but only to the extent that the flow of federal dollars continues. Even without the organisation, the state is prospering and is building on its capacity to support high technology industries, especially information technologies. North Carolina State University's Centennial Campus, for example, has attracted considerable investment from high-tech companies. The situation is perhaps most dire for the manufacturing extension programme, which was the centrepiece of NC ACTs efforts and was aimed at bringing technology to some of the state's older industries. Its federal funds depend on state match, which was reduced in 1999. This story, however, is still unfolding and politics, undoubtedly, will have as much to do with the outcome as strategic planning.

The Story of Virginia: Building a High-tech Image, Achieving a High-tech Presence

Virginia's innovation policy began in earnest and at significant scale in 1983, when Governor Chuck Robb formed a Task Force on Science and Technology. Based on a single but important recommendation, the Virginia legislature established the Innovative Technology Authority. It quickly formed a private, non-profit operating arm, named the Center for Innovative Technology (CIT), chartered and incorporated in 1984 and supported by state appropriations. CIT's four-fold mission was technology transfer, i.e. to enhance the ability of the state's universities to develop, transfer technology to industry, and license intellectual property; to expand knowledge pertaining to scientific and technological research; to encourage and provide specialised graduate education in science and technology; and to promote industrial and economic development. Therefore, it was highly research-driven and largely controlled by the state's research universities. Toward this end, it was expected to aggressively pursue federal R&D contracts and grants for its universities and industries. The CIT was expected to be entrepreneurial and aggressive, acting like a company, not a government agency. Its first president was selected from industry.

The state government appropriated $89 million between 1985 and 1993 in programmes. CIT's state budget averaged about $10 million per year between 1990 and 1996. In addition to its own staff, CIT operated through four research institutes (biotechnology, computer-aided engineering, information technology, and materials sciences) four technology development centres (fibre optics, bioprocess, power electronics, and semi-custom integrated systems) and seven university-based innovation centres, three of which housed new business incubators.

Being a mostly rural state, rural factions of the legislature also had to be satisfied, and the CIT quickly established outreach arms in its community colleges to bridge the inevitable gap between the remote and less technology advanced businesses and the research universities. In 1987, CIT formed the Economic and Technology Development Project within the state's community colleges. It initially placed its personnel at offices at nine of the state's 23 community colleges, working with college business and industry training staff, to assist industry in finding solutions to technical problems. After one year, the programme claimed to have started 201 projects, completing 86, saving businesses from $10,000 to $1.5 million each (Center for Innovative Technology 1988). In one of the state's more controversial acts, the state later appropriated another $21 million for the construction of a new building. It was controversial because a growing number of state legislators were already beginning to question the economic results of their investments and saw this as a symbol of unwarranted expansion. CIT's inability to adequately document positive results fuelled critics of public expenditure on R&D, and its influence on university research created tensions among competing universities and research centres. To address legislative concerns, CIT selected its new president not from industry but from politics – the former Republican Governor Linwood Holton. By restructuring and retrenching, he was able to satisfy legislative concerns and create a solid niche for CIT.

In 1992, the legislature, still not fully convinced that CIT was meeting the needs of industry, created a review committee to assess the 'Performance and Potential of the Center for Innovative Technology'. The committee found that although CIT was trying to be more responsive to the needs of industry by solving short-term problems and helping to commercialise technologies, the scale and scope of programmes serving high-tech industries and the state's industrial base were insufficient (Report of the Review Committee 1993). The state government, however, also took much of the blame by not giving CIT a large enough role in its economic development strategies. The Secretary of Economic Development was charged with developing a plan with CIT that took advantage of the state's technology resources.

About the same time the state's department of planning and budget was also reviewing the state's technology policies for technology diffusion and their ability to serve SMEs. This report was also critical of the state's efforts, charging that 'it had not developed a unified approach for industrial modernization', 'and found that 'overlap and duplication has made priority-setting and resource allocation difficult' and that 'there is no agency with clear responsibility for guiding the system' (Virginia Department of Planning and Budget 1993). Clearly, the state did not consider modernisation part of the CIT's domain. In fact in 1993 the state submitted a proposal to the NIST for support of the Virginia Alliance for Competitive Manufacturing (VACM), which was intended to provide the leadership and coordination. The proposal was successful but in the short period of time between NIST's decision to fund the VACM and the final contract a change in governors and political parties interrupted the process. The new political regime viewed VACM as the policy of the previous administration and therefore postponed accepting the federal funds.

In 1994, CIT president Governor Holton was replaced by a popular and prominent community college president, Dr Robert Templin, indicating CIT's willingness to move closer to the needs of the SMEs. The continuing restructuring under new leadership paralleled the changes in state technology policy, from technology transfer to technology diffusion, from large-scale R&D to modernisation of SMEs, and from targeting technologies to targeting industry clusters. CIT now focuses on five key industry clusters: aerospace and transportation, where the potential is believed to exist for the state to become an international leader and develop Spaceport Virginia; biotechnology and medical applications, a small but rapidly growing cluster; energy and environmental technologies with an estimated $400 billion global market; and information technologies and telecommunications, where it already has 4,000 companies. CIT is also a partner, along with advanced manufacturing technology centres associated with community colleges in southern and western Virginia, in the new Virginia Alliance for Competitive Manufacturing, finally created two years after the federal grant was authorised.

For the years 1995 and 1996, CIT announced that it had created or retained 5,571 jobs and 130 companies and created $161 million in 'increased competitiveness' for Virginia (Virginia's Center for Innovative Technology Innovations 1996). This assessment was a response to earlier criticism of CIT's failure to set precise economic goals and document achievement. A new strategic plan formulated in 1994 set out goals for 1995–97 of 6,000 jobs and 150 companies, and $100 million in competitiveness. Thus, CIT had already exceeded two of its goals and was near the third with a year to go.

For example, the state now has in total 11 technology development centres, most of which are supported in part by CIT, a NASA-funded technology transfer centre, a number of high-tech industry councils and a small business innovation research/technology transfer support programme. Most of the programmes receive a commitment for five years of funding after which they are expected to become self-sufficient based on industry sponsors (Coburn 1995).

As Virginia takes to technology and innovation, most of its programmes are still predicated on traditional recruitment goals. The investments are expected to pay off in the long term, but elected state officials look first at their success in bringing in immediate jobs. The recruitment of a large Motorola plant in 1995, for example, was credited to the state's technology resources and viewed as a seed for a Virginia version of Silicon Valley (Corcoran 1995). Economic development remains a matter of incentives, but technology and innovation resources are an increasing part of that package. Still, the number of high-tech jobs in the Commonwealth has been declining, along with total manufacturing jobs (Center for Innovative Technology 1997).

A more recent technology strategy of the Commonwealth and the CIT targets specific sub-state regions, examining their particular technology-based industries and resources, and fits programmes to their special circumstances. Thus far, the CIT has identified six such technology regions: Hampton Roads Region (the southeastern shore); Northern Shenandoah and Northern Virginia Region (the northernmost counties); the Greater Charlotteville Region (the home of the University of Virginia); the Greater Richmond Region (the state capital and population centre); Virginia's Region 2000 (a four-county area in the centre of the state with a heavy manufacturing base); and the New Century Region (the western counties, home of Virginia Tech).

One such region is a four-county, three-city, 2,000-square-mile area in central Virginia that formed a regional planning body called Region 2000. Anchored by the city of Lynchburg, this highly industrialised region of 210,000 inhabitants lacks any technological support infrastructure. It has no research university within its borders and few advanced technical education programmes. Both the University of Virginia and Virginia Polytechnic are within a two-hour drive, but in different technology regions and a bit too far to use or attend classes regularly.

In 1995, the Region 2000 area began a process of planning its long-term future. Since the area is near Research Triangle Park (RTP), local officials became intrigued by RTP's success. The stimulus for a technology plan was Region 2000's desire to explore the possibility of replicating RTP. Already the home of a number of high-tech businesses (e.g. Ericcson and B&W nuclear), Region 2000 considered policies that would enable it to attract enough additional high-tech businesses to become Virginia's own RTP. It would, of course, have to compete for this title with the state's three leading high-tech areas, the Washington DC suburbs, the state capital, Richmond, and Hampton Roads, home of a major shipbuilding industry on the state's eastern shore. It was that environment that led Region 2000 to contact CIT, and request and receive a grant to develop a technology plan, 'Regional Technology Strategies 1996–1997'.

Once the region assessed its strengths and weaknesses it became apparent that traditional manufacturing, not high-tech industry, was its bread and butter. But future success would hinge on its ability to move its companies toward higher-value-added manufacturing. This, in turn, would depend on their rates of innovation and improvement in technology and techniques. Although the region prided itself on the diversity of its economy, an industry location and employment analysis revealed concentrations and interdependencies, particularly in industrial machinery, electronics, and wood products.

Though lacking R&D, the region had the state's only community college able to carry out certifiable ISO 9000 training, an effective new business incubator, and a plethora of professional, trade, social, and civic organisations that provided social conduits for learning and building trust. Yet the region did not fully appreciate either its industrial strengths or its interdependencies. Its schools strongly encouraged youth away from industry and toward liberal arts courses and four-year colleges. The businesses overwhelmingly rated skill shortages and outmigration of youth as their major problem. This led a group of machining firms to form their own training centre. And despite the large number employed in manufacturing, the region did not have any state industrial or technology extension service, or CIT outpost to provide technical assistance. All were located outside the region.

To improve the region's ability to create, commercialise, and use technology, the plan recommended the formation under Region 2000 of a Technology Committee and a Manufacturers' Support Service. The plan was submitted to and approved by a commission that represented most of the region's leading education institutions, agencies, business sectors, and professional associations. As a result of the strength of its business leadership, the will of its political leaders, and support from the Commonwealth, the plan has been implemented much as intended. To its credit, in the summer of 1999 the region contracted for an assessment of its progress in implementing the plan and suggestions for new courses.

Principles of Effective US Technology and Innovation Strategies

The histories of technology and innovation policies in North Carolina and Virginia illustrate the scepticism and lack of commitment within state governments. Although the importance of technology and innovation to economic growth is well established in the US, their place in public policy is not, and the institutions created to support technology and innovation are only as secure as their most recent records of jobs created or equivalent accomplishments and the legislative strength of their champions. The legitimacy of government subsidies or incentives to accelerate technology and innovation in the private sector (except for those used to attract high-tech companies) is still regularly questioned, particularly when budgets are tight and pressures to reduce taxes high. The experiences of US states, demonstrated in part by the two southern states, incorporate a number of important lessons about the success and failure of regional technology and innovation policies.

Integrate Technology and Innovation into Regional Economic Development Agendas

In the United States, economic development is funded and carried out by states and their designated development agencies have the most stable funding streams and most extensive networks of practitioners. Technology and innovation strategies are most likely to achieve legitimacy among state elected officials if they can be woven into the 'conventional practice' of economic development agencies. But technology and innovation also can be accepted as economic development for the wrong reasons. States have relied for so long on recruitment that research, technology and innovation are often coveted as and converted into incentives rather than their direct value. Preoccupation with recruitment tactics turns technology and innovation into strategies for making places more competitive with other places instead of making businesses more competitive with other businesses, and the economic developers, not the industries, become the customers. Virginia seems to be taking greater steps to integrate the two than North Carolina, where the Department of Commerce remains at arm's length from technology and innovation.

Design Programmes to Be Demand-Driven

The best technology and innovation strategies are governed by industry, including SMEs, and driven by the needs of businesses and workers rather than the interests or expertise of service providers. This does not mean government takes a passive role. Good strategies use knowledge, information and leadership effectively to stimulate demand for technology among SMEs. However, it is often difficult to arrive at customer-driven solutions and solicit private-sector participation from SMEs. Small and mid-sized firms tend to be only marginally involved in strategic planning and governance and to under-value technology because, first, their owners and managers have too little time and resources to commit to public processes, second, many do not trust the public sector, and third, there are few regional or national associations that can represent their technical needs and interests. Unfortunately, labour, in most parts of the US, is too weak and relationships with business management too confrontational, to permit constructive dialogue, and consequently labour has nominal, if any, input. Demands are driven by business managers' needs.

Treat Regions as Systems of Interdependent Firms

Strategies that address the collective and interrelated needs of a region have had greater impact than those that address individual firms or problems. The best attempts improve the operation of the systems rather than the individual parts, and the more innovative are beginning to frame the system in terms of production, not the delivery of services. In a regional production system, the set of related firms is the central element, services are designed to address the needs of that system and firms are recruited that fill gaps in the system. The system can revolve around a set of related products, a core technology, a research capability, a set of unique skills or a natural resource. Technology and innovation strategies that address systems are more apt to optimise the use of a region's technical resources and produce the most synergy. Those that take this route often lead to a second stage of planning, empowering and helping the dominant or strategic clusters to develop their own specialised strategies. This strategy places a high value on social infrastructure and building trust and may support industry technology associations and councils. North Carolina's targeting of key industries and cluster hubs at some of its community colleges represents such an approach. Both North Carolina and

Virginia also invested in social infrastructure – North Carolina through its industry initiatives and support of industry associations and Virginia through its support of high-tech councils and business networks.

Obtain High-Level Endorsement, Scale, and Sufficient Time

When a well-respected or very high authority actively and enthusiastically endorses a strategy and promises a high level of support, things happen. Without this support, plans often fail to reach the implementation phase. Even when they do receive support, sometimes the authority to develop the plans is not accompanied by sufficient funds for implementation at any scale that can possibly make a difference in a region's economy, leading to under-funded pilot efforts that are unable to keep their promises and to frustration and competition among participants. Programmes are also given far too little time to show results. The US is better at devising innovative technology-based strategies than it is at building consensus and support, implementing at scale, and transcending political elections. Another important condition for success is an organisation that can do this at state-level. But continuity (at least until outcomes can be assessed) is very difficult to achieve. Both MCNC in North Carolina and CIT in Virginia were chastised by their respective legislatures first, for not proving economic impacts and, second, for not achieving self-sufficiency quickly enough.

Be Inclusive, Involving All Relevant and Impacted Segments of the Population

This is an argument for raising the priority of consensus-building. The more expansive and inclusive the base of support, the better the chance that the strategy will address the community's needs and priorities. This is difficult when one is addressing technology and innovation because active participants are over-represented by the best-educated segments of the population and most well-off regions. It is made more difficult because the US never developed the European concept of 'social partners' to regularly participate in strategic planning or policy-making. Membership in organised labour is low and, in most states, excluded from policy processes. To be more inclusive, some states create large commissions and working committees or take the issues into the field to engage a large set of actors. The US has a large, significant, and perhaps unique non-profit sector composed of organisations that are often involved in and assist with planning and implementation. Many of these non-profit organisations – which often receive government funding – take on functions generally assumed in Europe by the public sector.

Measure Impacts

The strongest programmes in the US have developed procedures for measuring and documenting their impacts – on the competitiveness of businesses, on the economies of regions and on the quality of life of individuals. The first of these currently receives the most attention. The MEP is developing a standard design for collecting information and evaluating impacts on businesses for two purposes in order to demonstrate the impacts of public investments on the global competitiveness of SMEs. Technology diffusion programmes prior to this national programme limited evaluations for the most part to scale of efforts such as numbers of companies visited, types of interactions, and income earned, and did not measure results such as cost–benefit ratios and impacts on sales, profits and employment. Some successful programmes also measure impacts on workers by looking for changes in earnings, promotions or quality of work. But such outcome measures are much rarer in the states because most technology and innovation programmes' effects on workers are derivative, not primary goals. Impacts on specific places, such as depressed or very rural areas, are measured only when programmes are funded by agencies that target these areas.

CONCLUSION

Most technology and innovations policies in the US are partnerships among federal, state and local governments and regional organisations, with federal agencies serving as catalysts and sources of funds, regional consortia acting as coordinators, and local governments taking advantage of opportunities – but with the states securely sitting in the driver's seat. Technology and innovation policy is constantly evolving and expanding in the US as new strategies emerge. It is also constantly defending its investments before sceptical legislatures and the Congress, which expect quicker and clearer results and high levels of corporate fees than technology and innovation are generally able to produce, or believe that free markets will be able to produce results more effectively than government interventions. North Carolina and Virginia are both states that want very much to be known for the quality of their science and technology establishments and industries, yet have not fully accepted and indeed embraced the programmes that have done much to contribute to this image and reality.

MAURICE AVERY[1]

11 Regional Innovation Strategies in Quebec: The Bas-Saint-Laurent Region

THE CANADIAN AND QUEBEC CONTEXT

In the past twenty years international economic exchange has become increasingly complex. Barriers to international trade have fallen, creating a more competitive environment that presents new challenges for industrialised countries. Canada's distinctive geographic and economic characteristics add to these challenges. Canada, including ten provinces and two territories, is the largest country in the world after Russia and has one of the world's lowest population densities. In 1994, Canada's population of 29,251,000 inhabitants covered an area of 9,976,100 square kilometres, equivalent to a density of 2.9 inhabitants/square kilometres. In Quebec, a population of 7,300,000 inhabitants represents one eighth of France's population, while its area of 1,522,000 square kilometres is three times larger than that of France.

More than half of Quebec's population lives along the St Lawrence River and is concentrated in the metropolitan regions of Montreal and Quebec City. At considerable distances from the urban centres, the outlying or 'resource regions' cover 89 per cent of the province's area and are populated by barely 13 per cent of its inhabitants. Located more than 400 kilometres to the east of Montreal, the Bas-Saint-Laurent is a resource region with a population of 209,100 inhabitants (2.9 per cent of Quebec's population) living on an area of 22,376 square kilometres.

The Canadian economy has long been tied to the exploitation of natural resources and based largely on primary traditional sectors including agriculture, forestry, mining and the fishery. Despite a significant diversification within the last thirty years that has been mainly confined to the major urban centres, the Canadian economy remains to a large extent dependent on natural resources. As a result, the industrial sector is closely linked to agrifood production, metallurgic production and the pulp, paper and wood industries.

For the past twenty-five years Canada has had a high unemployment rate. That trend continues today with a rate that is higher than those in many OECD countries. In 1994, the unemployment rate in Canada was 10.3 per cent, compared with 8.4 per cent in Germany, 8 per cent in Sweden and 6 per cent in the United States (OECD 1996). Possible contributing factors include the seasonal nature of some industries (e.g. fishery, forestry), a high level of debt, a restrictive monetary policy and a generous unemployment insurance programme.

Indicators of the Level of Competitiveness

Despite government efforts to diversify the economy and develop technology and innovation-based sectors, indicators related to R&D expenditures place Canada behind the industrialised countries of the OECD (table 11.1). In 1994, the ratio of gross domestic expenditures on research and development (GERD) to gross domestic product (GDP) was lower in Canada than in all other OECD countries except Italy.

TABLE 11.1: GROSS DOMESTIC EXPENDITURES ON RESEARCH AND DEVELOPMENT AS A PROPORTION OF GDP FOR SELECTED OECD COUNTRIES, 1986–94

	1986	1987	1988	1989	1990	1991	1992	1993	1994
Canada	1.48	1.43	1.38	1.37	1.46	1.51	1.55	1.61	1.61
France	2.23	2.27	2.28	2.33	2.41	2.41	2.42	2.45	2.38
Germany	2.73	2.88	2.86	2.87	2.76	2.61	2.48	2.43	2.33
Italy	1.13	1.19	1.22	1.24	1.30	1.32	1.31	1.26	1.19
Japan	2.75	2.82	2.86	2.98	3.08	3.05	3.00	2.94	2.90
Sweden	–	2.98	–	2.94	–	2.89	–	3.29	–
United Kingdom	2.34	2.22	2.18	2.20	2.23	2.16	2.18	2.20	2.19
United States	2.91	2.84	2.79	2.76	2.82	2.84	2.78	2.66	2.54

Source: Statistics Canada, 1996. *Service Bulletin Science Statistics*, Vol. 20, No. 6.

The contribution to R&D by Canadian enterprises confirms these results. Within the OECD, Canadian companies are among those that contribute the least to their country's research and development effort (approximately half, compared with two-thirds for all of the OECD countries taken together). However, a 1996 study by the Conseil de la Science et de la Technologie shows that the R&D expenditure/GDP ratio for Canadian enterprises increased from 0.60 to 0.90 between 1981 and 1993. The ratio for Quebec companies showed a greater increase during the same period, rising from 0.60 to 1.09.

This brief analysis indicates that the Canadian economy is lagging behind the average of the OECD countries. Disparities exist between the different regions in Canada and it is mainly the regions that are close to large urban centres that have undertaken a technological reshaping. For example, it is estimated that in Quebec 85 per cent of industrial R&D is carried out in the greater Montreal region (Conseil de la Science et de la Technologie 1996). This gives cause to question the effectiveness of national science and technology policies. In Canada and Quebec, programmes have been applied uniformly across the country and province. The often disappointing results of the implementation of these policies and 'across the board' programmes suggest that a review of these approaches is warranted, with particular consideration given to regional and local contexts.

The Bas-Saint-Laurent Region: Economic and Geographic Characteristics

The Bas-Saint-Laurent region is bordered by New Brunswick to the south, the St Lawrence River and 320 kilometres of coastline to the north, the Gaspésie-Îles-de-la-Madeleine region to the east and the Chaudière-Appalaches region to the west. It has an area of 22,376 square kilometres. During the past twenty years, the population of the Bas-Saint-Laurent has remained relatively stable, with a growth rate of almost zero because of the migration of young adults to the large urban centres (Montreal and Quebec City). In 1994, the population of the region was 209,100 inhabitants and represented 2.9 per cent of the population of the province of Quebec.

During this twenty year period, the rural areas gradually decreased in population as people moved to the region's medium-sized towns and cities. Today, the population is approximately equally divided between rural and urban agglomerations and distributed across 135 municipalities. A net population density of 9.4 inhabitants per square kilometre illustrates the extent to which the population is dispersed, a characteristic of Quebec's outlying resource regions.

The main job market indicators for the region are inferior to those of the province and point to the region's relatively weak economy. In 1994, the region's unemployment level was 15.5 per cent compared with 12.2 per cent for Quebec, and the active workforce for the region was 56.6 per cent while the province's rate was 62.5 per cent (Secrétariat au Développement des Régions 1995).

Classified as a resource region, the Bas-Saint-Laurent has an economy structured around the exploitation of natural resources. Forestry is one of its pillars, with 85 per cent of the region covered in forest. In 1993, this sector generated 7.8 per cent of the region's employment whereas it represented approximately 3 per cent of the employment in Quebec (Société Québecoise pour le Développement de la Main-d'oeuvre 1994). Food production also plays a significant role in the region's economy, generating 8.5 per cent of jobs compared with 4.2 per cent for the province. About twenty companies in the region's peat industry produce 50 per cent of Quebec's annual production which represents close to 20 per cent of the total Canadian production.

The transportation sector is experiencing significant growth in the region. In addition to a trucking industry with approximately 400 companies, the manufacture of transportation equipment for two distinct sectors has become an important industrial activity. These sectors include the rail transportation industry, involving a Quebec multinational, and the ship repair industry in medium-sized shipyards. These industries are important because of the R&D and subcontracting activity they generate.

Geographically, the region's location along the St Lawrence Estuary has contributed to the development of the field of oceanography, which represents the region's largest R&D sector. However, this R&D effort is confined primarily to the university institutions and research centres.

The economy of the region is primarily resource-based, with very little processing or manufacturing activity. In 1994, the primary sector generated 10.9 per cent of regional employment, compared with 3.7 per cent for the province as a whole (table 11.2). The secondary (manufacturing and construction) sector is less developed than the province's average, with 15.8 per cent of jobs compared with 22.5 per cent for Quebec. Finally, the service sector generates almost three-quarters of the region's jobs.

TABLE 11.2: SECTORIAL DISTRIBUTION OF EMPLOYMENT IN THE BAS-SAINT-LAURENT AND QUEBEC, 1994

Activity sector	(,000)	Region	Quebec
Primary sector	8.3	10.9%	3.7%
Secondary sector	12.0	15.8%	22.5%
- manufacturing	8.4	11.1%	18.1%
- Service sector	55.8	73.3%	73.8%
- transportation and other public services	5.7	7.5%	7.1%
- services			
- commerce	13.9	18.3%	17.3%
Total employment	76.1	100.0%	100.0%

Source: Secrétariat au développement des régions, 1995. *Les régions administratives, édition 1995*, Quebec.

With respect to the level of technological activity, measured by the average R&D expenditures over sales, the region shows a net deficit compared with the province. Only 1.1 per cent of manufacturing companies in the region operate at a high level of technology compared with 3.1 per cent province-wide (table 11.3).

Barely 0.7 per cent of jobs in the manufacturing sector in the Bas-Saint-Laurent region are classified in the high-technology category (8.9 per cent for Quebec), and 75.4 per cent of companies (66.3 per cent for Quebec) fall into the low-technology category and account for 67.7 per cent of the region's jobs (figure 11.1).

TABLE 11.3: THE MANUFACTURING SECTOR IN THE BAS-SAINT-LAURENT (BSL) REGION AND QUEBEC STRUCTURED ACCORDING TO THE LEVEL OF TECHNOLOGICAL ACTIVITY, 1995

	High level of technological activity	Medium-high level of technological activity	Medium-low level of technological activity	Low level of technological activity	Total manufacturing activity
BSL					
Companies	4	23	60	266	353
%	1.1	6.5	17.0	75.4	100.0
Employed	68	352	2,885	6,943	10,248
%	0.7	3.4	28.2	67.7	100.0
Quebec					
Companies	393	1,190	2,746	8,530	12,859
%	3.1	9.2	21.4	66.3	100.0
Employed	44,646	50,140	106,358	297,918	499,062
%	8.9	10.1	21.3	59.7	100.0

Source: Ministère de l'Industrie, du Commerce, de la Science et de la Technologie, 1996. *Profil économique de la région du Bas-Saint-Laurent* (01, 1996).

FIGURE 11.1: DISTRIBUTION OF JOBS IN THE MANUFACTURING SECTOR ACCORDING TO THE LEVEL OF TECHNOLOGICAL ACTIVITY IN THE BAS-SAINT-LAURENT REGION AND QUEBEC, 1995

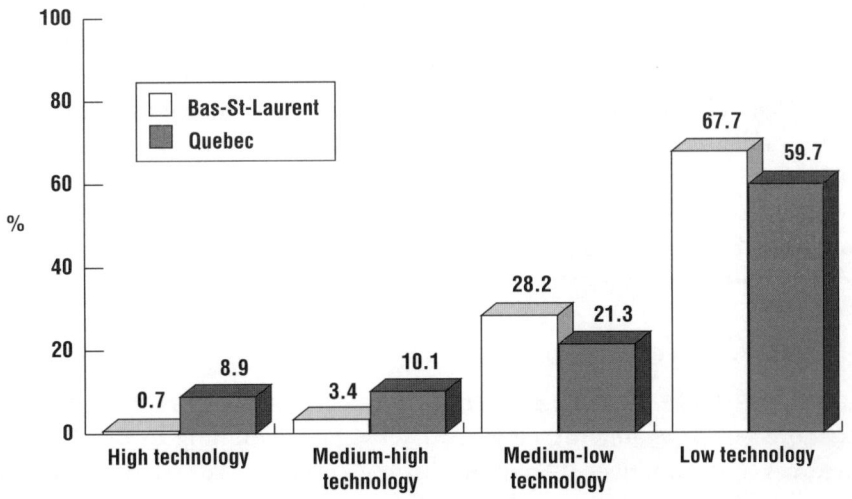

Given this technological lag, it is not surprising that the level of education among the Bas-Saint-Laurent population falls below the provincial average. There is a comparatively high proportion of people with less than nine years of schooling (25.5 per cent vs 20.1 per cent) and a comparatively low proportion of people with a university diploma (6.5 per cent vs 10.3 per cent) (OPDQ 1991). As these figures suggest, the difficulty companies face in recruiting personnel is in large part attributable to the lack of a qualified labour force in the region. For companies that want to become more technology-based, the figures have troubling implications.

A brief overview of the professional structure in the Bas-Saint-Laurent indicates that natural and applied sciences professionals and technicians represent 3.7 per cent of jobs in the region, compared to 4.9 per cent for Quebec. Professionals account for a large part of this deviation (1.2 per cent vs 2.5 per cent) owing to the notable lack of consulting firms in science- and technology-related fields.

Regional Development Approaches

Regional development in Canada, as in other federally structured OECD countries, consists of responsibilities shared between the federal government and the provinces. But, whereas the federal government considers a region to be a territorial entity that results from dividing Canada into geographic zones (the West, Centre, Ontario, Quebec and the East), each with their own economic characteristics, Quebec has divided its territory into 16 administrative regions which include 1,474 municipalities. These two views of how a region is defined go a long way towards explaining the different regional development approaches taken by the two levels of government.

The question of the share of powers between the federal level and the provinces is a delicate and still largely debated question. Very crudely stated, one can note that the provinces are responsible for their natural resources (energy, mines, woods, agriculture, etc.), training and education and culture. Health is under the responsibility of the provinces too, but under federal norms regarding quality and access to health services. Inter-provincial transport is under federal jurisdiction, while intra-provincial transport is under the authority of the provinces. Similarly, maritime fishing is a federal responsibility, while inland waters fall under the provincial authority. Some competencies, like regional development, are shared between the two levels, but agreement on the respective roles of each government tier is not complete.

The Federal Approach

In the mid-1980s, the federal government undertook a major restructuring of its approach to regional development, subsequently aiming to develop programmes and initiatives in response to the specific needs of the Canadian regions. Management was decentralised through the creation of four organisations, each targeting a specific region: the Atlantic region, Quebec, Northern Ontario and Western Canada.

Since 1991, the federal government's responsibility for regional economic development in Quebec has been assigned to the Bureau Fédéral de Développement Régional-Québec (BFDR-Q). This agency is responsible for defining the orientation of the government in matters of regional development, negotiating and managing agreements with the Quebec government and implementing support programmes designed to meet the needs of the province.

The Quebec Approach

The Quebec government has traditionally had an active regional development policy. In 1966 administrative regions were created (since modified in 1987) and provincial government departments were regionalised in order to make government activity more accessible to the population. Today, regional offices for government departments and agencies can be found in most of the sixteen administrative regions. In the education sector, many of the regions have access to a network of higher-education institutions (colleges and universities) and publicly funded research centres.

Since the beginning of the 1990s the government's efforts in regional development have intensified as greater responsibility has been assigned to the sixteen administrative regions for matters related to their own development. In 1992, the government restructured its regional development institutions and set up the Secrétariat au Développement des Régions (SDR) to be represented in each region by an assistant deputy minister who presides over the Conférence Administrative Régionale (CAR). This body coordinates government activity in the region with a focus on adapting the programmes and policies of the various departments and agencies to the requirements of each region. The government also established the Conseil régional de développement (CRD). The council is composed of elected municipal representatives, various development agents (including agents from the education sector), representatives of service organisations and Members of Quebec's National Assembly (MNAs). The CRD encourages collaboration within the region, defines the development strategy and manages a regional development fund.

ORIGIN OF THE REGIONAL STRATEGY

In 1992, within this new framework, the Quebec government launched a major exercise in strategic planning where each region was encouraged to formulate a development plan that identified the issues and problems related to the region's development and established a consensus on priorities. Responsibility for this task was assigned to the CRD. However, in many regions this process attracted very little interest from the industrial sector and in particular from technologically oriented small and medium-sized enterprises (SMEs). In fact, the regional plans offered very little in terms of strategies for the development of innovation and technology transfer within the private sector.

On this basis, the Conseil de la Science et de la Technologie du Québec (CST) proposed a 'science and technology' exercise to encourage the regions to include a stronger technology component in their existing development plans and to formulate strategies that would improve their innovation capacity. Furthermore, this pilot project would allow the CST to continue previous studies that had addressed the problem of regional technical development and also to test a methodology that could potentially be used more widely by the regions and other government departments. With this in mind, it was agreed that the experiment would be limited to three regions. The Bas-Saint-Laurent was identified early on as one of these regions, owing in large part to its leaders' strong expression of interest in the exercise. As of spring 1997 it was the only region to have completed the formulation of a strategy and to have proceeded with its implementation.

The Bas-Saint-Laurent region is an interesting choice for other reasons as well. It is a resource region where there is an alarming rate of unemployment and where the technological reshaping of the economy seems to pose particular difficulties. The geography of the region (a large area with low population density) and its sociological characteristics (low education levels and gaps in technical education) contribute to the difficulty of meeting the challenge of technological reorientation.

Despite these obstacles, the region also offers promising potential for innovation. A network of four colleges and one university is experiencing an accelerated rate of development in science and technology. The private sector is generating new technologically based companies and contributing to the renewal of traditional enterprises in strategic areas such as telecommunications. In 1994, thanks to the support of the entire region and their indication of such to the government, the university established a Faculty of Engineering. This faculty symbolises the region's technological awakening and is considered to be an invaluable partner to help the region face the challenges of the new technology era.

THE BAS-SAINT-LAURENT SCIENCE AND TECHNOLOGY REGIONAL STRATEGY

The primary objective of the strategy is the development of the technological capacity of the Bas-Saint-Laurent region. The strategy aims to identify ways of stimulating and accelerating changes that will allow the region to reshape its economy and to create conditions favourable to successful business performance. The strategy also experiments with a new approach to defining priorities of action. This approach is based on establishing a consensus among the very people who are involved in the development of science and technology in the region: the private sector, government departments and higher-education institutions. This bottom-up approach should contribute to the creation of a new culture, one where the region's key players in science and technology development take charge and where cooperation, partnerships and networks play a major role.

To summarise, the development of a strategic plan will permit:

- the implementation of a regional plan that emphasises the development of the region's technological capacity;

- the establishment of a consensus and common vision shared by key players in the region around the issues of technological development;

- the emergence of the private sector as the leader in the development of the region;

- the establishment of a regional consensus on priorities of action;

- the creation of a new regional culture where science and technology are among the region's priorities for development;

- the recognition of regional priorities that translate into government policies on science and technology.

The Process

At the regional level, the exercise was carried out under the responsibility of the CRD who assigned the task to the strategy committee. Chaired by a company executive, the committee consisted of representatives from government, higher education (colleges and universities) and the private sector. The CST and the various government departments acted in an advisory capacity and provided support in keeping with the spirit of the approach to have private-sector leaders take charge of the process.

The strategy committee identified the following steps in the elaboration of a strategy (see figure 11.2):

- Prepare an up-to-date assessment of where the existing strategic development plan stands.

- Prepare an assessment, based on a SWOT (strengths, weaknesses, opportunities, trends) analysis, of where the region stands in terms of its science, technology and research development capacity and formulate an initial diagnosis.

- Hold a workshop to confirm the assessment and to gather input from industry and other sectors on conditions favourable to the technological development of the region.

- Prepare a preliminary strategy based on the results of the consultation and the assessment that describes avenues for development in the region.

- Consult with the CAR about the diagnosis and the actions proposed by the committee.

- Prepare a final report describing the regional science and technology strategy that includes information about government assistance programmes for research and development and which makes reference to the international context.

FIGURE 11.2: STEPS FOLLOWED IN THE FORMULATION OF THE REGIONAL STRATEGY

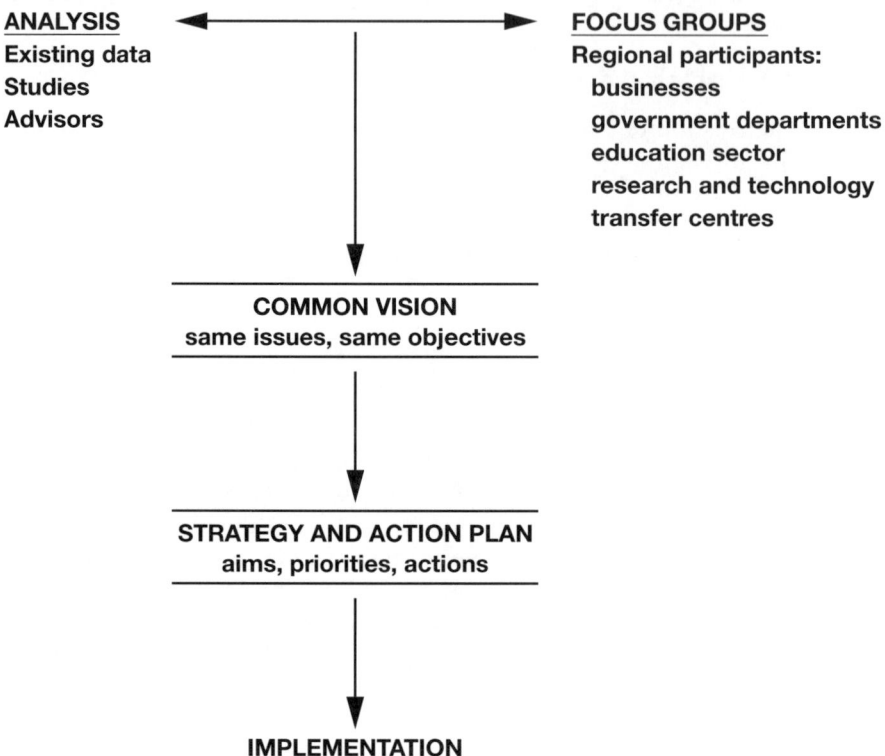

Source: Secrétariat au développement des régions (1995). *Les régions administratives, édition 1995.* Quebec: SDR.

Research and Development in the Region

The analysis carried out under the RTP yielded the following elements about the R&D situation of the region.

Compared with the province, the Bas-Saint-Laurent region falls well behind in research and development. Although the population represents 2.9 per cent of the province's total, the regional GERD represents only 1 per cent of provincial expenditure. In terms of R&D expenditures per inhabitant, the region spends $132 while the province spends an average of $387. With respect to the number of people employed in research per thousand in the active work force, Quebec's figures are more than double those of the region's (table 11.4).

In the region, more than half of the R&D expenditure occurs in government organisations compared with 10.5 per cent for the province. Only 27.6 per cent of R&D expenditure occurs in private enterprise in the region, compared with 59.1 per cent for Quebec (table 11.5; figure 11.3).

To summarise, technological innovation and R&D efforts in the Bas-Saint-Laurent region are confined primarily to higher education institutions and public research centres. The economy is strongly tied to the natural resource sector, where R&D activities are mainly carried out in agriculture and marine-related sectors.

The marine sector is the most active, owing in large part to the region's strategic position along the St Lawrence Estuary. Four organisations, including a federal government institute, a college and two university institutions, have developed a range of research activities related to the fishery, oceanography, hydrography and aquaculture as well as marine and intermodal transportation. These activities represent approximately two-thirds of all R&D expenditures in the region and involve more than half of the researchers. The university also offers programmes at the master and doctoral levels in marine resource management and oceanography, while the college offers training in marine navigation.

TABLE 11.4: ESTIMATES OF GROSS DOMESTIC EXPENDITURES ON R&D IN THE BAS-SAINT-LAURENT AND QUEBEC (REGIONAL AND PROVINCIAL GERD), 1992–93

	Regional GERD ($,000,000)	People employed in R&D	Regional GERD/capita	People employed in R&D/1000 active workforce
BSL	27.9	359	$132.4	3.92
Quebec	2,770.9	27,682	$386.5	8.18
BSL/Quebec	1.0%	1.3%		

Source: Conseil de la science et de la technologie according to data from the Bureau de la statistique de Québec, Ministère de l'Éducation and Statistics Canada.

TABLE 11.5: ESTIMATES OF GROSS DOMESTIC EXPENDITURES ON R&D BY SECTOR IN THE BAS-SAINT-LAURENT REGION (REGIONAL GERD), 1992–93

	Industrial R&D	University R&D	Government R&D	
			Provincial	Federal
	$,000,000	$,000,000	$,000,000	$,000,000
BSL	7.7	4.9	0.4	14.9
Quebec	1,637	843.9	76.0	214.0
BSL/Quebec	0.5%	0.6%	0.5%	7.0%

Source: Estimates prepared by the Conseil de la science et de la technologie based on data from the Bureau de la statistique de Québec.

FIGURE 11.3: DISTRIBUTION OF RESEARCH AND
DEVELOPMENT EXPENDITURES BY SECTOR

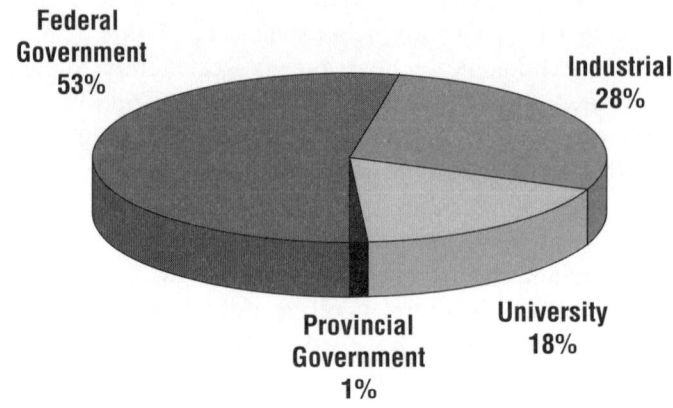

Federal
Government
53%

Industrial
28%

University
18%

Provincial
Government
1%

Agricultural research is concentrated primarily in the western part of the
region where important research activities and technology transfer take place
in the peat industry. Training in agricultural food production is also offered at
the college level.

Despite a comparatively low level of research and development, the Bas-
Saint-Laurent region has a critical mass of research infrastructure and activity.
However, three main weaknesses of the region continue to impede development: an under-qualified labour force, an insufficient number of partnerships
between educational institutions, research centres and private enterprise, and
a lack of specialised services available to businesses.

Guidelines Proposed by the Region: The Consultation

With the report on the current status of the region in hand, the Strategy
Committee decided to hold a day of consultation involving the key players in
science and technology from the region. Participants were invited to exchange
ideas and participate in the following activities:

- Provide a reaction to the assessment on the state of the region and
  identify their needs in terms of human resources and the availability
  of support for R&D and innovation.

- Identify the major directions and primary issues that could serve as
  a basis for creating a context that favours innovation (common
  vision of development).

- Propose actions to support a strategic development plan.

A major objective of this consultation was that the technology-based SME
sector should be strongly represented, with members of this sector at the forefront of the discussion. This objective having been achieved (more than 40 per

cent of the participants came from private enterprise), the conclusions of the consultation formed the basis of the science and technology strategy for the Bas-Saint-Laurent region.

Propositions Concerning the Strategy

The various comments and suggestions formed the basis for a science and technology strategy for the Bas-Saint-Laurent region. It was proposed that the central objective of the strategy should be to reduce the major disparities in the areas of research and development, technology transfer and work force training as identified in the regional assessment.

In order to ensure the attainment of this objective, several specific objectives were identified:

- Promote a common vision of development for the region which is based on knowledge.

- Make risk capital available in the region and administer it.

- Make maximum use of the network of businesses (SMEs) and institutions in the region.

- Adapt professional and technical training to the needs of private enterprise.

- Create and make specialised services available such as fostering, incubator facilities and expertise exchanges.

- Give priority to development projects that use and integrate new technology.

- Improve and adjust where necessary the administrative practices of research and technology transfer centres to improve support for regional technological development.

The steps formulated to put the plan into action aim to achieve the above objectives and are based on the following facts:

- The region has within its businesses, research centres and institutions the basic potential for innovation to flourish in strategic and high-performing sectors.

- The region has access to an important local resource in the form of a well-structured telecommunications sector.

- The region suffers from a lack of leadership on the part of its institutions and businesses for scientific and technological development.

The Strategy Committee felt that in order to build on the potential of the region and address an existing weakness it was essential to identify individuals or groups who would have the responsibility for spearheading the science and technology development process. The committee formulated its proposed actions on the basis of this premise. The eleven proposed actions are:

- Make scientific and technological development a regional priority.

- Create a regional science and technology development committee whose mandate will be to carry out those actions most likely to reduce disparities related to workforce training, R&D, technology transfer and the establishment of a context favourable to technological innovation. To ensure viability, at least half of the members of the committee should be representatives from private enterprise.

- Facilitate access to risk capital for technological development through the creation of a regional fund to support R&D, technology transfer activities and high-technology projects.

- Adapt workforce education and training to respond to the needs of private enterprise.

- Encourage the formation of innovation networks. Considering the important role that networks play in the development of science and technology, it is essential to learn about existing networks and encourage networking in other sectors with potential for technological development.

- Encourage higher-education institutions and research centres to simplify their administrative procedures in order to better respond to the needs of private enterprise.

- Develop specialised services in the region including incubator facilities, fostering, and specialised advisory services in order to permit companies to benefit from professional services that they would be otherwise unable to access.

- Taking into account the current fiscal constraints at all levels of government, manage financial support programmes at the regional level in such a way that priority is given to projects with technological content.

- Create a technology transfer centre for the marine sector.

- Ensure greater association between the institutions, research centres and businesses operating in the fishery science and marine sectors.

- Request that the Science and Technology Development Committee follow up on government decisions related to the funding of R&D and the maintenance of research infrastructure in the region.

IMPLEMENTATION OF THE STRATEGY

Immediately following its adoption, implementation of the strategy began with the creation of the Science and Technology Development Committee to be chaired by the head of a company and composed of an equal number of company executives from various sectors across the region and of representatives of Bas-Saint-Laurent regional development organisations (Ministère de l'Industrie, du Commerce, de la Science et de la Technologíe, SDR, BFDR-Q, higher education institutions and research centres, etc.). The tools used to implement the strategy include an annual action plan and yearly evaluations.

Networks

The establishment of networks was identified in the regional strategy as a key element. It was determined that in the short term three networks should be established in the following areas: transportation, recycling of biomass by-products and development of products from marine biological substances. The committee also put forth the idea of developing an action plan for the information technology (IT) sector. In addition, a new partnership was established between the university (mainly its science and engineering departments) and the private sector of the region through the creation of a corporation for the technological development of SMEs.

The Transportation Network

This network was launched through the initiative of the private sector and as a result of the Science and Technology Development Committee's discussions about how manufacturing companies can remain competitive in the face of high transportation costs due to markets outside the region. The creation of the transportation network was facilitated by the fact that all the basic requirements deemed essential for implementing a network were met:

- an interest expressed on the part of manufacturing companies to improve their level of competitiveness;

- the presence of research expertise at the college level in the field of transportation and a willingness of the experts to establish a partnership with the companies;

- a context that creates an opportunity for a partnership to develop (threatening situation).

This network, which has been financed in part by a special fund created for the region (the Technology Fund) and by the Regional Initiative Fund, has led to the establishment of a regional observatory on transportation. This body has a mandate to propose cost-optimising strategies for the transportation of merchandise.

The Biomass By-products Network

This network gathers together business people and researchers interested in the development of value-added biological by-products. It grew out of a pilot project on the processing of pig waste and wood shavings into compost. The creation of this network was dictated by the regional context and involves industries such as pig-farming and wood-processing. These industries have enormous economic potential but they generate by-products that are harmful to the environment and expensive to eliminate. Biotechnology now exists, however, that can treat these residual materials and produce new value-added products while eliminating environmental risks.

One feature of the network is that it unites different economic sectors of the region. Pork producers and wood-processing factories provide the raw materials to be treated by the technology while users of the compost include farmers and growers. At the heart of this network is a partnership between business people and university researchers that is based on the use of biotechnology. The features that have helped the Science and Technology Development Committee put this network in place include a strong interest from the partners, an obvious socio-economic opportunity, promising technology, and potential benefits for the region.

The Marine Biomass Product Development Network

The marine sector provides the region with a comparative advantage. At present several 'bio-industries' are expressing considerable interest in the sector because of the enormous potential it offers for biologically active and therapeutic substances. Research projects in this field are now underway at the university institutions in the region. Health-related organisations have also expressed strong interest in exploring avenues that could lead to the development of new anti-cancer products. A regional association has already taken a leadership role through its support of research teams in this sector. The marine sector shows promise. It is maximising the region's natural resources as well as its expertise in biology, pharmacology and biotechnology towards the development of a new regional industry.

The Information Highway Committee

The region's Information Highway Committee, consisting of representatives from various other sectors such as culture and tourism, helped bring a more global perspective to the Science and Technology Development Committee's objectives and concerns about information technology. The committee's work also brought the region's plan in line with the objectives of the Quebec government's policy on the information highway. The Bas-Saint-Laurent region is one of the first to have completed such an exercise. The Information Highway Committee also served as a springboard for a project (judged as high priority by the committee) to create a regional website for the internet. This project will serve as a vehicle to promote the region's technological resources and achievements and as a working tool for the SMEs of the region.

The Corporation for the Technological Development of SMEs

The corporation is an interesting spinoff from the Science and Technology Development Committee's activities. The university and businesses of the region joined together to create a corporation with a mission to promote innovation and technological development in the SMEs of Eastern Quebec. This objective is to be achieved by ensuring that the businesses of the region have access to the physical resources and expertise at the university's engineering faculty and by orienting students' practical training towards the needs of SMEs.

Funding

From the beginning of the exercise, it was clear that the region faced a financial challenge with regard to support for industrial R&D and innovation. The region's R&D expenditures fall below provincial levels, and a large proportion of the funds are granted to university researchers for projects that often have little connection to private enterprise. The university's engineering faculty holds promise for attracting funds in partnership with industry but it has only recently been established. Finally, the creation of a new regional fund did not seem to be a short-term possibility.

The region was able to make use of a federal government fund established as compensation for the elimination of a programme designed to support the transportation industry in Eastern Quebec. The studies as well as the diagnosis presented in the strategy documents, which underlined the region's difficulty in developing innovation, convinced authorities to use this money to encourage and help industry become more competitive. An important tool for private enterprise, the Technology Fund of 20 million Canadian dollars over five years, serves to support R&D projects and equipment purchases in industry. Because of the programme's matching grant rules the fund, at the end of the five-year period, will potentially generate a minimum of 50 million Canadian dollars for industrial R&D and innovation. Furthermore, as a result of making science and technology a priority in the region, SMEs have access to the Regional Initiative Fund, which is managed by the CRD (3.6 million Canadian dollars per year). Several projects initiated by the networks have been financed by these two funds and include the transportation observatory, the pig waste composting project and a major R&D project on peat.

Private enterprise also has access to a large risk capital fund managed by public companies created for this purpose by the Quebec government. Société Innovatech-Quebec, serving Eastern Quebec, manages a fund of 60 million Canadian dollars designed specifically to support innovation in industry.

Reports show that businesses are responding positively to this new environment in which various funds have been made available to them. However, a proactive attitude on the part of the strategy committee is necessary to promote the funds and ensure that SMEs take maximum advantage of them for technological development and innovation.

IMPACTS OF THE STRATEGY

From the beginning of the exercise, it was clear that success was not guaranteed. But after only one year of implementation, results are apparent even if they are not measurable by the usual indicators of innovation and R&D. Table 11.6 summarises these impacts by identifying the major achievements.

CONCLUSION

Still perceived today as a region that contributes little to the innovation system in Quebec, the Bas-Saint-Laurent is the first region in the province to have developed and tested a new approach to regional technological development that is based on the mobilisation of regional leaders. It is important to note that initially, a rather unfavourable assessment of the region, which took into consideration its socio-economic and geographic characteristics, presented many challenges.

The region's chances for success relied on certain assets that were recognised early in the exercise. Among these was the fact that the region had just successfully completed a strategic planning exercise that had drawn together several key players in the region around a joint project that involved making choices and setting priorities. In addition, it was possible to identify at the beginning of the exercise a core of leaders who believed in the importance of scientific and technological development. Finally, it was recognised that the region, its institutions and many of its SMEs have the ingredients and the potential to generate an environment for innovation.

The positive results after the first year of implementation provide interesting information about the validity of the approach and the activities carried out. Some of the elements that contributed to success can be described as follows:

- The approach to the development of the strategy was kept flexible and constant attention was paid to ensuring that leaders in the industrial sector made their opinions known and assumed a leadership role in the process.

- The strategy was based on an accurate evaluation of the strengths and weaknesses of the region and a precise assessment of its science and technology capacities, all of which contributed to an efficient consultation in the region and well-targeted proposed actions.

- The strategy focused on a limited number of promising avenues of development and avoided an overly wide approach.

TABLE 11.6: THE IMPACTS OF THE STRATEGY ON
SCIENTIFIC AND TECHNOLOGICAL DEVELOPMENT

Themes/Challenges	*Achievements/Impacts*
A regional culture with numerous government programmes in place to support development and a private sector that is reluctant to take charge.	Development of leadership and a regional vision of development priorities; active participation by company leaders on the Science and Technology Development Committee and in the networks.
Region lags behind in R&D efforts.	New fund to help businesses become more competitive ($20 million/5 years); R&D made a priority by the Regional Initiative Fund $3.6 million/year); funds for the Corporation for Technological Development of SMEs ($1/2 million/year).
Technological development has a low priority in the region: very little second and third stage processing.	Technology has now become a priority for the region and several innovative technology transfer and R&D projects are underway.
Harmonisation of the two levels of government in the region.	Federal and provincial government agencies in the region are working more closely together and are participating in joint activities with the region's SMEs.
A low density of enterprises across a large area makes collaboration among SMEs difficult.	Three networks in strategic sectors are established; the Science and Technology Development Committee develops good collaborative relationships.
Urgent need to develop the information and telecommunications field by making full use of the presence of the head office of a major telecommunications company in the region.	The Science and Technology Development Committee is chaired by the president of this company; the committee on information technology established a plan of action for the region in this sector and activities were initiated (regional website).
Inadequate system of innovation: little relationship between institutions and SMEs.	Creation of structural projects including: Corporation for the Technological Development of SMEs (university-SMEs); observatory on transportation (college-SMEs); major project on composting (university-SMEs).
Companies need qualified labour and customised training programmes.	Implementation of a committee on training, including institutions and industry, with a mandate to propose projects.
Lack of knowledge about R&D programmes and the various support services available to SMEs for technological development.	'Technology' workshops geared towards SMEs.
A regional approach to technological development is a low priority for many of the Quebec government departments concerned.	New government policy to integrate a regional dimension into its action plan.

- The CRD, at the beginning of the process, assigned responsibility for the strategy to one person, thus ensuring a continuous presence during the implementation of the action plan and tracking of the various projects. An agreement between the university, the CRD and the BFDR-Q was put in place to share financial responsibility for this initiative.

- The Science and Technology Development Committee was established immediately after adoption of the strategic plan and the leaders of ten companies in the region agreed to sit on the committee (making up 50 per cent of the total membership), thereby guaranteeing a balanced representation of the private sector; in this way the strategy expanded the traditional, restricted circle of university academics and government employees into a network where the private sector plays a central role.

- By appointing representatives to the Science and Technology Development Committee, several institutions (universities and colleges) and organisations (SDR, MICST and BFDR-Q) of the region became actively involved in supporting the actions of the committee.

- The exercise was guided by two primary concerns that were shared by all members of the Science and Technology Development Committee:

  - that a common vision should be established within the committee and that the various partners should work together (private sector, government and higher education);

  - that the committee's actions should respond to the expressed needs of the companies involved.

- The exercise of formulating and implementing a regional strategy is being funded by the various partners. Most of the costs incurred to develop the strategy were assumed by the Université du Québec, the Conseil de la Science et de la Technologie and the SDR, while the costs related to the implementation of the strategy, in particular the costs of coordinating the activities, are being shared equally by three of the partners. They include the CRD, the BFDR-Q and the Université du Québec.

The Leadership of the Private Sector

Probably the most significant aspect of the approach in the elaboration of the RTP in the Bas-Saint-Laurent was the chief concern to bring the SMEs to play a central role in a process dominated by studies, analysis and discussion forums. Traditionally this type of exercise offers little appeal to the private sector because it is viewed as time-consuming, theoretical and not very efficient.

The sustained interest and the willingness of the SME representatives to play such an active role is best explained by the care taken in adjusting the whole of the exercise to their expectations. Apart from the fact that the information (studies, analysis, etc.) transmitted to the members was very carefully prepared and limited to the essential data, the representatives of the private sector were given all the opportunity to express their views and their suggestions were given the most consideration. This was achieved because the representatives of the education and government sectors acted accordingly, giving up their traditionnal attitude of defining the agenda and leading the debates. Furthermore, in order to keep a balanced representation with the private sector, the institutional and governmental participation was limited to the departments viewed as essential to the process.

Other factors also played an important part in bringing the SMEs to express their leadership. Among these, some relate specifically to the context of the Bas-Saint-Laurent region:

- Many leaders of SMEs in the region are of a new generation: some follow the family tradition, through reshaping and modernising of the existing enterprises, while others have started new technology-based enterprises; but a number from both these categories have gone through higher education in administration and/or in technology-related areas, and therefore are very sensitive to the challenge of the new economy.

- The leaders of these technologically active enterprises were aware of the advantages of the RTP exercise, confident that it could bring better understanding of their needs from the other sectors of the community and that it could give them better access to the regional expertise, ultimately enhancing their capacity to innovate; this was also expressed in terms of their interest to gain access to national and international technological networks and centres through the regional expertise. This latter factor is particularly important for the many SMEs in sectors related to the natural resources of the region (forestry and wood, agriculture, peat, etc.): these SMEs rely on the regional environment to help them go through the technological mutations;

- The present context in Quebec and in Canada, with renewed political support to regions and with the implementation of structures and policies in line with this political shift, is most favourable to regional initiatives that lead to customised measures aimed at regional development. In the Bas-Saint-Laurent, a region that has for many years demanded such policies, this new context is viewed by the private sector as a good opportunity for changing the regional dynamic of the economy, especially at a time when the government is also reviewing its programmes in support of the SMEs.

- The elimination in 1995 of an important programme designed to support the transportation industry in Eastern Quebec, which includes the Bas-Saint-Laurent region, led the members of the industrial sector to realise the fragility of their position on the national and international market and to evaluate the importance of improving their level of competitiveness through R&D and innovation. Therefore the proposition prepared and submitted to the government authorities by the strategy committee, and which led to the Technology Fund (see 'Funding'), was greeted by the industrial representatives as more than an encouraging result and proof of the validity of the strategic approach.

A Cultural Change and Conflicting Visions

In addition to the involvement of the private sector, other aspects of this exercise are also worth mentioning. For instance, this was to some extent an upsetting experiment, because of its approach based on a new and different dynamic between the usual actors in regional development. Especially for government departments, the RTP process meant redefining the *modus operandi* at both the central and regional levels. The interactive approach that characterised this strategic exercise was an occasion to experiment with different visions of regional development. The importance of science and technology in regional development, the role of central vs. regional bodies, the choice of the sector and/or the organisation best suited to lead the process, are just a few issues that came up during the exercise.

For instance, it seemed important to those proposing the methodology that the CRD, because of its mandate relative to regional coordination, be given responsibility for the RTP exercise. This meant a change in culture for the region and in particular for this council, which rarely dealt closely with science and technology issues and therefore never developed day-to-day relations with the SMEs from the industrial sector. Traditionally such issues are addressed by departments with a science and technology mandate or with sectoral mandates. Nevertheless, bringing the CRD to play a central role was seen as the only way to eventually bring a change in the regional priorities in favour of science, technology and innovation for the SMEs.

In line with the above, it is interesting to note that the idea to engage in a RTP came from outside the CRD, even though this council had previously led exercises in regional strategic planning. The impulse came from the university sector in collaboration with the Conseil de la Science et de la Technologie du Québec (CST), an organisation that has great credibility in Quebec. The suggestion came because it was felt that the previous exercises led by the CRD failed in the science and technology component and did not sufficiently integrate the private sector in the process. The willingness of the Secrétariat au Développement des Régions (SDR), the department responsible for the

CRDs, to participate actively prompted the CRD to engage in the process and to accept responsibility. However, the initiative taken by the CST to initiate and experiment in RTP exercises did not create much enthusiasm in certain government departments, especially at the central level. Indeed, some departments view their responsibility in science and technology as exclusive and not to be shared by other organisations. Therefore, a process that includes new participants in the science and technology arena, and develops a new dynamic between the main actors of regional development, means that the traditional roles of these actors may be redefined. Such a process can prove quite disturbing to some. On the other hand, it must be stressed that at the regional level, the RTP process rallied all the main actors and that a very sound and close working relationship was established within the strategy committee.

This illustrates the differences, within government, in the vision on regional development and in the ways the related issues should be managed. Some support a decentralised and regional approach, encouraging the regions to work towards greater regional autonomy, while others have a more centralised and less 'customised' approach to regional issues. The RTP can be viewed as an interactive exercise that allows firms and agencies to deal openly with these issues and, it is hoped, to help bridge the gap in the vision of regional economic development between the various key players.

NOTES

1. This chapter has been written in collaboration with André Lemieux, doctoral student in Urban Studies at the Université du Québec à Montreal. Maurice Avery is responsible for the regional science and technology strategy for the Bas-Saint-Laurent.

12 The New Wave of Innovation-Oriented Regional Policies: Retrospect and Prospects

This book started with a plea for a more anthropocentric view of regional development: the intangible social, organisational and relational dimensions, and the values of trust and reciprocity that we place at the heart of the 'learning regions' challenge, all point to the crucial role of human factors when we are reflecting on ways and means to improve the situation in less-favoured regions (LFRs). After all, the development of new cognitive maps, the overcoming of rigidities and the implementation of learning mechanisms are works of human beings, whatever their specific environment.

Yet this focus on the human factor does not mean that our socio-economic faith should be left entirely in the hands of psychotherapists, who should help individuals to behave more in accordance with the new paradigm! First, because institutions are assigned a key role in supporting the transformation of any region's potential assets into real opportunities for progress: that of promoting an environment conducive to learning and cooperation among firms and public and private organisations in the region. Second, because market mechanisms are not denied under this view, rather, they are acknowledged as the main backdrop for economic activities, despite the fact that they are regarded as insufficient to cope with the serious problems faced by LFRs.

When economists (and others) reflect and advise on regional innovation policies, it is clear that they should broaden their view and become more creative. Indeed, the new vision of the socio-spatial dynamics of innovation, as described in the first chapter of this book, is both difficult to translate into operational guidelines, and hard to tackle with traditional analytical tools. This is understandable since this framework is difficult to reconcile with traditional economic thinking and thus with the standard policy recipes associated with it. Therefore, advances in policy-making appear mainly as a trial-and-error process. The aim of this book is precisely to collect lessons from a representative sample of these cases and enrich the strategic view with practical experience.

It is the purpose of this final chapter to confront the ideas developed in the first chapter – about how a coherent regional innovation policy could be conducted if it is to address the key development challenges of LFRs – with the reality of policy-making in the regions of the EU and North America. We include also in this assessment the reflections on the case of Central and Eastern European (CEE) countries, which provides us with an interesting benchmark on the EU situation, in so far as regions in the CEE suffer from problems present in the LFRs of the EU, but in a much more extreme form. A better interaction between theory and practice is, in our view, the best way to achieve progress on both sides and ultimately to improve the effectiveness of policies for innovation-based development in LFRs.

The following five sections discuss how far the pilot RTP exercises and related operations have added to our understanding of regional innovation systems and strategies.[1]

THE CHANGING ROLE OF THE STATE: PROMOTING REGIONAL DIALOGUE

As we saw in chapter 2, the RTP/RIS scheme developed by the European Union had the chief objective of launching strategic discussions within the EU regions around the promotion of innovation. This was expressed in the injunction to 'build a regional consensus' in each region so as to create a strategy and action plan to reinforce innovation. One important institutional innovation in the scheme – the creation of a Steering Committee – was made compulsory with this aim in mind.

In the light of the various experiences analysed in this book it appears that, instead of a real 'consensus', what these operations have achieved can be more adequately defined as higher degrees of *transparency* and *inclusiveness* in the policy-building process. A search for consensual views on each element of the regional innovation strategy is a utopian task, beyond the reach even of the best-organised regions. As was notably made clear in the Central Macedonian case, the real world is full of tensions between diverging interests and it is not realistic to expect that a solution satisfying all could be reached on every topic. On the contrary, correcting errors from the past very often means taking painful decisions that can never win unanimous approval. The stories of the RTPs in the EU and similar exercises in North America all showed that the main value-added of these operations was to open a new framework for discussing possible futures in terms of raising innovation in the region. They also showed that targeting consensus might end up in constructing feeble strategies, which would gather a wide, but at the same time weak and meaningless support. Therefore, developing a *high-quality and open regional dialogue* is a more appropriate goal for regional innovation policies than trying to reach a regional consensus, and it is also one compatible with the search for a focused strategy and action plan.

In line with the theoretical view outlined in chapter 1, the implementation of RTPs and related exercises shows that, in order to open and foster this dialogue, a number of ingredients are necessary. The first relates to the *presence of a well-endowed and legitimate animateur, stimulating and organising the multilateral dialogue.* The second concerns the *need to overcome rigidities of institutions and individuals* which prevents them having new conversations. The third is the need for an *innovative and strategic capacity* within the public sector itself.

First, most of the case studies collected in this book highlight the necessity of devoting time and resources to the intangible task of 'animating' the regional actors, a task systematically underestimated at the start of the operations, not least by the European Commission. Some regions called it a 'project champion' (as in Wales) and all pointed out the necessity for this agent to receive the backing of the regional authorities, if the latter did not take on this role themselves. In cases where the role of animation was delegated to external bodies (such as in South Brandenburg, where the exercise was consultancy-led), this was seen to be a danger, since it could easily weaken the commitment of regional actors and their sense of ownership of the whole exercise. The complex process of an RTP necessitates both a focal point and various places for regional interaction, all converging towards the animateur. In regions where this leadership was too weak, the construction of a real strategy was made difficult and the exercise ran the risk of ending up with a mosaic of projects, with no clear priorities or coherence between them, and a lack of broadly defined goals for the region. When the region lacks the institutional legitimacy to engage in this role, the risk is greater.

When the importance of this role was finally recognised, when new regions entered into the RIS/RITTS scheme, efforts were devoted by the Commission to support the regional animateurs in their role: training and exchange of experience sessions, delivery of tools such as 'goal-oriented project planning' techniques, a self-monitoring guide and customised guidance by the EC project officers – all aimed at supporting this role of animateur by the regional authorities or their delegates.

Experiences also showed that this role of animateur should be based on a clear wish from the regional leaders to enter into the exercise, as was the case in the Bas-Saint-Laurent region in Quebec. Indeed, the case of Castilla y León showed that, when the operation is imposed in a top-down fashion, there is great difficulty in starting the exercise and finding leaders committed to the success of the project. Only when regional leaders felt they had some ownership of the exercise could it really begin in earnest.

Second, the experiences in the regions made it clear that weaknesses in the competence of institutions and individuals are at the heart of their development problems. In South Brandenburg, for example, the analysis conducted under the RITTS reached the conclusion that the lack of linkages among firms, and between firms and their environment, was a key problem.

Generalised 'distrust' in this region or the 'absence of a spirit of collaboration' in Central Macedonia were held to be the main barriers to innovation. Most of the chapters reported that one main success of the RTP operation was to foster new cooperation between local actors. The weakness of local actors relates also to the lack of any tradition of strategic thinking or reflexivity, as reported notably in the case of Lorraine, where the RTP was said to have forced regional actors 'to think'. What these experiences illustrate is that, in order to become more innovative, regions should be able not only to learn but also to *unlearn* their past practices.

What are the means at the disposal of the regional authorities to foster dialogue and overcome rigidities? The regional experiences described in this book have combined demonstration mechanisms (through flagship projects in the final phase, as in Wales or Central Macedonia, or pilot projects right from the start, as in Limburg) with strategic planning tools (meetings, workshops, panels, consultations, etc.). In addition, studies of the various elements of the innovation system have been initiated and their results injected into the process. A key element in this array of techniques was the use of '*mirror*' techniques, as in Limburg, where sets of actors are confronted with the views of another set (e.g. support-providers with their clients). This has proven to be a valuable method to help regional actors enter into this necessary learning–unlearning process. Using RTP-labelled projects is another technique used, with two types of result: first, it helps give flesh to an operation that would otherwise be perceived as an excessively abstract exercise, and thus attracts the interest of actors most concerned with 'real things'; second, it also creates an image of a region that is moving and able to undertake new, ambitious projects. This second role seems most important, if we come back to the main challenge of 'opening minds' within the region: it has often been diagnosed that what lagging regions were lacking most was entrepreneurship, the belief that they were able to act on their future and take initiatives for themselves. The absence of 'reference models' is one bottleneck on this road, and one that the RTP projects can address.

Third, the case-studies gathered in this book show that, in order to design regional innovation policies adapted to the challenges faced by the regions today, there is a need for empowerment of the regional animateur, working to foster a regional dialogue and to break barriers impeding individual progress and hampering communication between actors. However, this is not going to produce the intended effects if the regional authorities lack an innovative spirit themselves and do not consider themselves as 'cooperative partners', in charge of 'showing the way' to other actors, as has been argued in the case of Limburg. Typically, most exercises encountered a difficulty in achieving inter-services dialogue and cooperation within regional administrations, or attaining a degree of international openness from public bodies. The task of promoting an innovative spirit among civil servants and regional administrations is every bit as important as promoting innovation in the corporate sector.

SUBSIDIARITY AND COOPERATION: TOWARDS MULTI-LEVEL GOVERNANCE

The principle of subsidiarity – that is, the adequate allocation of roles and responsibilities between the various tiers of government involved in regional innovation support – finds different applications according to the extent of powers devolved to the regions.

At one extreme, the cases of Lorraine in France or Wales in the UK illustrate the complexity of the task when regional authorities do not have much freedom to build a specific policy according to perceived regional needs: constant interaction is needed with the national authority and the policy developed is the result of a negotiation between central and regional governments. In this kind of region, one result of the RTP was that regional authorities felt empowered and more clearly committed to the goals set under the strategy, where the bottom-up character was more intense than usual. At the other extreme, in the autonomous Spanish region of Castilla y León, the RTP process could start only when the regional authority took control of the process: thereafter its autonomy allowed it to manage the exercise with a high degree of freedom. Between the two extremes, we find cases like the Bas-Saint-Laurent region of Quebec, where the discussion on the allocation of responsibilities between the various layers of authorities was vivid during the RTP: the tension between advocates of centralised and decentralised approaches was present throughout the RTP debates. In all cases, the necessity of empowering the regional animateur emerged as a key feature of the RTP exercise.

But the question of subsidiarity also encompasses the following one: which is the most appropriate territorial unit to focus on when designing innovation strategies rooted in local needs? Previous Community initiatives such as STRIDE have shown the limits of a strategy based on narrowly defined economic zones, often lacking both critical mass and institutional legitimacy to enter into meaningful strategies. The problem of the leakage of the benefits of the policies across the borders is hampering initiatives, as the chapter on the US has shown. In the latter case, this problem has led regional actors to develop multi-state programmes, which is certainly a possibility for EU regions to investigate further. With the RTP scheme, this limitation has been tackled, since in most cases regions with an institutional identity have been selected as pilot projects. In the largest regions, such as Wales or Castilla y León, the need to take into account the specificity of subregions has been met by specific actions addressed to parts of the region.

In the least-favoured regions of the EU – Central Macedonia for example – the Structural Funds have become a major instrument for orienting the development of the regions and for selecting programmes and projects. In this case, the RTP is directly linked with national and European policy through this instrument, which has a built-in mechanism of coordination between the various government tiers concerned. In other regions, the issue of *mainstreaming* the results of the RTP is a more difficult one. In the case of South

Brandenburg or Wales, for example, where the RTP exercise was led by an organisation that lacked the power and legitimacy of other regions, the question of the permanence of the RTP process becomes an issue.

The RTP experiences show that there is a dialectical role for the EU in the sphere of regional innovation policies. On the one hand it is clear that a stimulus from above may be very helpful to introduce new practices in policy-building in the regions, to influence the underlying conceptual framework behind the schemes, to help regions entering into international cooperations and exchanges of experiences, and to offer a new legitimacy to regional authorities' actions. On the other hand, however, there is a fundamental need to respect the diversity of the regions, to let their endogenous dynamics unfold – in a word to act in the spirit of subsidiarity. The challenge for the EU is thus to stimulate innovation in LFRs without interfering with the specific processes of strategy building on the ground – a subtle mix of hands-on and hands-off approaches.

In practice, the allocation of roles to the various governmental tiers for the management of regional innovation policies can be summarised as follows:

- To the region belongs the (major) role of creating an adequate spirit for fostering innovation within the productive as well as the public sectors – that is, that of organising and making best use of available resources through the fostering of co-operative learning mechanisms, specific to the regional situation. According to the level of autonomy of the region, this role can go far in terms of establishing support instruments and organisations fine-tuned to the needs of the enterprises.

- To the central state belongs the (fundamental) duty to set up favourable conditions for innovative activities to prosper: endowment of the nation and the region in terms of public research centres, development of an adequate education system, and definition of an appropriate legal, administrative and fiscal framework for industrial and services activities. Equally important, the central state can also help to disseminate good practice to other regions in the country, as already happens in a number of EU member states covered by the RTP pilot actions.

- To the EU level belongs the (critical) task of stimulating innovative practices with regard to the above roles, notably through providing benchmarking tools, fostering exchanges between regions and supporting inter-regional learning mechanisms geared to both the process and the content of innovation-oriented regional policies.

Clearly, this vision of subsidiarity in the field of regional innovation policies does not end up with a naive celebration of the local nor with a blind belief in globalisation abolishing the relevance of the smaller territories. Complementarity and cooperation are the key words here.

AN INTERACTIVE PERSPECTIVE ON INNOVATION SUPPORT POLICIES

Broadly speaking, all regional innovation strategies studied in this book start from the recognition of a similar problem: various public instruments have been put in place in the regions to favour technological development and innovation in SMEs, but access to these structures and use of the tools they propose are rather limited, as only a small number of firms become customers of the proposed schemes. In parallel, private support schemes classically target the more advanced firms – those already engaged in innovative activities. The result is that the rest of the economy, composed mostly of firms broadly categorised as technology-followers, is still largely untouched by the support system. All the RTP studies in this book have consistently come to the same conclusion: there is a mismatch between the type of support offered and the real needs of companies, and the main problem is the *absorptive capacity* of firms with regard to the support offered.

In the case of Central and Eastern European countries there is a more basic flaw: they have neglected the role of the firm as a source of technology and innovation, and, accordingly, have laid an emphasis on extramural R&D as a source of innovation. The majority of efforts is thus devoted to building bridges between the research world and the production sphere, notably through R&D support and technology transfer policies, while the key lies in the capacity of the firm to manage innovation, which means having access to finance, commercial and economic information, or adequately trained personnel, developing entrepreneurship and creating meaningful linkages, adapting organisational and human resource practices, etc.

If the task is to design new schemes to support innovation in the regions, it is necessary to develop them in such a way that they respond to the real needs of the enterprises; that is, they have to be thought of in what may be called a 'demand-led' fashion, though this needs to be qualified because firms may know what they *want* but not what they *need.*

What the policies described in this book aim at is *a synthesis between the real needs of companies and the possibilities of the support system.* Indeed, depending on the tradition of public action, the state of existing support mechanisms, the openness to change on the part of service-providers, etc., similar demands will receive different responses in the various regions. Building regional innovation strategies is a path-dependent process, hence pure 'demand-led' policies are a fiction. Most important, and more realistic, is that *interactive* support is developed, as argued in the first chapter of this book. The various activities of the RTPs where suppliers were confronted with their customers, directly or indirectly, create new possibilities for more interactive support systems.

A thought-provoking example of an interactive support instrument to innovation originates from the US experience, where the North Carolina state chose to coordinate its agencies and resources around a cluster-based strategy, with the unexpected result of a 'dinosaur' industry receiving support because it had been more proactive than others in submitting plans to the government. In this way, public money provokes and responds to an expressed demand, and is reoriented according to strategic plans instead of following a 'ticket desk' procedure.

Interactivity should be encouraged not only between support providers and their customers, but also between firms themselves: the above-mentioned US case was based on the provision that the region was treated as '*a system of interdependent firms*'.

As has been pointed out in the Limburg case, it is absolutely crucial in this 'interactive' policy perspective that the enterprises themselves realise that they are at the centre of the problem, and also at the core of the solution. When the enterprises have progressed along this path, it becomes possible for them to be associated with the exercise and to play an active role in it.

Nevertheless, the interactive policy approach does not really tackle the problem that many companies lack the organisational and managerial capabilities and competencies to identify their real needs, to enter into cooperative projects, and to define coherent strategies, which prevents them from interacting with support providers and with other companies. Therefore, such interactive policies need to be complemented by awareness-raising, monitoring and tutoring schemes to awaken companies, as witnessed by the development of audits, training and tutoring schemes, exchanges of personnel or demonstration schemes in the regions.

Another key requirement under this interactive view of innovation support is to acquire a broader vision of innovation, with technology seen as a necessary but not sufficient ingredient for support policies. This was a major achievement of the regional endeavours described in this book, through the fostering of dialogues between users and suppliers of those services, but also through the development of a knowledge-based approach to building policies: what the experiences in this book suggest is simply that there is no point having the main actors entering into a dialogue if they are not well informed about the discussion topic. This means basically two things. First, that enterprises need a better understanding of the support available and that support providers are better informed about innovation barriers and stimuli in firms. Second, that firms and support providers learn about their peers: this is often a weak point in larger regions.

Letting neutral observers write analyses of the regional situation, in terms of firms' needs, coherence of the support system, and general technological and industrial trends, has proved to be an excellent means of starting the process for two main reasons:

- First, it provides (often for the first time) a sound, coherent, and readable basis of information and an objective assessment of the baseline situation, which is necessary to start the dialogue on an informed basis.

- Second, it inevitably contains germs for discussions, by introducing controversial judgements and evoking the possibility of changes in the established order. It acts therefore as a stimulus for the regional dialogue.

As an illustration of the above elements, table 12.1 lists the typical themes focused on by the strategies developed under the RTPs. With few exceptions, each item in this list is present in the majority, if not all, of the cases studied in this book.

TABLE 12.1: MAJOR STRATEGIC AXES DEFINED IN RTPS AND SIMILAR OPERATIONS

Strategic Axes for Regional Innovation Policies
Bridge the gap between HEIs and industry
Identify and support clusters of enterprises
Raise demand for innovation in SME's
Increase demand for skilled people in SME's
Increase supply of adequate human resources for innovation
Build a permanent Advisory Board for policy
Provide adequate finance for innovation
Raise awareness of innovation
Adapt training and further education to SMEs' needs
Organise co-operation between supply organisations
Foster the attractiveness of the region for high-tech companies
Support external orientation of SME's
Strengthen the technology transfer offer (in Objective 1 regions)
Develop support tools for the observation of SME's needs
Develop non-technical support to innovation

ENDOGENOUS–EXOGENOUS BALANCE IN THE DESIGN OF REGIONAL INNOVATION STRATEGIES

Two aspects should be dealt with under this theme of synergising the local and the global in the building of regional innovation policies. First, there is the question of introducing both dimensions in the *content* of the policies to be developed, and second, there exists the problem of combining internal and external forces in the *process* of building such policies.

As regards the first question, one should note an evolution of thinking throughout Europe: in the past, numerous policy schemes have aimed at attracting external investment in the hope of replacing failing industrial sectors so as to recreate an industrial basis in more promising industries.

However, disappointing results from inward investment have nurtured a belief that fostering the internal capacities of the regions should be at the core of the development of these regions. Policies targeting local forces have followed, as was the case notably with the STRIDE initiative. The RTP scheme proposed by the European Commission is very much in line with this view on the potential for endogenous development of the regions.

Today, we have come to realise that both the exogenous-pull and endogenous-push approaches, rather than being mutually exclusive, should aim to be complementary: using local assets to embed external inputs in the regional tissue, and tapping external sources to stimulate local firms.

The RTP experiences in EU regions and elsewhere have shown in a number of cases the difficulty of this combined approach: in South Brandenburg or Lorraine, for example, the idea of involving large multinational companies received little support. In contrast, in regions where large foreign-owned firms were already involved in relations with the local firms, the former have been involved in the exercise, as in Limburg for example.

As regards the second question, it is clear that regional innovation policies of the new wave intend to renew the *process* as well as the content of policies in the regions. This means inevitably putting into question habits, customs and policy instruments, altering some of them and inventing new ones. Doing this in closed circuit is very difficult because any system tends to work towards its survival: the *status-quo* forces are usually the strongest in organisations as well as in individuals. This is the reason why the RTP scheme, while focusing on the gathering of local forces, also stresses the importance of entering in inter-regional learning mechanisms.

Table 12.1 illustrates the wide overlapping of priorities between the regions in terms of strategic axes for a sound innovation policy. Of course, the regions mentioning common themes in their plans do not intend to develop them in a similar way, neither do they all stem from the same history with regard to these policy lines. Nevertheless, the convergence between the regional strategies for a number of key orientations, as described above, provides large support for the view that there is wide scope for inter-regional cooperation between the regions involved in RTP-like exercises.

In the studied regions, the international learning aspect has been tackled through the enrolment of foreign consultants, as in South Brandenburg or Lorraine, or national ones with international experience, and also via the organisation of open events in order to bring in, for shorter periods of time, specially briefed international experts in general meetings (in Wales) or in focused seminars (in Limburg, South Brandenburg and Lorraine). Both mechanisms show the need for brokers and personal contacts in the international exchange process: it is very difficult for regional delegates to enter into direct dialogue with their peers at the start of a project. Indeed, few direct exchanges could take place, during the development phase of the RTP, between the regions involved in the exercise, like the network events organised 'from above', in a rather anonymous fashion. At the international level too, the need for trust and social capital is fundamental for learning mechanisms to take place and develop. If this is ignored, distrust and sceptical attitudes take the place of the intended open interregional exchanges. Clearly, the RTP cases have a long way to go in this direction.

When the strategy is written and the action plan starts to be implemented, that is, when the regions have 'done their homework', the room for direct exchange seems to widen, because the discussion can become more focused and relationships forged on the basis of identified common interest. There are a number of signs that inter-regional projects are being developed between the first RTP pilot regions.

Perhaps the clearest role of the European Commission during the implementation of the RTPs relates to the promotion of these inter-regional learning mechanisms – not least beyond the frontiers of the EU, as the cases on North America demonstrated. It can reasonably be said that, without the impulse of the Commission, few, if any, moves towards exchanges of experiences between regions engaged in similar exercises would have taken place. This role should not, however, be reduced into one of promoting 'best practices', understood as standard, or universal, ways of doing policy. Indeed, the diversity of the experiences prevents them being replicated in other environments. Promoting cross-border learning is very different from transferring tools across borders.

A CONTINUOUS POLICY-MAKING PROCESS: THE TEMPORAL DIMENSION

The 'model' for building an RTP, as proposed by the Commission, was initially interpreted by the pilot regions mainly as a linear process: starting with the definition of a workplan, moving to the analysis phase, from there to a debate on the strategic directions of the RTP, from strategy to an action plan, following this with the launching of actual projects and finishing with an evaluation and monitoring system.

In reality, however, the regions did not follow such a linear process: feedback from one phase to another, considerations pertinent to later phases while the region was officially in earlier ones (and vice versa), inversions between phases, etc. can be noticed in many regions. This seemingly 'irrational' way of working happens because the building of an RTP is an evolutionary process, path-dependent and rooted in the history of policy building and in the institutional and techno-economic context of the region: the RTP is therefore at best an inflexion in a pre-existing trajectory, but never a completely new strategy, wiping the slate clean.

An operation like the RTP cannot be terminated at the end of the EU project: the *temporal dimension* is an important element to be taken into account in this process. Building a focused regional dialogue takes time, and it is necessary to 'give time to time' to let trust relations grow and develop. Building knowledge of the regional innovation system, defining a strategy based on an inclusive debate, and implementing actual projects cannot be achieved in the twinkling of an eye. Also, the timescale needed to see the results of investments in immaterial innovation support is usually longer than the one needed to see results from traditional, more visible investments in infrastructure.

This is not to deny that there is a need to keep the momentum with the RTP exercise to ensure it does not degenerate into a 'no-end' process. In this respect, the formal 'end' imposed by the EU on the RTP exercise is a good thing. However, it may be risky to stop the stimulus from above and from the regional partnerships, at the very moment when the new regional dynamics may be about to deliver their more concrete results. The continuity of inter-regional exchanges and peer-pressures, orchestrated by the Commission, might be a decisive way to maintain the energy induced by the RTP experiences in the regions.

This evolutionary character also points to the need for reflexivity, of a constant revision of the means and objectives defined at one point of time in the RTP exercises, as we saw very clearly in the Central Macedonian and Limburg cases. To this end, the development of *monitoring and evaluation* indicators and systems, which was somewhat neglected in the 'official' RTP periods, are necessary. The latest moves towards the setting up of Regional Innovation Observatories illustrate this point. It is the expression of their wish to pursue the 'knowledge-building' part of the RTP in the future.

The pursuit of the 'focused dialogue' aspect of the RTP is translated in most regions into a desire to establish a permanent advisory body, as a continuation of the RTP Steering Committee. Maintaining coherence in the innovation support system implies the need to review periodically the efficiency and effectiveness of the actions and projects supported, to ensure they do not fade out in a collection of projects with dubious synergetic effects on the innovation capacity of the region.

To ensure the continuity of the 'strategic' exercise and its transformation into real actions in the region, the main challenge faced by the regions at the end of their the RTP pilot actions is to bridge the gap between the new culture brought in by RTP and the traditional culture prevailing in the rest of the policy community. Notably, when the authorities in charge of managing the Structural Funds have not been associated closely with the exercise, the danger of building up isolated and short-lived exercises is real. Here again, we touch upon the very critical issue of raising competencies and favouring more open and creative attitudes within the public sector, so as to *mainstream* the RTP dynamic in the larger Structural Funds programmes.

CONCLUSION: REGIONAL INNOVATION STRATEGIES IN THE 21ST CENTURY

Although it is impossible to summarise each RTP studied in this book in one sentence, one might try to pinpoint that the main value-added of these approaches, taken together, is that they have helped to:

- provide a detailed monitoring of the functioning of the regional innovation system (Central Macedonia);

- support a collaborative and inclusive form of learning-through-strategy-making in the region (Wales);

- give voice to the private sector in the design of policies (Bas Saint-Laurent);

- foster the cooperation between regional actors (South Brandenburg);

- rationalise the supply of support to enterprises (Castilla y León);

- introduce a new vision of innovation at the heart of the policy agenda (Lorraine);

- favour a learning process from regional policy-makers (Limburg).

Thus, the actual cases of regions having entered into a strategic exercise to define their regional innovation-oriented policy have shown that *building knowledge networks, learning mechanisms and social capital* is a necessary complementary asset to the economic factors traditionally thought to influence economic development.

It is striking to note that the fundamentals behind the new approach proposed have never been questioned in the regions working along those lines, even when these were coming 'from above'. Neither did we find any fundamental divergence of views from outside the circle of EU regions, as it has been shown that in North America the same values were at the core of the exercises carried out with the same aim, and that implementing regional innovation strategies in Central and Eastern European countries would have to be guided by the same principles. What is more, the same approach is now spreading to other policy circles in some of the regions (Central Macedonia, Wales, Bas-Saint-Laurent), especially in the field of the Regional Information Society Initiative (RISI).

An important conclusion here is that the evolutionary character of the RTP implies that there is no such a thing as an optimal system of innovation: those systems are place- and time-specific, and in constant evolution. Therefore, innovation policies can only be built and evaluated in relation to the situation to which they refer: there is no one-size-fits-all model for policy-building in this area of innovation support. On the contrary, the *diversity* of approaches should be favoured, as a source of new ideas and practices able to enrich any region wishing to augment its learning capacity.

All this leaves us, however, with two crucial questions:

- Can public action foster the creation and development of social capital in the regions or is the latter a prerequisite for successful public action?

- Is this going to respond to the challenge of job creation in less-favoured regions?

The first question refers to the circular reasoning in theories that claim that 'innovation occurs because there is a favourable milieu, and the milieu develops where there is innovation'. The question is thus: is there an entry point in the circle for public action? The case of Central and Eastern European countries provides an interesting benchmark situation for EU regions in this respect, since almost all preconditions are lacking there for achieving successful regional innovation policies in the sense we advocate here. The basic problem has been identified as coordination failure and the absence of social capital. The way out of such a situation, or the entry point for public policies, is the need to identify potential network animateurs and use them as stimuli for building cooperative relationships between local actors. In the light of the various experiences in this book we would argue that, if properly managed, regional innovation strategies of the new wave could help to create such necessary conditions in the regions most in need of them.

The second question is an equally difficult one. It should be clearly stated here that innovation policies do target the problem of employment because they tackle the question of the competencies of firms and regions. And there is no way around the fact that the creation of durable jobs depends on a strong economy. But it should also be recognised at the same time that the number of jobs created in more innovative firms will in most cases be insufficient to absorb the mass of unemployed workers left over by the restructuring of declining industries and the effects of the globalisation of the economy, or that this will occur with unacceptable time-delays. Regional innovation policies are not a *direct* solution to the job creation imperative, and should be complemented by other public policies, notably targeting local employment possibilities to make the transition less painful. It might be the case in a number of regions that conducting more efficient innovation policies would lead to devoting less money to the system, since the immaterial aspect of policy-building is relatively cheaper to implement than building unused facilities. Money saved in this area could be used to support job-creation in other areas.

Finally, this book has been about regional innovation strategy, which involves a subtle combination of the exercise of power and the art of dialogue, a mix between the acquisition of knowledge and the development of intuitive understanding of human relations, a dialectical exercise that involves being open to the world and taking care of local well-being.

While we argued earlier that the state (regional, national, European) should not be emasculated, since it should use power to take proactive steps to contribute to a sound framework for innovative practices, we would like to add here that it should also be feminised, in the sense that approaches to policies and attitudes within decision-making circles should borrow more from the set of typically feminine attributes, such as a disposition to enter into dialogue and a capacity to value people for their human qualities rather than their image or status. These intangible qualities have yet to receive the attention they deserve in literature on development.

NOTE

1. Throughout this chapter, we use RTP to mean all types of RTP-like operations referred to in this book, thus also RITTS and similar policies outside the EU.

REFERENCES

Alden, J (1996) 'The Transfer from a Problem to Powerful Region: The Experience of Wales', in Alden, J and Boland, P (eds) *Regional Development Strategies: A European Perspective.* London: Jessica Kingsley.

Amin, A and Thrift, N (eds) (1994) *Globalization, Institutions and Regional Development in Europe.* Oxford: Oxford University Press.

Amman, R J C and Davies, RW (1977) *The Technological Level of Soviet Industry.* New Haven and London: Yale University Press.

Aoki, M and Rosenberg, N (1987) *The Japanese Firm as an Innovating Institution.* Department of Economics, Stanford University, California.

Arnold, E and Thuriaux, E (1997) *Supporting Companies' Technological Capabilities.* Brighton: Technopolis.

Auriol, L and Radosevic, S (1996) 'R&D and Innovation Activities in CEE Countries: Analysis Based on S&T Indicators', paper presented at the OECD Conference on 'The Implementation of OECD Methodologies for R&D/S&T Statistics in CEE Countries', Budapest.

Axelrod, R (1984) *The Evolution of Cooperation.* London: Penguin.

Aydalot, P (ed.) (1986) *Milieux Innovateurs en Europe.* Paris: GREMI.

Bachtler *et al.* (1995) *Synthesis of Agreed Single Programming Documents in Objective 2 Areas* (1994–96). Report to DG XVI. European Commission. Brussels.

Bagnasco, A (1977) *Tre Italia. La Problematica territoriale dello sviluppo economico italiano.* Bologna: Il Mulino.

Boekholt, P (1994) *Methodologies to Identify Regional Networks and Clusters*, presentation for European Commission DG XIII–RITTS workshop, Luxembourg.

Camagni, R (ed.) (1991) *Innovation Networks : Spatial Perspectives.* London: Belhaven.

Cantwell, J (1995) 'The Globalization of Technology: What Remains of the Product Cycle Model?' *Cambridge Journal of Economics*, 19/1, 155–74.

Carolina Hosiery Association (1995) Hickory, N C, *Preserving Hosiery Manufacturing in North Carolina: Strategies for Modernization Through Technologies.*

CDTI (1995) *Sistemas Regionales de Innovación, Cuadernos CDTO no.5.* Madrid: CDTI.

CDTI (1996) *El sistema de innovación en Castilla y León, Cuardernos CDTI no.5.* Madrid: CDTI.

CEC (1994) *Regional Technology Plan Guide Book*, 2nd Edition. Brussels: CEC, DG XVI/DG XIII.

Center for Innovative Technology (1988). *Higher Education Economic and Technology Development Pilot Program: Building Virginia's Economic Base Through Technology Transfer: Year One Report.* Herndon, VA: CIT.

Center for Innovative Technology (1997) *Technology Plan for Virginia: High Performance Manufacturing Materials.* Herndon, VA: CIT.

Chabbal, R (1992) *OECD Programme on Technology and Economy.* Paris: OECD.

Cohen, W and Levinthal, D (1990) 'Absorptive Capacity: A New Perspective on Learning and Innovation', *Administrative Sciences Quarterly*, 35, 128–52.

Confederation of British Industry and NatWest Technology Unit (CBI/NatWest) (1997) *Innovation Trends Survey*, issue 8. London.

Conseil de la Science et de la Technologie (1996) *L'aide fiscale à la R-D: un outil important pour le développement des entreprises du Québec.* Memoire presented to the Commission sur la Fiscalité et le Financement des Services Publics. Quebec.

Cooke, P and Morgan, K (1991) 'The Intelligent Region – Industrial and Institutional Innovation in Emiglia-Romagna', *Regional Industrial Research Report No 7.* Cardiff: Welsh Development Agency.

Cooke, P and Morgan, K (1992) *A Regional Innovation Strategy For Wales.* Cardiff: Department of City and Regional Planning, University of Wales.

Cooke, P and Morgan, K (1994a) 'Growth Regions Under Duress: Renewal Strategies in Baden-Württemberg and Emilia-Romagna', in Amin, A and Thrift, N (eds), *Globalization, Institutions and Regional Development in Europe.* Oxford: Oxford University Press.

Cooke, P and Morgan, K (1994b) 'The Creative Milieu: A Regional Perspective on Innovation', in Dodgson, M and Rothwell, R (eds) *The Handbook of Industrial Innovation.* Aldershot: Edward Elgar.

Cooke, P and Morgan, K (1998) *The Associational Economy: Firms, Regions and Innovation.* Oxford: Oxford University Press.

Corcoran, E (1995) 'Planting a Seed of Silicon: Experts See High Tech Nurturing Role for Virginia', *Washington Post*, 13 April, p. B.5.

Cordelier, S and Poisson, E (eds) (1996) L'État de la France 1996–1997. Paris: La Découverte.

COTEC (1997) *Innovación en las Pymes: factores de éxito y relacion con su supervivencia. Estudio bibliografico 1987–1995*, Serie Estudios no.7, Madrid.

Cronberg, T (1994) 'The Perm Region's Approach to Defence Conversion – And Why Regional Initiatives Do Not Seem to Succeed in Russia', paper presented at the workshop on the Conversion of the Russian Defence Sector. Moscow.

Dankbaar, B (1993) *Research and Technological Management in Enterprises: Issues for Community Policy. Overall Strategic Review.* Monitor-Sast Project no.8. Brussels: European Commission.

Dankbaar, B and Cobbenhagen, J (1998) 'In Search of a Regional Innovation Strategy for Flanders', paper presented at the Learning Region Conference, Tilburg University, 26/27 March 1998.

de Vet, J (1993) 'Globalization and Local and Regional Competitiveness', *STI Review*, 13, 89–121, Paris: OECD.

Department of Trade and Industry (1993) *Competitiveness: Helping Business to Win.* London: HMSO.

Dertouzos, M L, Lester, R K and Solow, R M (1989) *Made in America: Regaining the Competitive Edge.* Cambridge, MA: MIT Press.

Doeringer, P and Terkla, D (1990) 'How Intangible Factors Contribute to Economic Development', *World Development*, 18, 9, 1295–1308.

Dosi, G, Freeman, C, Nelson, R, Silverberg, G and Soete, L (eds) (1994) *Technical Change and Economic Theory.* London: Pinter.

Dosi, G, Pavitt, K and Soete, L (1990) *The Economics of Technical Change and International Trade.* New York: Harvester-Wheatsheaf.

DRI/McGraw Hill (1995) *America's Clusters.* Lexington, MA: DRI/MacGraw Hill.

EBRD (1995) *Transition Report 1995: Investment and Enterprise Development.* London: European Bank for Reconstruction and Development.

EBRD (1996) *Transition Report: Infrastructure and Savings.* London: EBRD.

Economist Intelligence Unit (1996) *Assessing and Measuring Progress in the Transition*, EIU Country Forecast, 2nd quarter. London: EIU.

Edquist, C (ed.) (1997) *Systems of Innovation: Technologies, Institutions and Organizations.* London: Pinter.

European Commission (DG XII) (1992) *Archipelago Europe*. FAST Prospective Dossier no.1.

European Commission (1992) *White Paper on Growth, Competitiveness and Employment: The Challenges and Ways Forward into the 21st Century*. Brussels.

European Commission (1993) *Cohesion and RTD policies*. COM (93)203 of 12 May 1993.

European Commission (1994a) *Competitiveness and Cohesion: Trends in the Regions*. Brussels.

European Commission (1994b) *European Report on Science and Technology Indicators*. Brussels.

European Commission (1995) *Cohesion and the Development Challenge Facing the Lagging Regions*. Regional development studies no.24. Luxembourg.

European Commission (1995) *Green Paper on Innovation*. Brussels.

European Commission (1996) *First Report on Economic and Social Cohesion*. Brussels.

European Commission (1997) *Guide to Regional Innovation Strategies*. Luxembourg.

European Parliament (1995) *Opinion of the Regional Policy Commission Submitted to the Budget Commission on the Draft Budget*. Strasbourg.

Foss, N (1993) 'Theories of the Firm: Contractual and Competence Perspectives', *Journal of Evolutionary Economics*, 3,2, 127-44.

Gabor, R I (1997) 'Too Many, Too Small: Small Entrepreneurship in Hungary – Ailing or Prospering?', in Grabher, G and Stark, D (eds).

Glasmeier, A (1991) 'Technological Discontinuities and Flexible Production Networks: The Case of the World Watch Industry', *Research Policy*, 20, 469–85.

Glasmeier, A, Hall, P and Markusen, A (1983) *Defining high-technology industries*, Working Paper 407. Berkeley, CA: Institute of Urban and Regional Development, University of California.

Grabher, G (ed.) (1992) *The Embedded Firm: On the Socio-Economics of Industrial Networks*. London: Routledge.

Grabher, G (1995) *The Disembedded Regional Economy: The Transformation of East German Industrial Complexes into Western Enclaves*, in: Amin, A and Thrift, N (eds), *Globalization, Institutions and Regional Development in Europe*. Oxford University Press.

Grabher, G (1997) *Adaptation at the Cost of Adaptability? Restructuring the Eastern German Regional Economy*, in Grabher and Stark.

Grabher, G and Stark, D (eds) (1997) *Restructuring Networks in Post-Socialism: Legacies, Linkages, and Localities*. Oxford: Oxford University Press.

Granovetter, M (1985) 'Economic Action and Social Structure', *American Journal of Sociology*, 91, 3 (November) 481–510.

Gulacsi, G (1993) *'The Place of Small Enterprise Development in Contemporary Economic Policy'*, in Public Policy Institute Foundation.

Hanson, P (1995) 'Regions, Local Power and Economic Change in Russia', in Smith, A (ed.), *Challenges for Russian Economic Reform*. London: Royal Institute of International Affairs.

Hanson, P and Pavitt, K (1987) *The Comparative Economics of Research, Development and Innovation in East and West: A Survey*. Chur, England: Harwood Academic Press.

Hare, P and Oakey, R (1993) *The Diffusion of New Process Technologies in Hungary: Eastern European Innovation in Perspective*. London: Pinter.

Hausner, J, Kudlacz, T and Schlachta, J (1997) *Regional and Local Factors in the Restructuring of South-Eastern Poland*, in Grabher and Stark.

Henderson, D (1995) *A Review of Innovation and Technology Support Infrastructure: The Key Issues*, Report prepared for RTP Wales.

Hernandez, C and Del Olmo, R (1994) 'Investigación y Desarrollo en Castilla y León: Análisis y orientaciones estratégicas', in Hernandez, A (ed.) *La estructrura Socioeconomica de Castilla y Leon en la Unión Europa*. Valladolid, Spain: Universidad de Valladolid.

Hill, S and Munday, M (1994) *The Regional Distribution of Foreign Manufacturing Investment in the UK*. London: Macmillan.

Hirschman, A (1958) *The Strategy of Economic Development*. Yale: New Haven Press.

Hirschman, A (1970) *Exit, Voice and Loyalty: Responses to Decline in Firms, Organizations and States*. Cambridge, MA: Harvard University Press.

Hodgson, G (1996) 'Varieties of Capitalism and Varieties of Economic Theory', *Review of International Political Economy 3*, (381–434).

INSEE (1997) *La France et ses Régions*. Paris.

Jeffery, C (ed) (1996) 'The Regional Dimension of the European Union,' *Regional and Federal Studies*, 6, 2.

Jones, D R (ed) (1986) *Building the New Economy: States in the Lead*. Washington, DC: Corporation for Enterprise Development.

Justman, M and Teubal, M (1996) 'Technological Infrastructure Policy (TIP): Creating Capabilities and Building Markets', in Teubal *et al.*

Kirkow, P (1997) *'Economic Change in Novosibirsk Province: from Depressed Rust Belt to Siberia's Financial and Distributional Centre?',* Russian Regional Research Group, Centre for Russian and East European Studies, Working Paper no.6. University of Birmingham.

Komninos, N (1992), 'Science Parks in Europe: Flexible Production, Disintegration and Technology Transfer', in Dunford and Kafkalas (eds), *Spatial Implications of Competition and Regulation in the New Europe*. London: Belhaven.

Komninos, N (1993), *Technopolises and Development Strategies in Europe* (in Greek). Athens: Gutenberg.

Komninos, N (1997) *The Innovative Region: The Regional Technology Plan of Central Macedonia.* Athens: Gutenberg.

Kuznetsov, Y (1997a) *Can Private-Public Collaboration Solve Mexican Growth Riddle? Concept of Social Capital in Growth Theory.* Washington DC: World Bank, mimeo.

Kuznetsov, Y (1997b) *Knowledge Assessment: Alternative Concept and Pilot Projects.* Washington DC: World Bank, mimeo.

Lagendijk, A (1996) 'Spatial Clustering at the Cross-roads of Territorial and Industrial Development: A Review', paper presented at the EUNIT Seminar on The Territorial Dimensions of Innovation, Dortmund, 21–23 May 1996.

Landabaso, M (1992) 'Política regional comunitaria, I&D regional y nueva cooperación y organización institucional', in *Economía Industrial* no.287, Madrid.

Landabaso, M (1993) 'The European Community's Regional Development and Innovation: promoting 'Innovative Milieux', in Practice', *European Planning Studies*, vol.1, no.3. London.

Landabaso M (1997) 'The Promotion of Innovation in Regional Policy: Proposals for a Regional Innovation Strategy, *Entrepreneurship and Regional Development*, 9, pp.1–24. Taylor & Francis.

Levi, M (1996) 'Social and Unsocial Capital', *Politics and Society*, 24, 1, 45–55

Lorentzen, A (1996) *'Crisis, Institutions, and Technological Change in the BAZ County, Hungary',* paper presented at the 8th General EADI Conference, Vienna.

Lorenz, C (1995) 'In Two Minds', *Financial Times*, 10 November.

Luebke, P (1990) *Tarheel Politcs: Myths and Realities.* Chapel Hill: University of North Carolina Press.

Luger, M I and Goldstein, H A (1991) *Technology in the Garden; Research Parks and Regional Development.* Chapel Hill: University of North Carolina Press.

Luhmann, N (1979) *Trust and Power.* Chichester: Wiley.

Lundvall, B A (ed.) (1992) *National Systems of Innovation. Towards a theory of innovation and interactive learning.* London: Pinter.

Lundvall, B A (1994) 'The Learning Economy: Challenges to Economic Theory and Policy', paper to the European Association of Evolutionary Political Economy Conference. Copenhagen, October.

Making Manufacturing & Technology Work in North Carolina: Strategies for a Competitive Future. (1995). A Report of the North Carolina Alliance for Competitive Technologies, Research Triangle Park, NC, December.

Maskell, P *et al.* (1998) *Competitiveness, Localised Learning and Regional Development.* London: Routledge.

Merton England, J (1982) *A Patron for Pure Science: The National Science Foundation's Formative Years, 1945–57.* Washington, DC: National Science Foundation.

Ministére de l'Industrie (1996) *L'Industrie dans les Régions 1996–1997.* Paris.

Ministére de l'Industrie, du Commerce, de la Science et de la Technologie (1996a). *Profil économique de la région du Bas-St-Laurent* (01). Quebec.

Ministére de l'Industrie, du Commerce, de la Science et de la Technologie (1996b). *La conjoncture économique des régions du Québec en 1995.* (Quebec). Direction des Communications.

Ministre délégué aux affaires régionales (1992). Développer les régions du Québec. Quebec.

Morgan, K (1994) *Reversing Attrition? The Auto Cluster in Baden-Württemberg,* working Paper no.37. Stuttgart: Centre for Technology Assessment.

Morgan, K (1996a) 'The learning region: institutions, innovation and regional renewal', *Regional Studies,* 31, 5, 491–503.

Morgan, K (1996b) *The Information Society: opportunities for SMEs in Objective 2 regions.* European Commission, Brussels.

Morgan, K (1996c) 'Learning By Interacting: Inter-Firm Networks and Enterprise Support', in OECD (ed.) *Networks of Enterprises and Local Development.* Paris: OECD.

Morgan K (1997) 'Institutions, Innovation and Regional Renewal. The Development Agency as Animateur', Conference on Regional Futures: Past and Present, East and West, Gothenburg, Sweden, May.

Morgan, K and Henderson, D (1997) 'The Fallible Servant: Evaluating the Welsh Development Agency', in Macdonald, R and Thomas, H (eds) *Nationality and Planning in Scotland and Wales.* Cardiff: University of Wales Press.

Morgan, K and Sayer, A (1988) *Microcircuits of Capital: Sunrise Industry and Uneven Development.* Cambridge: Polity Press.

Murray, R (1987) *'Flexible Specialisation in the Third Italy',* *Capital and Class,* no.33, Winter.

Murray, R (1991) *Local Space: Europe and the New Regionalism.* Manchester: Centre for Local Economic Strategies.

Murray, R (1992) 'Towards a Flexible State', in Murray, R. (ed.) *New Forms of Public Administration,* Institute of Development Studies Bulletin, 23, 4.

National Governors' Association (1983). *Task Force on Technological Innovation, Technology & Growth.* State Initiatives in Technological Innovation. Washington, DC.

Nauwelaers, C (1996) *Promotion of Innovation and the Information Society Under Community Structural Policy: General Report.* Brussels: CEC, DGXVI; Ministry of Economy, Technology and European Affairs of the State of Saxony-Anhalt.

Nauwelaers, C and Reid, A (1995a) *Innovative Regions: A Comparative Review of Methods of Evaluating Regional Innovation Potential.* Luxembourg: European Commission, DG XIII.

Nauwelaers, C and Reid, A (1995b) 'Methodologies for the Evaluation of Regional Innovation Potential', *Scientometrics,* 34, 3, 497–511.

Nauwelaers, C and Cobbenhagen, J (1996) *Building Regional Innovation Strategies: RTPs in an Evolutionary Perspective,* Maastricht Economic Research Institute on Innovation and Technology, Working Paper 2/96–017.

Negroponte, N (1995) *Being Digital.* London: Hodder & Stoughton.

Nelson, R (1991) 'Why Do Firms Differ and How Does It Matter?', *Strategic Management Journal* 12, 61–74.

North Carolina State University (1996) *The North Carolina Manufacturing Competitiveness Survey.* Final Report. Research Triangle Park: NC NBS ACTs.

Nooteboom, B (1996) *Towards a Cognitive Theory of the Firm.* Groningen University: School of Management and Organization.

OECD (1969) *Science Policy in the USSR.* Paris: OECD.

OECD (1992) *Technology and the Economy: The Key Relationships.* Paris: OECD.

OECD (1993) *Territorial Development and Structural Change*. Paris: OECD.

OECD (1994) *Politiques et problémes régionaux au Canada*. Paris: OECD

OECD (1994) *Industry in the Czech and Slovak Republics*. Paris: OECD.

OECD (1995) *Review of Industry and Industrial Policy in Hungary*. Paris: OECD.

Office de planification et de développement du Québec (OPDQ) (1991) *Bilan socio-économique 1990, région du Bas-St-Laurent*. Quebec. Service des communications de l'OPDQ. Quebec: OPDQ.

Office for National Statistics (1996) *Regional Trends: 1996 Edition*. London: HMSO.

Office of Technology Assessment (1984) *Technology, Innovation, and Regional Development*. Washington, DC: Government Printing Office.

Office of Technology Assessment (1990) *Making Things Better: Competing in Manufacturing*. Washington, DC: Govermment Printing Office.

Olson, M (1965) *The Logic of Collective Action: Public Goods and the Theory of Groups*. Harvard Economic Studies. Cambridge, MA: Harvard University Press.

OST: Observatoire des Sciences et des Techniques (1994) *Science et Technologie: Indicateurs 1994*. Paris: Economica.

OST: Observatoire des Sciences et des Techniques (1996) *Science et Technologie: Indicateurs 1996*. Paris: Economica.

Oughton, C and Whittam, G (1997) 'Competition and Cooperation in the small firm sector' *Scottish Journal of Political Economy*, 44. 1.

Patel, P and Pavitt, K (1991) 'Large Firms in the Production of the World's Technology: An Important Case of Non-Globalization', *Journal of International Business Studies* 22, 1–21.

Pelikan, P (1994) Can the Imperfect Innovation Systems of Capitalism Be Outperformed?, in Dosi, G *et al.* (eds).

Peteri, G (1993) 'From the "Enterprising" Local Government towards Local Economic Development', in Public Policy Institute Foundation paper.

Phelps, P and Brockman, P (1992) 'Science and Technology Programs in the States', unpublished Paper for the National Governors' Association.

Piore, M (1995) *Beyond Individualism*. Cambridge, MA Harvard University Press.

Piore M, and Sabel, C (1984) *The Second Industrial Divide: possibilities for prosperity*. New York: Basic Books.

Polanyi, M (1966) *The Tacit Dimension*. London: Routledge & Kegan Paul.

Porter, M (1990) The Competitive Advantage of Nations. London: Macmillan.

Public Policy Institute Foundation (1993) 'Private Sector Development and Local Government in Hungary', *Papers and Proceedings of the Conference Organized by the Centre for International Private Enterprise and the Public Policy Institute Foundation, Eger (Hungary)*. Budapest.

Putnam, R (1993) *Making Democracy Work*. Princeton University Press.

Radosevic, S (1994a) *National Systems of Innovation in Economies in Transition: Between Restructuring and Erosion'*, paper presented at the conference 'Research Co-operation with Countries in Transition' Vienna, Austria, Six Nations Programme.

Radosevic, S (1994b) 'Strategic Technology Policy for Eastern Europe', *Economic Systems*, 18, 2, December, 87–116.

Radosevic, S (1996a) Restructuring of R&D Institutes in Post-Socialist Economies: Emerging Patterns and Issues, in Webster, A. (ed.) *Building New Bases for Innovation: The Transformation of the R&D System in Post-Socialist States*. Cambridge: Anglia Polytechnic University.

Radosevic, S (1996b) 'Divergence and Convergence in R&D and Innovation Between East and West?', paper presented on the Fifth Freiberg Symposium on Economics: 'Innovation and Transformation', August 1996, Freiberg; mimeo.

Radosevic, S (1997a) 'Strategic Policies for Growth in Post-Socialism: Theory and Evidence Based on Baltic States', *Economic Systems*, 21, 2, June.

Radosevic, S (1997b) 'Strategic Technology Policy in Post-Socialism', in Hirschhausen, C (ed.),
    *New Neighbours in Eastern Europe - Economic and Industrial Reform in Lithuania, Latvia and
    Estonia*. Paris: Écoles des Mines.

Rees, J and Lewington, T (1990) 'An Assesment of State Technology Programs', in Schmandt, J
    and Wilson, R (eds) *Growth Policy in the Age of High Technology: The Roles of Regions and States*.
    London: Unwin Hyman.

Report of the Review Committee (1993) *The Performance and Potential of the Center for
    Innovative Technology*, Senate Document no.16. Richmond: Commonwealth of Virginia.

Rosenberg, N (1976) *Perspectives on Technology*. Cambridge University Press.

Sabel, C (1994) 'Learning by Monitoring: The Institutions of Economic Development', in Smelser,
    N and Swedberg, R. (eds) *Handbook of Economic Sociology*. Princeton University Press.

Schoenberger, E (1994) 'The Firm in the Region and the Region in the Firm', paper to the Harold
    Innes Conference, June, Toronto.

Schulze, K P (undated) 'Erfolge und Schwierigkeiten bei der Förderung innovativer
    mittelständischer Betriebe', presentation paper. TINA, Brandenburg.

Scott, A (1988) *New Industrial Spaces. Flexible Production, Organisation and Regional
    Development in North America and Western Europe*. London: Pion.

Secrétariat au développement des régions (1995) *Les régions administratives*, édition 1995.
    Quebec: Gouvernement du Québec.

Segal Quince Wicksted Limited (1994) *Survey of the Innovation Infrastructure in Central and
    Eastern Europe*, A Report to SPRINT, EC-DGXII, Brussels.

Simonian, H (1997) 'Carmakers' Smart Move,' *Financial Times*, 1 July.

Société québécoise de développement de la main-d'oeuvre du Bas-Saint-Laurent, de la
    Gaspésie/Iles-de-la-Madeleine (1994) *Plan régional de développement de la main-d'oeuvre
    1994-1997*, Février. Quebec.

Soete, L and Arundel, A (eds) (1993) *An Integrated Approach to European Innovation and
    Technology Diffusion Policy: A Maastrich Memorandum*. Brussels: European Commission.

Southern Technology Council (1989) *Turning to Technology: A Strategic Plan for the Nineties*.
    Research Triangle Park, NC: Southern Growth Policies Board.

Spielkamp, A (1997) 'Innovation as a Transfer Result of Cooperation Between the Business and
    Academic Communities', paper presented at the International Conference on Industrial
    Policy for Europe, London, 26–27 June.

Statistics Canada (1996) *Service Bulletin Science Statistics*, vol.20, no.6.

Storper, M (1995) 'The Resurgence of Regional Economies, Ten Years After: The Region as a
    Nexus of Untraded Interdependencies,' *European Urban and Regional Studies*,2, 191–221.

Statistics Canada (1996) *Service Bulletin Science Statistics*, vol.20, no.9.

Storper, M (1997) *The Regional World: Territorial Development in a Global Economy*. New York:
    Guilford Press.

Storper, M and Scott, A (1995) 'The Wealth of Regions: Market Forces and Policy Imperatives in
    Local and Global Context,' *Futures, 27*, 505–26.

Sutherland, D (1997) *Small and Medium Sized Enterprises in the Russian Regions: Employment
    Constraints and Incentives,* University of Birmingham, Russian Regional Research Group,
    Centre for Russian and East European Studies, Working Paper 7.

Teubal, M (1997) 'A Catalytic and Evolutionary Approach to Horizontal Technology Policy
    (HTP),' *Research Policy*, 25, 8, January, 1161–1188.

Teubal, M, Foray, D, Justman, M and Zuscovitch, Y (1996) *Technological Infrastructure Policy: An
    International Perspective*. Dordrecht: Kluwer.

TINA Brandenburg (1993) *Regionaler Innovationsverbund CITI '99 – ein technologieorientiertes
    Entwicklungskonzept für Südbrandenburg*.

van Zoon, H (1992) *Towards Regional Innovation Systems in Central Europe,* Forecasting and
    Assessment in Science and Technology (FAST), FOP 308. Brussels: European Commission.

Virginia Department of Planning and Budget (1993) *Industrial Modernization in Virginia*. Richmond: State Government.

Virginia's Center for Innovative Technology Innovations, 'CIT Continues Progress Toward Three-Year Goals', October 1996.

von Hirschhausen, C (1996) *Du Combinat a l'Enterprise: une analyse de la nature du Combinat socialiste et des restructurations industruielles post-socialistes en Europe de l'Est*. Paris: Ecole des Mines.

Webster, A (ed.) (1996) *Building New Bases for Innovation: The Transformation of the R&D System in Post-Socialist States*. Cambridge: Anglia Polytechnic University.

Wegner, M (1993) *Die neuen Bundesländer in der EG*. Baden-Baden: Nomos Verlaggesellschaft.

Welsh Affairs Select Committee (1995) *Fourth Report, Wales in Europe, vol. 1, Report of Proceedings of the Committee*. London: HMSO.

Welsh Development Agency (1996) *Wales Regional Technology Plan: An Innovation and Technology Strategy for Wales; Consultative Report*. Cardiff.

Whittington, D (ed.) (1985) *High Hopes for High Tech: Microelectronics Policy in North Carolina*. Chapel Hill: University of North Carolina Press.

Williamson, O (1985) *The Economic Institutions of Capitalism*. New York: Free Press.

Winter, S (1988) 'On Coase, Competence and the Corporation', *Journal of Law, Economics and Organization*, 4, 1, 163-80.

World Bank (1996) *World Development Report 1995: From Plan to Market*. Washington, DC: World Bank.

World Bank (1997) *World Development Report 1997: The State in a Changing World*. Oxford: Oxford University Press.

Wulf-Mathies, M (1995) 'Community Structural Policies and Employment,' paper to Informal Council of Ministers Responsible for Regional Policies and Spatial Planning, Madrid, 30 November.

INDEX

Page numbers in italic indicate reference to a table or figure.